Bell's Weekly Messenger, April 15, 1832

Britain in Europe
Prospects for change

Edited by
JOHN MILFULL

 Routledge
Taylor & Francis Group
LONDON AND NEW YORK

First published 1999 by Ashgate Publishing

Reissued 2018 by Routledge
2 Park Square, Milton Park, Abingdon, Oxon, OX14 4RN
711 Third Avenue, New York, NY 10017, USA

Routledge is an imprint of the Taylor & Francis Group, an informa business

Copyright © John Milfull 1999

All rights reserved. No part of this book may be reprinted or reproduced or utilised in any form or by any electronic, mechanical, or other means, now known or hereafter invented, including photocopying and recording, or in any information storage or retrieval system, without permission in writing from the publishers.

Notice:
Product or corporate names may be trademarks or registered trademarks, and are used only for identification and explanation without intent to infringe.

Publisher's Note
The publisher has gone to great lengths to ensure the quality of this reprint but points out that some imperfections in the original copies may be apparent.

Disclaimer
The publisher has made every effort to trace copyright holders and welcomes correspondence from those they have been unable to contact.

A Library of Congress record exists under LC control number: 98074841

ISBN 13: 978-1-138-60913-6 (hbk)
ISBN 13: 978-1-138-60931-0 (pbk)
ISBN 13: 978-0-429-46066-1 (ebk)

Contents

Preface		viii
1	Introduction: Australia, the New Britain and the New Europe - an Identity or Three? *John Milfull*	1
I	**PREHISTORIES**	
2	English Historiography and the Invention of Britain and Europe *Conal Condren*	11
3	Enlightenment, Cosmopolitanism and Nationalism *John Gascoigne*	28
4	The Strange Case of British Music *Roger Covell*	36
II	**PREVIOUS ENGAGEMENTS**	
5	Perceptions of Britain in Wilhelmine Social Democracy *Dick Geary*	49
6	The Intellectual Connections between British and European Economists in the 1920s: Cambridge and Geneva on International Economic Policies *Grant Fleming*	66
7	The British in the Rhineland *Heidi Zogbaum*	79

III A NEW BRITAIN IN A NEW EUROPE?

8 Britain, the European Union and National Identity 91
   Peter Shearman

9 New Europe, New Labour:
   British European Policy Reconsidered 103
   Helen Wallace

10 The Sources of New Labour 113
   Rodney Smith

11 Public Opinion, Sovereignty and the European Union 135
   Elim Papadakis

IV NATION AND REGION

12 Scotland and the New Regionalism 157
   James Mitchell

13 An England of the Regions in a Europe of the Regions? 171
   John Murphy

14 Regional Inequality: the New Germany and the European Union 190
   Hans Joachim Meyer

V REFRACTIONS

15 Europhobia in the New Tory Historiography 207
   Andrew Bonnell

16 "Grass Roots": Eric Cantona, Jürgen Klinsmann and the
   Europeanisation of English Football 226
   Andy Smith

17	Afterword: Studying "Britain" *Michael Wilding*	248

Notes on Contributors   252

Preface

This book was conceived before Tony Blair's landslide victory in the British elections, at the height of the controversy about Britain's future role in Europe. The conference which brought the contributors together was held in its immediate aftermath, when the reorientation in policies on integration and internal devolution was already taking shape. Two years later, it is gratifying to see how many subsequent developments were signalled and anticipated, while many of the issues raised remain to be addressed.

My warmest thanks are due to Jim Potts, Director of the British Council in Australia, and Countess Ute Baudissin, Director of the Goethe Institute Sydney, both model citizens of a New Europe - Jim for his immediate enthusiasm for the project, from our very first meeting, and his support for Helen Wallace's visit, and Ute for making one of the world's most attractive conference venues available to us, for her legendary hospitality and for enabling Hans Joachim Meyer's participation. This exemplary cooperation is not only reflected in the comparative and cosmopolitan focus of the book; it marks a future direction for European Studies in Australia, in which the focus on national cultures is increasingly replaced by a broader view of the complex interactions between region, nation and Europe's role in the world.

My thanks are also due to the Delegation of the European Commission in Canberra, for sponsoring William Wallace's visit; to Helen and William, for their leading role in our discussions; to the Faculty of Arts and Social Sciences of the University of New South Wales, for its generous support; and to my wife Helen Milfull, whose eagle eye was of invaluable assistance in the last phase of the preparation of the manuscript. I hope that the book will stand as a fitting memorial to an enormously enjoyable and productive conference, and as a prelude to a new and mature engagement with British and European Studies in Australia.

Sydney, December 1998   *John Milfull*

1 Introduction: Australia, the New Britain and the New Europe - an Identity or Three?

JOHN MILFULL

Growing Up

Parenthood is one of the most difficult tasks, both for the parents and the parented, that we have inherited from the Enlightenment tradition and its redefinition of family and education. The autonomy and freedom, the *Mündigkeit* which is its ideal goal is coupled with an equally revolutionary emphasis on the "caring family" which, like Freud's psychoanalysis, creates new and deeper bonds to be transcended, in their turn, in a relationship of mutual acceptance and tolerance of the "selfness" of the other, ex-parent and ex-parented. We are all familiar, from our deepest personal experience, with the often tortuous ambivalences of dependency on both sides. And many of us share the Utopian vision of a genuine "adult" and equal friendship in which we can somehow reward one another for the long haul of growing up with an open, unfettered communication between the selves which have been shaped and transformed in the process.

    Australia and Britain are both currently engaged in a difficult phase of "transference", redefining themselves, externally and internally, in terms of a rapidly changing global situation in which the "New" that is programmatically attached to "Labour", "Britain" and "Europe" seems less a statement of fact or even intention than of necessity. Equally, Australia's reorientation to the Asia-Pacific is not a matter of choice, but simply a recognition of realities which could no longer be ignored. But if Britain is part of Europe and Australia belongs in the Asia-Pacific, what are "Britain" and "Australia"? It is impossible to separate the compulsion towards "external" redefinition from the redefinition of what it is that is being reorientated, not only because the factors that lead to the compulsion have already had a decisive impact on the character and composition of our societies, but because the old definitions were premised on realities that no longer exist, the parental conditions of Empire. It is not surprising that cries of betrayal have been heard on both sides, from the cracked record of Aussie complaints about Britain's (unwilling) complicity in the absurdities of the CAP to the accusations of *lèse-majesté* with which Fleet Street has peppered Australia's attempts to discover its "self". And the "ambivalences of dependency", as I have termed them above, have always presented a Pandora's Box of Oedipal nasties to be fired off in both directions, in a display of post-colonial "sledging" of which the Australian cricketers are uncontested masters, no doubt because they are only too aware who taught them the Great Game.

This is the kind of childish behaviour to which parents, too, are all too susceptible. But the relations between Britain and Australia, between parent and parented, are far too complex to be resolved in an adolescent slanging match. As Jim Potts, the British Council's Director in Australia, persuasively argued at the conference where the idea for this book had its genesis,[1] there are some very significant credits in the ledger of Empire, often the very values in whose name the ex-imperial parent is attacked. A Republican movement in Australia which is essentially anti-British, or perhaps more accurately, anti-English, will miss the whole point of "growing up", the liberation from cringe and condescension, with their attendant aggressions, to a mature friendship between people who still have a lot to talk about, who can define and defend common values in the new and different environments in which they increasingly function and honour their shared past with productive alliances in the present and future. Blaming your parents or your children for your own sins of omission and commission leads nowhere.

The "(In)visible Anglo" - Home and Away

But Australia and Britain are not individuals, [English] parent and [Anglo-Australian] child; they are diverse and relatively *disunited kingdoms*. Most curious of all: as Norman Saadi Nikro writes in a recent dissertation, while there is no doubt that Australia exhibits a dominant "Anglo" culture, Anglo-Australians have been "de-ethnicised" within a self-styled multicultural society in which only non-Anglo-Australians are "ethnic" and represent a [problematic] "cultural variability", while "Anglo-Australians [predominate] as the major signifier of Australian nationality" and "cultural unity":

As long as Anglo-Australian forms of identification are not
regarded as particular ethnic cultures, then their peculiarities will
remain abstract generalisations dominating the Australian cultural
and historical landscape.[2]

These "abstract generalisations", which stand in marked opposition to the history and diversity of Anglo-Australian communities - Nikro warns against "underestimating the violence perpetrated on [Anglo-Saxon culture]" - are the key to "structures of power that have much to do with the maintenance of binary oppositions that measure cultural diversity from the standpoint of cultural unity defined by a(n) (in)visible Anglo-Australianness".[3] In the last analysis, they are a relict of the ideology of Empire which corresponds neither to present geopolitical nor social realities, and condemn Anglo-Australians to an unfortunate mix of arrogance and cringe to mask their crippled identities, while presenting the ever-increasing non-Anglo contingent with a troubling vacuum at the centre of "cultural diversity". It is, after all, a parental ideology which has survived the departure of the parent and an unimagined reconstitution of the family. Its most obvious manifestation is the extraordinary difficulty Australian foreign policy has faced in projecting an Australian position which is at once adult and autonomous and free of the delusions of Empire - a mixture, again, of insecurity and over-compensatory arrogance which quotes the condescensions of imperialism without the power base that gave rise to them. To embrace Australian independence means, above all, to come to terms with the reality of a minor power whose only real hope of "influence" in the international scene of the future can stem from its successful development of an innovative, culturally diverse and productive society which will act as a bridge between Europe (in the broadest sense) and Asia.

But the "(in)visible Anglo" is (not) at home in Britain just as much as in Australia. As Krishan Kumar writes:

All subjects of the Empire might be designated 'British", but that
paradoxically served only to emphasise the distance separating the
British of Great Britain, the colonisers and carriers of "the white
man's burden", from all the other British of the British Empire. The
imperial connection promoted the sense not just of difference but of
superiority, even of uniqueness. For the British people must be most
powerfully and peculiarly endowed if so small an island could
become the ruler of the greatest empire since Rome.

There was one other consequence of the imperial contribution to
Britishness. The Empire drew more closely together the different

> ethnic groups inhabiting Britain, English, Welsh, Scottish, Irish. They were joined in common governance of the far-flung empire. They were also united, one might say, by their equal share in the plunder of empire...
>
> Britishness was undermined by the end of the empire and by Britain's decline as a world power. Lacking the stimulus and the bracing influence of a world role, Britishness capitulated in the face of an assertion of Scottish, Welsh and Irish nationalism. England, the core nation, stood exposed, no longer protected by a surrounding carapace of Britishness.[4]

The post-colonial debate needs to be directed back at the metropolitan culture not only in the sense Edward Said advocates in *Culture and Imperialism*, to uncover the hidden role of colonialism and the colonised in the shaping of British society, but to penetrate to its crucial "pilot project", the process of internal colonisation within Britain itself.

It was in this light, fresh from our discussions on regional inequality and devolution in Britain and Europe, that I first read Nikro's acute comment on the "abstract generalisations" to which a de-ethnicised dominant culture has been reduced in Australia. What, after all, is "British culture"? Simply "devolving" its Scots, Welsh and Irish components, however desirable or expedient it may be, will only address the most blatant legacies of internal colonisation. The relics of social and cultural imperialism, in England and elsewhere in Britain, reach far deeper and coexist awkwardly with a new economic order which, well before Blair, had already begun to jettison the illusions of Empire and world Anglo dominance for autonomy and pragmatic partnerships. It was perhaps the ultimate paradox of Thatcherism that it was able to mobilise, in the name of modernisation, both a deep-seated antagonism towards an [English] establishment which stretched well beyond the traditional élites, but still clung to the hierarchies of Empire, and a crude post-imperialist chauvinism among social groups who had once served as cannon-fodder for Empire and whose gains from the type of modernisation pursued were transient at best. *Sidere mens eadem mutato*, "the same mind under a different star", reads the depressing motto of the University of Sydney; there are inescapable parallels with the Australian situation discussed above, where radical economic change coexists with a troubling vacuum at the cultural centre. In Thatcherite mode, John Howard, the current Australian conservative prime minister, constantly attacks a 'black armband view' of Australian history which seeks to uncover and address the wrongs of the past, while himself presiding over an even faster erosion of shared social values and the structures in which they had found expression.

Perhaps successful reform and reorientation demands, above all, the coming to terms with past failure, the abandonment of false national pride? Last year, I welcomed the Spanish Ambassador to Australia, Emilio Fernandez-Castaño, to a lecture with what I thought a suitably diplomatic reference to David Ringrose's thesis of the "myth of [Spanish] failure",[5] only to be told with great elegance and at some length that failure was the really constructive force in history, and that Spain's current resurgence in Europe sprang, above all, from "freeing [it]self from the past". "History", as a former Vice-Chancellor of UNSW once put it to me, "can sometimes be a positive disadvantage." I am sure Tony Blair would agree. But "freeing oneself from the past" demands, above all, an insight into its failures and its injustices which alone can serve as the basis for genuine reform. To parody Walter Benjamin, the real task of the historian is to explode the false continuities of history and expose the unfulfilled promises of the past which lie buried under its rubble heaps. I wish the "New Britain" luck and courage in the attempt.

Filling the Gap

There may be valid, even obvious, political reasons for New Labour's rejection of history, especially recent history, but as Rodney Smith writes below, it cannot last. Ultimately, Britain will need to rewrite its history, to review it from the perspective of a New Britain and a New Europe and uncover past alternatives which can be made productive in present and future. This is a project far too large for a book of this kind, but it nevertheless has some suggestions to make; for instance, to part the Red Sea of British exceptionalism in the quest for a time before "Britain" and "Europe" were invented, when English, Scots, Welsh and Irish artists and scientists held pride of place in a European "republic of letters". The impoverishment which followed the embrace of Empire and insularity is only more obvious in music; like the reality of the colonised, the links with Europe were driven underground (my Professor of English at Sydney University wrote in the margin of an essay in which I had quoted Goethe: "Do not parade your knowledge of foreign cultures"!).

But for all the attractions of Enlightenment universalism, there may be more future in unearthing histories and stories of a different kind, reaching from soldiers of occupying armies to football fans and progressive economists. If "Europe" and "Britain" are to acquire real content, it will not be on the level of sublime abstraction, but of lived lives. When Siegfried Kracauer spoke of the need for "sensuous concepts" (*sinnliche Begriffe*), he might have been criticising the "fleshlessness" of Eurospeak.

Citizenship and Identity

"Do you mean", a colleague of mine asked a visiting apologist for European integration, "that the Germans will stop being German?" I wanted to add: "or Swabians, Saxons, *Berliner* or Upper Franconians?" and butt in with a resounding "No!". My visitor simply looked pained - his whole motivation and argument had been misunderstood. But the misunderstanding is symptomatic, and often enough encouraged by a false rhetoric of European unity, a phrase which should not be allowed out in public without its complement "in diversity".

How could there ever be a European *identity*? And if there could, what kind of atrocious homogenisation would it involve? Europe itself, as Agnes Heller has written,[6] is hard enough to define, even geographically; but there can be no doubt whatever that what makes Europe "European" is above all a rich and extraordinary cultural diversity which even national borders define quite inadequately, a diversity of ethnicity, social strata, language, religion, of land- and cityscape.

The source of the misunderstanding arises in the confusion of *citizenship* and identity. In a remarkable article, James Donald[7] has pointed out that there is a fundamental difference between citizenship, which has, of necessity, a universalising, abstract tendency, and identity, which is constituted by the often multiple environments in which we grow up, live and work. However noble his motivation may have been, Jürgen Habermas's concept of "constitutional patriotism", born from the fear of a New German nationalism, thus remains a contradiction in terms; we may value, and even feel a strong commitment towards, the principles of good citizenship, but they do not create identification, through their very generality they even tend to inhibit it. For all the bad press he received after German unification, Günter Grass was on surer ground with his 1967 vision of a "communicating plural",[8] a Germany which resisted the future seductions of "national unity" by building on the strengths of West German federalism, a federalism which, as Hans Joachim Meyer writes, is not about surrendering rights, but protecting them. It remains a major historical irony that the rapid unification process Grass, like the rest of us, did not foresee and found hard to digest, did the "right thing for the wrong reason". In the haste to absorb and delegitimise the GDR, five new East German states (*Länder*) were created and granted accession to the Federal Republic under Article 23 of the Basic Law, which was never intended for this purpose. The convention to draft a new constitution for a united Germany called for by Article 146 was never held. In the mean time, it seems as if it is precisely, and only, on the level of the new East German *Länder* that the economic, social and psychological problems of unification may be resolved. If it is too difficult, and even inherently dangerous, to try and define a "German identity", I, for one, have no problem with the persistence of that successful strategy with which the bulk of West Germans made do for so long, as *Münchner*, *Berliner*, Bavarians or Swabians and citizens of Europe.

The dangers may be less obvious, but is it really much easier or more useful to define a "British" identity? For most "Britons" (the term can only survive in abbreviation as "Brit", returned to the warmth of the street) it is probably the most difficult and least productive form of identification. Regional and group identities survive all attempts to repress them, and I can only agree with Donald that a) we all need such identifications, transient and "fuzzy" as they may be, and b) the answer is not to "absorb" them, but to embark on the far more complex and productive task of affirming them and relating and reconciling them to a broader concept of citizenship. This citizenship may, indeed, be better defined as "European" than British, if the British government(s) can finally take up the challenge and fight for the realisation of their own proud, if slightly damaged, democratic traditions in the governance of Europe. They will find many allies. But "citizenship" will remain only an abstract and vulnerable concept unless "subsidiarity", that appalling term which conceals the most vital signpost to European unity, is given a human face. As in Italy and Spain, devolution and regional autonomy are not just a stratagem, but a pre-condition for survival and the emergence of trust in the process of integration, British, German, Italian and European. And integration is surely both necessary and inevitable; the point is to ensure its quality and success. I hope that Australia may play its part, with Britain *in Europe*, in a dialogue on the *New Federalism* without which, I suspect, none of our countries will succeed in retaining some sense of humanity and social justice amid the challenges that lie ahead.

Notes

1. *Britain in Europe*, a cross-disciplinary conference organised by the Centre for European Studies, University of New South Wales, in collaboration with the British Council, the EC Delegation and the Goethe Institute Sydney, 25-27 July 1997.
2. Norman Saadi Nikro, *Shifting Margins, Imaginary Journeys: Writing Migrant Experience*, Ph.D. thesis, University of New South Wales 1997, p. 234.
3. *ibid.*
4. Krishan Kumar, "'Britishness and 'Englishness': what prospect for a European identity in Britain today?", in *British Studies Now*, anthology issues 1-5, The British Council 1995, p. 88, 93.
5. cf. David R. Ringrose, *Spain, Europe and the "Spanish miracle," 1700-1900*, Cambridge University Press, 1996.
6. Agnes Heller, "Europe: An Epilogue?", in *The Idea of Europe. Problems of National and Transnational Identity*, ed. B. Nelson et al., New York/Oxford: Berg 1992, pp. 12-25.
7. James Donald, "The Citizen and the Man About Town", in Stuart Hall and Paul du Gay (eds.), *Questions of Cultural Identity*, London: Sage 1996, pp. 170 - 190.
8. Günter Grass, "The Communicating Plural" (1967), in *Two States - One Nation?*, San Diego: Harcourt Brace Jovanovich 1990, pp. 62-75.

I

PREHISTORIES

2 English Historiography and the Invention of Britain and Europe

CONAL CONDREN

> And Samson went and caught three hundred foxes, and took firebrands, and turned tail to tail, and put a firebrand in the midst between two tails.
>
> And when he had set the brands on fire, he let *them* to go into the standing corn of the Philistines, and burnt up both the shocks, and also the standing corn, with the vineyards and olives.
>
> JUDGES 15, 4-5

> Historye will tell ... as your Matie to well knowes, For Indeed, though theye looke divers wayes, with their heads, yett theye are tied together like Samsons Foxes by theyr Tyles Carienge the same fierbrandes off Covetusnes & Ambition, to putt all Into a Combustion whersoever theye coume, thatt will nott Submitt to them.
>
> WILLIAM CAVENDISH, 'Advice' c. 1660,
the 'Welbeck' MS, ch. 2

It is easy to be spuriously paradoxical about the compromised alterity of Britain in Europe: Britain is both in and distinct from Europe, each in a sense is the other's ambivalent Other. This shimmer of post-modernist indeterminacy arises because, as I have expressed it, we have an invitation to the careless use of abstract classifications such as Britain and Europe; and because the paradoxicality of the statement exploits the tendency to reify relational predicates of sameness/difference, self and other as abstract, absolute and negating categories. It is a process that can only terminate in self-contradiction. The sense lying behind the parody of post-modernist perplexity is that the notions of Britain and Europe are mutually informing. Yet, Britain's involvement in Europe is not simply a matter of location on any single vector of assimilation or integration. There is a degree to which the notions of Britain and Europe have been created, or at least manipulated in tandem, each being used in conjunction with the other for often diverse requirements of positioning.

There is, I suspect, a certain polemical convenience in the distinction between British / Anglo American philosophy as opposed to continental / European philosophy, a matter almost of *ad hominem* pigeon-holing that allows a denigrating avoidance of the postulated 'other'. In practice, I am told, outside America the most vibrant centre of British analytic philosophy (it certainly isn't Britain) is Italy--a mere foreign fashion perhaps, a minor stab in the European philosophical back? Yet if were are to look at the seminal figures of British and analytic philosophy, several hailed from the vicinity of Vienna and worked in a straight Kantian tradition. So, to an extent, one form of philosophy must needs invent the other to emphasise a sense of self. In contrast to such isolating bifurcation lies the homogenising, or deeply integrating notion of *The* Enlightenment Project as an overarching enterprise of the modern European philosophical mind; this loses Britain in Europe, but at the high price of ignoring the complexity and diversity of Enlightenment thought, as it was found in, say, David Hume's Scotland. At either extreme, if we pursue philosophy back to the early modern period, a projection of British and European identities is decreasingly helpful. My comments on philosophy are only for the purpose of initial orientation, illustrative of the sort of terrain I wish to cover, but sufficient, I hope, to indicate that my main focus of attention does not exhaust the general issues of myth-making and identity.

Looking at the broader historiography of Early Modern England, I want to sketch in some of the changes in relationship between Britain and continental Europe, an expression used here only to designate an arbitrary geographical identity. The untidy sweep that follows is an attempt to map some of the wayward movement of the tied notions of Britain and Europe, always on the move through the waving corn-fields of academic and political debate. And like Samson's foxes, they have been partly the creatures of mythic imagination, torchbearers against the philistine.

At the risk of sounding unduly like a 'new historicist' of English literature, I shall light my way with an anecdote. In 1996 I visited Bruges, a city I remembered only from the glow of late childhood. I went partly to reactivate some spoken French, to arrive in the veritable epicentre of non-French speaking, - even Francophobic - Belgium, as I am assured, everyone else in the world knows. The Bruggers would speak German, Dutch and English with alacrity, but I would have been better off going back to Britain, to Jersey to practice French. And had I wanted to speak Flemish, heaven forfend, I could have gone to Hull, Heaven forfend some more, where, I was told, by a local bus driver, the authentic dialect of a handful of Hull fisherfolk, if that is what Brussels now deems them to be, was a version of off-shore Netherlandish.[1]

This cautionary and humiliating tale encapsulates simply enough the seductive dangers of any Britain / Europe dichotomy. The old adage of international relations has left a linguistic print: your neighbour is your enemy, your enemy's enemy is your friend. This maxim, for example, is a pretty reliable guide to the patterns of alliance in fourteenth and fifteenth century Tuscany. More immediately to the point, Scotland was England's enemy, so France's friend; Burgundy was England's ally because she was France's foe. In historical perspective, Britain fragments into countries and regions, in Early Modern England, country often meant county. In Britain's Civil Wars, once seen as the first of the great modernising Revolutions of European (therefore world) History, it is salutary to recall that the Clubmen of Yorkshire, England's largest county, nearly kept both sides out of their country. 'Nothing to do with us'. By the same token, until relatively recently the Clubman phenomenon, a third force in many counties, was excluded from the narratives of the Civil Wars. 'Nothing to do with the world's first great Revolution'[2] The sort of valiant localism manifested by the Clubmen is, I am sure, true of the land mass, 'The continent' we now accept as Europe. It is certainly still true of Italy, and probably of Germany as well. Because of much more fragmentary alliances and identities, there have always been bits of what is now called Britain in Europe, and not just because, as Sir Humphrey once put it, we have to be there to cause trouble. That is why everyone was there, one of the success stories of the western world.

Like so many of the terms and concepts on which the historian now relies, the notion of Europe as a cultural identity, even an agent at large, was partially a creature of polemical debate and is now sustained, explored and adapted largely by political imperatives. If asked to date its beginnings, I'd be hesitant to go much beyond the French Revolution.

The early stages of the Revolution were seen from England as a French emulation of what England had done in 1688, an assimilation of the alien to the familiar. But it was more than this; Richard Price's emphatic sermon on the subject went so far as to claim that the French were only completing the work that had been left undone by the English revolutionary settlement of a hundred years earlier. This was close to suggesting a common project of political civilisation.[3] As a fear of the previous century's civil wars being re-opened began to increase, however, Edmund Burke replied, fighting sermonic fire with doses of brimstone. In the *Reflections* he provided a dramatised polemic designed to underscore how much was being destroyed by the forces of barbarism the French had unleashed. Burke, a man for whom hyperbole was always an idiom of understatement, thus had a rhetorical or ideological interest in projecting a myth of cohesive European civilisation under threat no less than Price saw it as being advanced. For Burke, as a corollary of the danger of destruction, it was the duty of Britain, a legatee of that portentous inheritance, to stand firm. On either side, what was being inculcated through polemical exuberance was almost a sense of a shared movement of civilisation dramatically culminating in the present and to which, for example, Kant only added when he wrote, that the Revolution had been greeted with universal moral approval.[4] Even if here, universal might too harshly be translated as Enlightenment Königsberg, the claim implicitly projects shared criteria of moral approbation suggesting a prior sense of civilisation, just as Price and Burke assumed universal standards of judgement projected from differing senses of Englishness. Such diametrically opposed affirmations of a sense of European/ English/ British civilisation are not necessarily disinterested bits of evidence for its obvious independent pre-existence. They may have been intimations of a need to create or at least consolidate it. Such writers, in short, projected a contemporary sense of civilisation backwards in order to give depth, significance and urgency to their political hopes and fears for the future.

But the one thing that we can be sure of as arising from the Revolutionary period was a distinctive political vocabulary which became as English and British as it was European. As I have argued elsewhere, it is the projection of this post-Revolutionary semantic structure back into a world that had neither its terms nor their equivalents, that has had a massively anachronising effect on the study of early modern political discourse.[5] I will only suggest here that in this process of projecting our own semantic world of liberalism, individualism, radicalism, left, right and so forth, we can also take notions of Britain and Europe too far.

European civilisation, certainly as it is now often imagined and hoped for, is a child born by fear out of massaged past, and Britain has a similar pedigree. As Denys Hay has demonstrated, until around the fifteenth century Europe was little more than a cartographic expression.[6] The largest unit in which people lived as members of a civilisation was Christendom, and Britain and England were unequivocally part of it. Local senses of culture, distinctiveness, legitimacy were all informed by a sense of being Roman and Christian, and it is simply wrong, though undeniably convenient, to see this sense terminating with what we now call the Middle Ages, an era duly to be superseded by the Renaissance and the Modern world. That particular set of related epochal terms is part of the problem of projection. The Middle Ages/ Renaissance/ Modernity grouping comes together only with the French post-revolutionary nationalist Michelet, again for at most quasi-historical reasons. They are still only of ambivalent historiographical use.[7] When, for example, Machiavelli raised his head to consider the politics of his world beyond his beloved *patria*, Florence rather than Italy, he wrote not of Europe but of Christian states and republics, and was reflecting on the sorry state of Christendom.[8] When later Thomas Hobbes surveyed the ruinous scene in the aftermath of the Reformation's wars of religion, he too wrote in terms of the crises of Christendom.[9]

Christendom extended forward more vibrantly and pervasively than we often think. Only gradually, unevenly, during the eighteenth century did it become restricted to the geographical space of continental Europe, and then become equated for some, via a commitment to a republic of letters, with a notion of Europe. Thus we do additional disservice by the retrospective extension a European cultural identity to occlude or replace that earlier sense of civilisation. Certainly, if the 'Idea' of Europe is extended back almost to the Rape and the Bull, as by Denis de Rougemont and in some moods J. M. Roberts, we will, of course, see the whole and much theorised articulation of a sense of Christendom as really an expression of something else, namely European culture, hypostatised, latent like Grendel emerging from his lair, gradually becoming more modern: like us, with us and about our future.[10] To process the past thus is myth-making on a grandly whiggish scale.[11] But that, of course, is the point; heritage not history. Yet such diachronic Eurocentrism, the manufacture of a European tradition and its placement into, or even beyond, the crumbling resilience of Christendom is hardly a unique phenomenon. It only exemplifies a more widespread need to symbolise present values and inscribe a privileged vision of the future on what is left of the past.

Ernest Gellner, descanting upon Eli Kedourie, has remarked that it is nationalism that invents nations;[12] as Eric Hobsbawn has also pointedly argued, nationalism has additionally been a creative form of governmental control once the nations have been invented.[13] Abstracting from the themes explored by such writers, one can suggest two complementary processes of political invention at work. Spatially, there is the need to identify aliens, enemies and sundry forms of the Other to give a sense of distinctiveness. In this way, denigration is often a means of asserting, making (not discovering or 'finding') an identity. This is why the rhetoric of 'searching' for an identity (literally a confused enterprise) is often code for denigrating an uncomfortably proximate 'other'. Temporally, there is the need to co-opt an exemplary heritage to provide a lien on legitimacy, to illustrate contemporary fears, values and aspirations and to ward off not just political foes, but any lurking subversive sense that there may be no trajectory to human affairs at all.

In plotting a grand European tour back into the pasts of various continental cultures we are no more than donning the historiographical clothes of the nineteenth-century nation makers, who like J. R. Green and Arthur Freeman and M. H. Carré after the second world war, began their histories of England in the vicinity of Rome.[14] As no doubt part of the motivation behind the invention of Europe has been to create something that will transcend the nastiness of nationalist politics, my point is not a carping one. The Union may be a consummation to be wished, albeit with the sustenance of myth.

Rather, my point, historiographically speaking, is that Europe is altogether a more problematic and elusive cultural category than we might think. And for good or ill, this is itself something which may be exploited in process working through the contentious issues surrounding future membership of the EU. The mythic image has had a distinctly western emphasis, seeming to subsume or leave vaguely on its eastern almost Asian margins societies now wanting to stake a claim to European identity. A similarly occluded sense of contingency holds for the notion of Britain and indeed even England, which as Alistair McLachlan has argued, is too easily construed as a given in accounts of its past.[15]

Most broadly, for a long time Britain, Great Britain, like Europe, was a geographical expression. England certainly has a more autochthonous identity because by the fifteenth and sixteenth centuries it had a relatively cohesive administration and legal framework and more dialect than language diversity; but its extent was still marginally uncertain. And the content given to the evocation of England and Englishness might well shift with the alien against which it was measured. The notion of a foreigner in early modern English was particularly extensive, as was that of an 'alien'. The former might well refer to someone from a neighbouring parish, the latter indiscriminately label someone from across the county border, river or the sea.[16]

Britain as a political entity, but certainly not as a cultural identity, is largely a seventeenth century problem, partly brought about by a multi-staged and variable unity of distinct kingdoms.[17] It was England's dominance of the British Isles, after the foreign invasion that opened the civil wars (Rangers 7, Oxford United nil) that allowed England to be construed and projected effectively as Britain by a process of homology, or what I have called subsumptive synonymity, a common process in the political semantics of the seventeenth century.[18] Expressed more symbolically, England's subsumption of the British Isles is the story of the transformation of Arbuthnot's satiric and pacific image of John Bull in 1712. Originally John was England, his sister Peg was Scotland.[19] Within 100 years, he was bellicose Britain. And it is not a little embarrassing to note that, until recently, there were some English historians who could use England and Britain interchangeably for earlier times - A. L. Rowse and, more recently, Christopher Hill have shown as elegiac a grasp of geography as John of Gaunt with his sceptred Isle girt by sea.[20]

I suspect that once the identities of Scotland and Wales, having helped give a shape to Englishness, had become part of the expanded Englishness of Great Britain, there may have been a greater emphasis on the delineating need for a continental other, generally a geographical Europe. Usually, however, the familiar foes and points of contrast are more precise, a Spain, Holland or France, with Europe, when it is mentioned, having an arbitrary, local and variable content.

Ranke's *History of England in the Seventeenth Century* is a substantial exception, but generally, one is hard pressed to see a sustained continental context for accounts of seventeenth-century England in nineteenth and twentieth century historiography of England/Britain.[21] It is not, however, the absence of the European continent that is as significant as its typical status. It appears characteristically as background, appendage or problem. Britain's involvement, frequent enough, is a matter of intervention in the markedly external. The European continent is significant, as a theatre, a means of showing Britain's status and significance. Nineteenth and twentieth-century school text books have exhibited these lineaments of relationship most extremely, but in seeking to provide a consolidating political education, they only firmed up the lines taken from several generations of scholarship.[22]

There is nothing unique in this. Peter Parley's World History for children, portrays every episode from the creation in 6004BC as a series of prefaces to the revolution of 1776, the significance of which is ratified by the addendum of Simon Bolivar's victories in South America.[23] The culmination of the sort of history I have in mind is the parodic bathos of *1066 and All That*.[24]

It is the kind of relationship between Britain and Europe entailed by such histories, even in their more sophisticated forms, that historians such as John Reeve have so strongly reacted against.[25] It is not that Europe simply looms larger in the background. And the change is not, principally, I think, because of the European Community. It is not to be explained, as it were, in terms of the culturally broadening consequences of the English seeking holidays on the Costa del Chips. Neither is it the result of beer hunting in Bruges (the truth will out).

I want to suggest, rather, that post-war revisionism encouraged a qualitatively significant shift of perspective. From being seen as problem, appendage or background, Europe has become a context for understanding the early modern British Isles. By background I denote incidental surroundings, or backdrop to one's focus; by context I refer to any such surroundings which are held to be of direct explanatory significance, and so as essential to understanding a given identity.

It must be accepted that 'revisionism', another historiographical term taken over from political and ideological debate, is a dubious term. Even in the present limited context it refers to no cohesive movement but is, as Glenn Burgess has put it, more of an amorphous generational trend, an intensification of a conventional enough feature of academic discourse, the critical appraisal of what is seen as orthodox.[26] Such qualifications notwithstanding, around the 1960s something does begin to take shape as an increasingly focussed reaction against strong, indeed orthodox, historiographical traditions formed in the nineteenth century. These traditions had been both patriotic and teleological, patriotic in the strong sense of celebrating the enduring value of a national identity and in the weaker one which perceived a Britain or England playing a part on a wider stage as it lead the way to modernity. To this trajectory had been attached structural, largely Marxist explanatory models and eschatologies.[27] Roughly by the Second World War the important questions seemed to be (to put the matter a trifle sharply) whether the culmination of the British story lay in a constitutional democracy (a good thing), a capitalist industrial empire (a bad if necessary stage of a thing), or a little bit of both (a problematic thing). Even in a weak sense, then, patriotic historiography and its Marxist variants had been whiggish and more generally anachronistic. On all sides, if the story was not about us and where we were going, it was not worth telling.

The materials on which such histories were based had been hugely augmented during the nineteenth century and had become more useable with the development of archives, libraries and a class of professional archivists to organise them.[28] In this respect, Britain was not unique, or indeed even in the historiographical vanguard, which should alert us to the fact that the unearthing of such materials was not merely serendipitous. It was part of the "underlabouring" process of nation-building and heritage creation to which I have already referred.

It had, however, the unintended consequence of unleashing a huge diversity of primary sources which constantly threatened to undermine the traditional exemplum history (celebratory or tragic) political élites and would be political élites wanted told. The sheer wealth of the past made it increasingly confusing and contentious. Similarly, there developed a distinct sense of historiographical identity. History writing, more and more in the hands of professionals (such F. W. Maitland, Sir Charles Firth, S. M. Gardiner), began to assert, and philosophers (most notably F. H. Bradley and Wilhelm Dilthey) to theorise, doctrines of intellectual responsibility beyond or besides the traditional moral requirements of exemplum history in which, to use Vosius' expression, the past was 'philosophy teaching by examples', and the historian a hand-maid to morality.[29] In its place was put an ideal of disinterested critical scholarship, the study of the past for its own sake, with an overriding emphasis on scrupulously detailed attention to the evidence in order to avoid anachronistic accounts of it.

Twentieth century historiography, certainly that of the British Civil War period, has seen a continuingly tensile relationship between the requirements of traditional exemplum history, which have given the history of England/Britain its whiggish, patriotic and Marxist shapes, and newer historicist idioms and expectations, which have provided the rationale for periodic revisionism. To put it a little unfairly, whiggish exemplum history has provided the framework around which histories of England/Britain can be constructed; historicism the means of criticising the attempts of others to do the same thing. We can see something of this tension in the early stages of historiographical professionalisation. Arthur Freeman quite correctly criticised George Grote's account of Athenian politics for its construal of the agora in terms of parliamentary party divisions; yet he saw the essence of Victorian England in the age of Edward I and was even apt to find the rudiments of national identity in pre-conquest England.[30] More immediately, the nub of the difference between Geoffrey Elton and his *bête noir* J. E. Neale, was this: Elton brought the full armoury of historicist criticism to Neale's thesis that Queen Elizabeth was the heroic moderniser of Britain, only to dethrone and replace her with the even earlier Thomas Cromwell and his modernising 'bureaucratic' revolution.[31] Similarly, as Alistair McLachlan has recently pointed out, both Elton and E. P. Thompson, unlikely passengers in the same railway carriage, shared a belief that some sort of reified Englishness was a motor for history, and a history of reverberating significance.[32] It is this which is so often seen to have been played out on the European stage, especially in historiography of the more popular sort, by writers such as G. M. Trevelyan and Sir Winston Churchill, and Sir Arthur Bryant.

Over the last thirty years the historicist strand of early modern historiography has become clearly, if only academically dominant. This is not a claim that historiography is now properly autonomous and politically sanitised, and indeed, like any history, it remains subject to the unintended consequences of political usage. My point is that the emphasis on detail, particularity, an enhanced suspicion of teleological narratives and a much greater caution in the application of borrowed social theories, all underwritten by a systematic desire to avoid anachronism, have altered the relationship of Europe to England and Britain. To repeat, continental Europe is now less backdrop, problem or stage set, than necessary context, and that too is becoming more particularised.

Part of the explanation lies in the shift from printed to manuscript materials from the 1950s, both in intellectual and general political history. This itself may have something of a social explanation. With the story of

Britain or England and its civil wars so well and often told, what were increasing numbers of students going to work on? Many were shunted to the unexplored micro-level of county history, and so once again newly available evidence upset old pictures. England, let alone Britain, could cease to look like a cohesive historical entity. The printed word is apt to suggest a much broader audience than the manuscript, which can give a very different sense of what people thought important, or what they thought they belonged to. Once entrenched in the machinations of the Cheshire gentry, Europe is unlikely to appear only as a dichotomised Other, let alone a problem for England. The foreigner is likely to be the man from northern Shropshire. The explanatory or motivational power of class allegiance and the principles of sovereignty alike become elusive in a turmoil apparently explicable in simpler if less edifying terms. The men of Myddle in Shropshire seemed to have gone with the first army to arrive in their village.[33] So the status of the civil wars has slipped from being a monument marking European advance to a mess of miscalculation and uncertainly contingent, even minimal, outcomes, and the whole more clearly tied to earlier religious wars than the shape of things to come.

The intellectual, especially political intellectual history of the period tells a similar story perhaps more clearly. The history of political thought, now accepted as one of the most invented of traditions, was beginning to be revealed as of little explanatory value for most thinkers routinely placed in it by twentieth-century political theorists. Yet the attempt to provide an improved context, initially for John Locke, led relentlessly away from England or English political thought to Holland and back to Reformation France.[34] It has since led to the localised politics of London.[35] Holland was important because it was a safe haven for Locke and his co-religionists when they had failed to topple a crypto-Catholic King. Locke's world was still crumbling Christendom. Algernon Sidney, who lost his head in 1683, had earlier been one of those important republican figures who had urged a formal joint sovereignty, that is a single state of Holland and England (and possibly Scotland) to save Christendom.[36] The materials now available on Sidney make it impossible to contain him within the confines of a concept of England. As Jonathan Scott has shown at length, he was a true and energetic cosmopolitan fighting for what was left of reformed Christendom, taking his republicanism from Florence and ancient Rome and his experience as a diplomat in Holland.[37]

So, too, with that ornament of the Parisian intellectual establishment Thomas Hobbes:- his major work was written in France and translated into Latin at the request of an intellectual following on the continent, where arguably he was better understood.[38] It is no coincidence that the modern rediscovery of Hobbes took place largely in Weimar Germany. Perhaps the most synoptic illustration of the shift can be found in the work of John Pocock. The first version of his *Ancient Constitution and the Feudal Law* was published in 1957, during the earliest stages of the revisionism I am concerned with. Pocock virtually relied upon a notion of the common law mind which he took to distinguish England from the continent. When he came to revise the earlier work, he accepted that this was itself in need of some revision.[39] Recently a comparative ancient constitution project was established on a Hull-Budapest axis.[40]

How significant has this shift of emphasis been? It has not been the discovery of a European culture; the sense of élite cosmopolitan culture was of educated Christendom. Instead, Europe as context has been a matter of seeking more necessary and specific discursive networks and localities. And Britain may be contracting to the recent past in which its formation is itself an illustration of historical contingency. As Kenneth Morgan has remarked of the *Oxford Illustrated History of Britain* (beginning conventionally enough with Rome), there is no simple story to be told, no emerging or underlying character, this is not the world of *1066 and all that*.[41] In effect, we have just all the contradictions you would expect of any long inhabited land mass, fascinating to the historian, less easily packaged for the use of the politician.

But overall we see a shift of emphasis, not a total departure. Historiography continues to exhibit a variable balance of political and historiographical propensities, sometimes the former encoded in the latter, as when Colin Davis tried to deconstruct the Ranters, that mythic vanguard of the Old English Revolution, only to find himself accused by a member of the Old Left of being a Thatcherite.[42] He replied with talk of gulags. In the light of such a controversy, it might be tempting to claim some convenient deep political structure for all revisionism. This, however, is no more helpful than to claim for it the status of a fixed doctrinal and purely historiographical school, rejecting the orthodoxy of the Other.[43] Socialists such as Willie Lamont, Liberal Democrats such as Conrad Russell, Tories such as Jonathan Clark can all wear the dubious revisionist hat to no detriment to their historical seriousness and standing. Each in different ways marks the intensification of the historicist momentum which must in some sense always be revisionist. So, if looked at merely politically, the whole phenomenon quivers on the edge of dissipation, fragmenting into revisionists post, present and proto. Nevertheless, in the present context, there is something that differentiates revisionist propensities from the many who have written copiously on England, Britain and Europe. It is the willingness above all else to evoke anachronism as a criterion of historiographical demarcation and to reject explanations eschewing inconvenient detail. What has been created is a well entrenched and heavily invested Maginot line against the exemplary energies that have traditionally sought to assimilate past to present for the purpose of offering an image of the future. Naturally, those more concerned with the future of Britain and Europe than with the fragmented past of Christendom and its myriad sub-communities will outflank it, for revisionist historiography, like the disciplined French army, has its limits. The revisionist emphasis on locality and contingency can hardly be expected to be immune from the massed bands of argument through heritage. This is especially so as, to repeat, historical argument of any sort may well provide the raw materials for the enrichment or re-working of a people's sense of its heritage. Such contingencies will remain at play regardless of whether revisionism is free of political motivation. Nevertheless, Samson's foxes, Britain and Europe, are still, as it were, tied together in the fields of Flanders: the historiographical barrier which can readily be seen to stand against the political imperatives of the mythic projection of Europe, has at the same time undermined the patriotic image of England or Britain strutting the European stage on its way to world domination before the First World War when, to quote *1066 and all That*, 'America became Top Nation and history came to a .'[44]

Notes

1   The direct route from England to Bruges is still by ferry from Hull. For a sense of the historic linguistic complexity of the region see C.A.J. Armstrong, 'The Language Question in the Low Countries: The choice of French or Dutch by the Dukes of Burgundy and their Administration', in J. Hale, R. Highfield and B. Smalley eds., *Europe in the Late Middle Ages*, (London: Faber, 1965), pp. 386-409.

2. On the Clubmen and their significance see J.B. Morrill, *The Revolt of the Provinces: Radicals and Conservatives in the English Revolution* (London, 1976).
3. Richard Price, *A Discourse on the Love of Our Country* (1789), pp. 39ff, 49ff.
4. Immanuel Kant, 'The Contest of the Faculties', in *Political Writings*, ed. H. Reiss, trans. H.B. Nisbet (Cambridge: 1991 edn), p. 182.
5. Conal Condren, *The Language of Politics in Seventeenth-Century England* (London, 1994), ch.5.
6. Denys Hay, *Europe The Emergence of an Idea* (Edinburgh, 1955).
7. Conal Condren, 'The Renaissance as Metaphor: Some Significant Aspects of the Obvious', *Parergon* n.s. 9 (1989), pp. 91ff.
8. N. Machiavelli, *Discorsi*, in *Il Principe e Discorsi* (Milan, 1973 edn), I. 12, p. 164: '...gli stati e le republiche cristiane...'
9. Thomas Hobbes, *Correspondence*, ed. Noel Malcolm, 2 vols. (Oxford, 1994), letter 37 'To William Cavendish'(1641), 1. p. 120.
10. J.M. Roberts, *A History of Europe* (Oxford, 1996). Initial caution, p. xi and the notion of peoples being in Europe, p. 9 gives way to the ancient Greeks among others being Europeans, p. 23.
11. Denis de Rougemont, *The Idea of Europe*, trans. N. Guterman (New York, 1966), where, to give but one example, Dante's vision of Christendom uniting the world under the Holy Roman Emperor in *De monarchia* is seen as an early plan for European union.
12. E. Gellner, *Nations and Nationalism* (Oxford, 1983); E. Kedouri, *Nationalism* (London, 1962), both at length.
13. E. Hobsbawm, *Nations and Nationalism since 1780,:Programme, Myth, Reality* (Cambridge, 1990).
14. J.R. Green, *A Short History of the English People* (London, 1874), and numerous editions thereafter; A. A. Freeman, 'The Continuity of English History', in *Historical Essays*, first series, (London, 1875) pp. 40ff; M. H. Carré, *Phases of Thought in England* (Oxford, 1949), esp. Introduction.
15. Alistair McLachlan, 'Patriotic Scripture: The Making and Unmaking of English National Identity', *Parergon*, 14 (1996), pp. 1ff., for a fine discussion.
16. Ian Archer, *The Pursuit of Stability: Social Relations in Elizabethan London* (Cambridge, 1991), pp. 131-40.
17. Conrad Russell, *The Causes of the English Civil Wars* (Oxford, 1990), ch.2.
18. *The Language of Politics*, pp. 57-8.

19 John Arbuthnot, *The History of John Bull* (1712), eds. Alan W. Bower and Robert A. Erickson (Oxford, 1976).
20 A. L. Rowse, *The Spirit of English History* (London, 1943); Christopher Hill, 'The Place of the Seventeenth Century Revolution in English history', in S.N. Mukherjee and J.O. Ward, eds., *Revolution as History* (Sydney, 1989), p. 24-5.
21 The point is well made by Jonathan Scott, 'The Peace of Silence: Thucydides and the English Civil War' in M. Fairburn and W. Oliver eds., *The Certainty of Doubt: Tributes to Peter Munz* (Wellington, 1996), p.91.
22 Valerie Chancellor, *History for their Masters, Opinion in the English History Textbook, 1800-1914* (Bath, 1970), lists 150 texts published between 1850 and 1914, pp. 143ff.
23 *Peter Parley's Method of Telling About the History of the World to Children* (Hartford, Conn., 1832).
24 W. E. Sellar and R.J Yeatman, *1066 and All That* (London, 1930, 1975 edn cited). It should be noted that this work is itself part of a tradition of comic and parodic history. But whereas works like Thomas Wright's *Charicature History of the Georges* (London, 1867) and Gilbert A'Beckett's *The Comic History of England* (London, nd. c1870) make fun of the subjects through comic evidence or elaborate frivolously on well known stories, Sellar and Yeatman satirise the historiography much more explicitly.
25 John Reeve, *Charles I and the Road to Personal Rule* (Cambridge, 1989), Introduction & ch. 9; 'The Politics of War Finance in an Age of Confessional Strife: A Comparative Anglo-European View', *Parergon* n.s. 14 (1996), pp. 85ff.
26 Glenn Burgess, 'On Revisionism: An Analysis of Early Stuart Historiography in the 1970s and 1980s', *The Historical Journal*, 33, 3 (1990) p. 617.
27 The collapse of this historiographical marriage of convenience and more specifically of the Marxist/Communist appropriation of whig traditions of political history, is finely charted by Alistair McLachlan, *The Rise and Fall of Revolutionary England: An Essay on the Fabrication of Seventeenth-Century History* (London: 1996).
28 Doris S. Goldstein, 'The Professionalisation of History in Britain in the late Nineteenth and early Twentieth Centuries' *Storia della storiografia*, 3 (1983), p. 3ff.

29   G. H. Nadel, 'The Philosophy of History before Historicism', in G. H. Nadel ed., *Studies in the Philosophy of History: Selected Essays from History and Theory* (New York, 1965) pp. 49ff; Vosius is quoted p. 67-8.

30   Arthur Freeman, 'The Athenian Democracy', *Historical Essays*, Second Series (London, 1880) p 154-5; cf 'The Continuity of English History', p. 40ff.

31   For some discussion of the tensions between traditional rhetorical history and professional historiography with especial reference to Elton, see Conal Condren, 'From Premise to Conclusion: Some Comments on Professional History and the incubus of Rhetorical Historiography', *Parergon* n..s., 6 (1988) pp.5 ff.

32   McLachlan, 'Patriotic Scripture', p.7.

33   Richard Gough, *The History of Myddle* ed. David Hay (Harmondsworth, 1981).

34   John Locke, *Two Treatises of Government* ed. Peter Laslett (Cambridge, 1960), Introduction.

35   Jonathan Scott, 'The Law of War: Grotius, Sidney, Locke and the Political Theory of Rebellion', *History of Political Thought*, 13, 4 (1992).

36   Jonathan Scott, *Algernon Sidney and the English Republic, 1623-77* (Cambridge, 1988) chs.6 & 8.

37   Scott, *Ibid.* and *Algernon Sidney and the Restoration Crisis, 1677-83* (Cambridge, 1991), at length.

38   Thomas Hobbes, *Correspondence*, 1, letter 77: Abraham du Prat to Hobbes, March/April 1656, and Noel Malcolm's comments, pp. xxxi-ii.

39   J.G.A. Pocock. *The Ancient Constitution and the Feudal Law: A Re-Issue with a Retrospect* (Cambridge,1987) p. xii & 255ff.

40   My thanks to Dr.Glenn Burgess for informing me of this.

41   Kenneth Morgan ed. *The Oxford Illustrated History of Britain* (Oxford, 1984), p. vi.

42   J.C. Davis, *Fear, Myth and History* (Cambridge, 1986); E. P. Thompson's review appeared in *The London Review of Books*, 9. vii.1987, pp. 9-10, with the controversy running on for several more weeks. To complicate matters, Davis was not abandoning explanatory models which might help give a clearer definition to the notion of revisionism, but using a social psychological one to subvert a Marxist one. For a more balanced assessment of Davis than Thompson was able to offer, see G. E. Aylmer, 'Did the Ranters Exist', *Past and Present*, 117 (1987), pp. 208-19; and Iain Hampsher-Monk, Review, in *History of Political Thought*, 8 (1987), pp. 553-57.

43 By one of those ironies of history, it is the legitimising effect of this sort of claim that has allowed its disingenuous appropriation by Holocaust revisionists. Once 'revisionism' has become historiographically legitimate it can become a cloak for a purely political enterprise.
44 Sellar and Yeatman, *1066*, ch.62 'A Bad Thing', p. 123.

3 Enlightenment, Cosmopolitanism and Nationalism

JOHN GASCOIGNE

'Storm on Channel, Continent cut off' — thus the nineteenth-century *Times* is supposed to have dismissed Europe as an outlining appendage of the British archipelago. But as the Chunnel now physically links Britain and Europe historians have become more preoccupied with the less tangible but nonetheless very real ties that once joined Britain to Europe and which still play a part in fostering a sense of a common European civilisation. The theme of this paper is, then, the way in which in the eighteenth century such common links survived the growth of a strong sense of a united *British* (as opposed to English, Scottish, Welsh or Irish) identity encapsulated in the growing prevalence of such national icons as the figure of John Bull or the boisterous rendition of that eighteenth-century hymn of national pride, *Rule Britannia, Britannia rules the waves*.

Behind the growth of such eighteenth-century patriotism (which has been recently examined by a number of historians notably Colley[1] and Wilson[2]) lay the increasing success of Britain in war and commerce for, in that age of mercantilism, the two were closely linked. Britain which, since the end of the Middle Ages had generally sought to avoid Continental entanglements, had, in the late seventeenth century, once again entered the cockpit of European Great Power conflict. Under the leadership of its foreign ruler, William III, Britain in the late seventeenth century and early eighteenth century began its involvement in a series of wars prompted by fear of French domination of the Continent. The Treaty of Utrecht in 1713 marked the immediate and largely successful end of the British goal of keeping in check the expansionist ambitions of Louis XIV but the conflict with France in one form or another rumbled on for most of the long eighteenth century and this 'Second Hundred Years War' did not really come to a definitive end until the defeat of Napoleon at Waterloo in 1815. Throughout much of this period, of course, Britain was ruled by the House of Hanover which brought with it contact with another area of Europe, the German lands,[3] and the sort of intellectual interchange which in the late eighteenth-century centred around the University of Göttingen, an institution which helped to redefine the purposes of the university.

For along with conflict with France went increasing engagement with its civilisation. As French replaced Latin as the *lingua franca* of European civilisation so, too, the English had to become more versed in the language and manners of the French and the Europeans more generally — especially as English was barely known in France until after 1715.[4] With the calming of the religious passions unleashed by the Reformation and still strong in the age of the Religious Wars of the seventeenth century went a growing openness to largely Catholic Europe. One manifest symptom of this was the growing prevalence of the practice of the Grand Tour as a form of elite education. The large number of well-born young travellers who brought back to England an appreciation of Continental art, manners, dress and even cooking provided a growing reservoir of understanding and even sympathy for Continental civilisation and some sense of a common European identity which embraced the British Isles.[5] By the end of the century Edmund Burke, that determined foe of the French Revolution, could nonetheless remark in his *Letters on the Regicide Peace* (1796) on the extent to which Europe possessed 'a system of manners and education that was nearly similar to all in this quarter of the globe' such that 'no citizen of Europe could be altogether an exile in any part of it'. Consequently, he continued, 'when a man travelled...from his own country, he never felt himself quite abroad'.[6]

Reciprocally, the French took an increasing interest in the English — particularly those French like the *philosophes*, Voltaire and Montesquieu who were looking for an alternative to the system of royal absolutism. It was an indication of a growing recognition that the cause of Enlightenment transcended national boundaries. For, as Gibbon put it: 'It is the duty of the patriot to prefer and promote the exclusive interest and glory of his native country but a philosopher must be permitted to enlarge his views and to consider Europe as one great Republic whose various inhabitants have attained almost the same level of politeness and civilisation'.[7] For the Enlightenment was a movement which sought to emphasise the cosmopolitan elements of European civilisation in the face of a growing trend towards the consolidation of state structures. One of the central endeavours of the Enlightenment was, where possible, to analyse the workings of society in the detached spirit of disinterested enquiry which had been so conspicuously successful in the natural sciences. In theory, then, the true Enlightenment thinker should be willing to stand back from his (or, more rarely, and more probably in France than Britain, her) own society and national loyalties to arrive at a better understanding of both its strengths and weaknesses through a sympathetic comparison with other societies and cultures. Hence the pioneering sociologist, Montesquieu, could claim that he was 'human of necessity' but 'French by accident'.[8] Ultimately, too, the Enlightenment's emphasis on universal laws of nature and a form of reason which transcended national and cultural divides tended to emphasise the points of similarity rather than the distinctiveness between different countries.

Such intellectual exchanges help to explain the fact that until the great watershed of the French Revolution the ongoing conflict with France lacked the ideological fervour of former ages despite the fact that hostile stereotypes of the French as a race of priest-ridden, downtrodden, wooden-shoe wearing, garlic-eating foreigners remained strong.[9] And, despite all this engrained hostility, by the late eighteenth century the mercantilist orthodoxy that one country's prosperity must be purchased by another country's impoverishment for the economy was a cake of fixed size began to soften under both the assault of the early political economists and, more compellingly, as a consequence of accumulated observation and experience. David Hume, for example, recognised that Europe was beginning to be bound together by common commercial ties — hence his claim that 'I shall venture to acknowledge, that, not only as a man, but as a BRITISH subject, I pray for the flourishing commerce of GERMANY, SPAIN, ITALY, and even FRANCE itself. I am at least certain that GREAT BRITAIN, and all those nations, would flourish more did their sovereigns and their ministers adopt such enlarged and benevolent sentiments towards each other'.[10] Such sentiments achieved some measure of practical political realisation with the Anglo-French commercial treaty of 1786 which lowered the tariff wall between the two countries out of a recognition that both could benefit from the freer passage of trade. Its successful completion led Pitt to urge his countrymen to abandon the belief 'that any nation could be unalterably the enemy of another'.[11] Ironically, within a few years the French Revolution with its potent challenge to the values and institutions on which old regime societies — including Britain — rested was largely to undo such attempts to bury the ancient conflict between Britain and France to an end.

But even during the period of the French Revolution the conviction that Britain and France belonged to a common civilisation was still kept alive with appeals to the ideal of a Republic of Letters which transcended national boundaries and disputes between nations. This notion of a Republic of Letters embodied in partially secularised form the older concept of a united Christendom which transcended national and regional boundaries by maintaining a common faith and civilisation in the face of dynastic conflict. Like the ideal of Christendom, too, it was strengthened by the ties of aristocratic kinship and common culture which linked together the different European states. After the devastation wrought by the wars of the seventeenth century engendered by a powerful brew of dynastic, religious and civil conflict between centralising monarchs and aristocratic intrigue the notion of a Republic of Letters offered some consolation to an intellectual elite weary of strife.[12] It provided some reaffirmation of a common civilisation which maintained some of the higher ideals which all Europeans could share irrespective of their political or religious affiliation.

As the common medium of Latin declined it also helped to create a sense that European intellectuals shared a common language of ideas if not a literal language and that the use of a widespread language such as French could transcend national purposes. Not that all citizens of the Republic of Letters were always in happy accord, for one of its roles came to be to provide common ground, in the form of journals or pamphlet literature, on which to conduct scholarly battles in which personal and intellectual grievances were inseparably intertangled. Such rivalries continued unabated into the eighteenth century when d'Alembert in his 'Reflections on the present state of the Republic of Letters' described the citizens of this putative republic 'fight[ing] over glory just as men without government or laws fight over acorns'.[13]

The ideals of the Enlightenment helped to maintain the cosmopolitan character of the Republic of Letters with the addition of a sense of social and political engagement which was often foreign to the scholarly *érudits* of the seventeenth century. Inevitably, however, such a sense of engagement often involved compromising international ideals for national ends — as is evident if one looks at the actions of Joseph Banks, President of the Royal Society from 1778 until his death in 1820.[14] Like Voltaire and Diderot, who had to balance their international sympathies with the need to win over individual would-be enlightened monarchs, so, too, Joseph Banks sought to combine his goal of contributing to a cosmopolitan world of science with his strong sense of British patriotism. As one of his obituarists remarked of him, though 'warm with national patriotism, Sir Joseph still considered himself a citizen of the world in the cause of science'.[15]

Along with Banks's endeavours to keep open the lines of scientific communication between France and Britain even while the two countries were at war went his activity in attempting to secure the release of men of science caught up in the toils of war. His most celebrated achievement in this regard was his successful intervention on behalf of the eminent geologist, Déodat de Dolomieu, who, after accompanying Napoleon to Egypt, was captured and held prisoner by the Court of Naples. His release in 1801 was largely due to the support of the British government urged on by members of the Royal Society led by its President. In his effusive letter of thanks Dolomieu linked Banks's actions with the 'enlightenment and philosophy disseminated by' the Royal Society which fostered loyalties which transcended national differences by 'mak[ing] common to all nations that blessed brotherly love which softens all political convulsions'[16] — in short that science and learning promoted fellow feeling within the Republic of Letters. When Banks acted as President of the Royal Society he was, of course, anxious to do all that he could to put science at the service of the British State but he was also aware of the importance of fostering an international audience for the Royal Society's deliberations. It was a tension which typified the situation of the Republic of Letters as it became more and more integrated with the world of the academies over the course of the eighteenth century and, as a consequence, its international loyalties were overshadowed by national interests. Scientific advance depended on the flow of information across national boundaries and so national interest and allegiance to a cosmopolitan Republic of Letters could coincide in linking British science with its larger European (and, in particular, French) community of fellow specialists.

The Royal Society, like other European scientific academies, from its beginnings consciously linked itself with a European-wide network of journals, corresponding fellows and international visitors which helped to make the academies natural custodians of the ideal of a cosmopolitan Republic of Letters. It was to this cosmopolitan world, which was linked together by the academies, that the citizens of the Republic of Letters looked for the rewards of prestige and fame. As the editor of the *Histoire de la République des Lettres en France* wrote in 1780 of the Republic of Letters: 'It is the empire of talent and of thought. The academies are its tribunals; people distinguished by their talents are its dignitaries'.[17] In this cosmopolitan world, which was largely held together by the academies, Banks, the longest serving of all Presidents of the Royal Society, naturally became a major figure. Existing academies recruited his good offices by making him an affiliate while new academies looked to him to help build up their legitimacy as fledgling members of the Republic of Letters. By his death in 1820 he was a member of some fifty foreign academies.

During the period of the Revolutionary Wars Banks continued to advance the claim that the world of science and learning could be regarded as a realm apart from that inhabited by warring nations. Thus a letter of 1802 to the French commissioner for dealing with prisoners-of war invoked the full rhetorical force of the language of the Republic of Letters: 'I agree with you Sir wholly, the cooperation of those employd in enlarging the Limits of human knowledge ought not to be interrupted by the enmity of their respective nations, the armistice of science should...be perpetual'[18] — a reference to the Peace of Amiens. Such fine sentiments were reciprocated from the French side later that year when Banks was thanked for sending an Australian natural history specimen to the Muséum d'Histoire Naturelle with a tribute to the worth of the 'Republic of Letters and sciences' as 'the most perfect of republics'.[19]

The academies with their cosmopolitan connections were, then, the major repository of the belief in the Republic of Letters. A related area where the international claims of science could be recognised without too much strain on national loyalties was in relation to exploration. This applied particularly in relation to the exploration of the Pacific which gathered pace in the late eighteenth and early nineteenth centuries. Some measure of international co-operation in this area was encouraged by the fact that in the Pacific the prizes were not sufficiently glittering to tempt rival nations into war over new territory. Such exploration, with its acquisition of new knowledge about both nature and humanity, was seen as the embodiment of the Enlightenment particularly since the relatively pacific exploration of the Pacific was contrasted with the earlier, more manifestly brutal Spanish subjugation of the Americas.

But though the frontiers of the Republic of Letters were kept open during the Revolutionary Wars inevitably the length, cost and ideological ferocity of the wars meant that the British more and more defined themselves against the French and, by extension, against Europe more generally.[20] Britain went into the nineteenth century with its insularity in many ways renewed and the cosmpolitan values of the eighteenth-century Enlightenment and Republic of Letters attentuated. The growth of the second British Empire which meant increasing trade and cultural contact with lands outside Europe was a further brake on Continental connections as, too, was the renewed strength of Protestantism in its Evangelical form. The British military victory over the forces of the French Revolution and its economic victory as the first industrialised nation heightened British complacency and its sense that Europe had more to learn from it than *vice versa*. The unravelling in the twentieth century of the conditions that made the nineteenth century 'the British century' have, however, laid the foundations for Britain to recapture some of that sense of a common European identity which began to take form in the eighteenth century before being largely extinguished by the Revolutionary Wars.

Notes

1. L. Colley, *Britons. Forging the nation 1707-1837*, (New Haven: Yale University Press, 1992).
2. K. Wilson, *The sense of the people. Politics, culture and imperialism in England, 1715-85*. Cambridge: Cambridge University Press, 1995.
3. J. Black, 'The European idea and Britain 1688-1815', *History of European Ideas*, 17 (1993), pp.442-3.
4. G. Bonno, 'La culture et la civilisation britannique devant l'opinion française de la Paix d'Utrecht aux "Lettres Philosophiques" 1713-1734', *Transactions of the American Philosophical Society*, n.s. 38 (1948), p.2.
5. J. Black, *The British and the Grand Tour* (London: Croom Helm, 1985).
6. T. Schlereth, *The cosmopolitan ideal in Enlightenment thought. Its form and function in the ideas of Franklin, Hume, and Voltaire, 1694-1790* (Notre Dame: Notre Dame Press, 1977), p.2.
7. ibid., p. 47.
8. Hampson, *The Enlightenment*, p.155.
9. M. Duffy, '" The noisie, empty, fluttering French". English images of the French, 1689-1813', *History Today*, 32 (1982), pp.23-4.
10. P. Gay, *The Enlightenment. An interpretation*. Vol.2 *The science of freedom* (London: Wildwood House, 1973), p.359.
11. J.S. Bromley, 'Britain and Europe in the eighteenth century', *History*, 1981, p.409.
12. D. Goodman, *The Republic of Letters. A cultural history of the French Enlightenment* (Ithaca: Cornell University Press, 1994), p.2.
13. Daston, 'Nationalism and scientific neutrality under Napoleon' in T. Frängsmyr, J.L. Heilbron and R.E. Rider (eds), *The quantifying spirit in the eighteenth century*, Canton, MA: Science History Publications, 1990, p.180.
14. In this section on Banks I am drawing on some material from Chapter Six of my book, *Science in the service of empire. Joseph Banks, the British state and the uses of science in the age of revolution* (Cambridge: Cambridge University Press, 1998).
15. anon, 'Memoir of Sir Joseph Banks', *New Monthly Magazine*, 14 (1820), p.193.
16. G.De Beer, *The sciences were never at war* (Edinburgh, 1960), p.242, Dolomieu, [30 April 1801] [French].
17. ibid., p.367.

18 Sutro Library, San Francisco, France 1:28, 26 Jan 1802?, Banks to Otto.
19 British Library, Add. 8099:245, Faujas de St.Fond to Banks, Oct. 1802 [French].
20 Black, 'The European idea and Britain', pp.445, 454.

4 The Strange Case of British Music

ROGER COVELL

People who like to oppose the transience of war and politics with the lasting qualities of great creative achievements of an artistic kind are apt to be distressed by history's lesson that art tends to follow the flag - the flag, in this instance, standing for military conquest or commercial prosperity. The city states of Burgundian Flanders and of fifteenth century Italy were glorious artistically in the wake of flourishing economy and political ambition. Elizabethan and Jacobean England took decisive steps towards maritime dominance and political unity in a period marked in that country by literary, theatrical and musical excellence.

The only period in which English music of official, ceremonious or high art status could be thought of as setting the pace in Western Europe was in the wake of Henry V's conquests in the first half of the fifteenth century, when the 'English countenance' (*contenance angloise*), with its tunefulness and consistent preference for sweeter harmonies (thirds and sixths) than the previously dominant Continental style, secured the admiration of Franco-Flemish composers and formed the basis of what became the characteristic musical sound of the Renaissance of the fifteenth and sixteenth centuries. The essence of this development seems to have been that English music by Dunstable, Power and other composers travelled to the European continent under the direct patronage of the music-loving king and his brother, the Duke of Bedford, and that it had time to be heard as part of the baggage of a conquering military establishment and resident garrison. At other times, British warfare on the continent, usually conducted by expeditionary forces, did not establish any lasting ascendancy or influence of an artistic kind, though it has done so, Heidi Zogbaum is suggesting, in the domain of sport.

Apart from the circumstances favourable to its dissemination, this all-conquering English style of the earlier fifteenth century was not in itself a radical departure from a familiar pattern of relationships between the music of an island and that of a continent. It did not represent an advance in style on previous Continental developments in music but the persistence of what seems to have been a traditional English preference for consonant tunefulness, based on practices of improvised polyphony. This tradition seems to have been observed as operating in English music for at least three centuries, possibly much longer, before it became the basis of a style widely esteemed and copied among Continental courts and their musicians. So what seemed to a Continental composer and theorist, Tinctoris (writing in around 1475) as a manner of inventing music refreshing enough to appear a totally new art, superseding all previous music and making that music appear of no account in contrast,[1] was really an aspect of insular conservatism, given the status of novelty by its indifference to the most advanced styles of recent Continental music and by an innate appeal which declared itself to a wider audience as soon as it was accompanied by the prestige of conquest. We note also from the musical chronicles of the time that, although the origins of the new style in English musical practice were well recognised, there was equally no doubt from the perspective of the later fifteenth century that Continental composers such as Dufay and Binchois were thought to have taken the essential qualities of that style and developed them far beyond their English exemplars.

By the time that Brahms was at that stage of his life when he was ready to be honoured for his creative achievement, Britain's, or more specifically England's, reputation as a "land without music" - that is, a land without a distinctive creative profile based on a recognisable national style in traditional music - was such that it has been claimed the Hamburg-born composer refused to travel to England to receive the honorary degree he was awarded by Cambridge University. The evidence of this is tenuous and debatable; and there are other explanations for Brahms's failure (on two occasions) to take up the invitation; but even if we take the story as no more than a rumour started by the British themselves and engendered by a British sense of inferiority, that in itself is significant. Certainly, Brahms was much more interested in musical history and in traditional music than most of his composing contemporaries and predecessors and was especially likely to find the reputed absence of what Germans by this time called 'folk music' a serious and off-putting fault in any country that aspired to more than cultural mediocrity.

The odd truth is that it was the English themselves who were the first to insist that they had no traditional music of any size or consequence. The most famous late eighteenth-century English historian of music, Charles Burney, whose works were read widely on the European Continent, had declared that England had no traditional tunes to call its own, as far as he knew, beyond about two or three; on another occasion he specifically doubted if there were as many as twenty-four. If this was the opinion of professional musicians in the metropolis, it draws attention to a split between the experience of a London upper and middle-class public and profession oriented towards the international styles of eighteenth century opera and concert music and the music sung and played in rural and smaller urban centres. A similar split developed during the years of the Austro-Hungarian empire between the musical awareness of upper and middle-class urban Hungarians and the musical practice of Hungarian villagers; but that is easily understood when we reflect that the Hungarian educated classes looked towards Vienna, the imperial capital, for advancement and for mastery of the accents of cultural distinction. The special achievement of London musical professionals and music-lovers was to adopt a provincial point of view - the belief that national character as well as excellence in music came from elsewhere in Europe - while being situated in an imperial or quasi-imperial capital. It is tempting to conclude that the early development of London as a leading music market in Europe impelled it towards the habits of international connoisseurship and the accompanying belief that the best of music was an imported luxury.

Just as upper-class and professional Hungarians were aware of a pleasing exoticism in their country's abundance of gypsy music, the music of the rest of the British Isles - outside England, that is - was accepted both in Britain and in Continental Europe as a marginal but delightfully characterful addition to official and international styles in music. Beethoven, Haydn, Weber and several other prominent Austrian and German composers arranged Scottish, Welsh and Irish airs for Scottish publishers; but no one seems to have asked whether there was any English traditional music of even comparable interest. This is easily explained. The action of Scottish publishers was an incident of cultural nationalism in which the recognition of a distinctive Scottish music, in particular, was a reminder that Scotland, despite its political union with England, was nevertheless not to be confused culturally with the dominant member of the partnership. Germany's interest in folk traditions of story, poetry and music, vigorously developed from the time of Herder onwards, was, among other things, a quest for cultural attributes that were essentially and definingly Germanic, in compensation for the manifest lack of German-speaking political unity. The English view seems to have been that possession of distinctive traditional music was not an issue for a country which was already the controlling element of a united kingdom.

As it happens, England's musical influence and achievements had been more extensive in the era of the enlightenment than most educated English musicians and music-lovers were aware. In opera, for example, England managed in the earlier eighteenth century to export a native tradition of ballad operas that became one of the foundations of the German singspiel. But this had been largely forgotten at a time - the later nineteenth century - when opera fanciers in Britain could not recall anything more internationally notable than the hospitality of London audiences to Italian operas composed by a German (Handel).

By the time Haydn and his music conquered London in the 1790s, the city seems to have been divided musically into two aesthetic factions: the ancient and the scientific.[2] Adherents of one school of musical thought and taste were at loggerheads with supporters of the other. The Ancients thought of music as having reached its summit in an earlier period and were addicted to its Handelian and pre-Handelian heritage. J.C. Bach and Haydn himself were, in contrast, among the most eminent practitioners of the scientific manner, which amounted in effect to the wholly contemporary music of the newly perfected Viennese classical style. Haydn was able to cross the barrier dividing these factions, as when he accompanied a prominent soprano in London in a performance of Purcell's famous scena of feigned madness, *From rosy bowers*; and Haydn was also receptive enough to what was distinctive in British music-making to be inspired by the massed choral singing he had heard in London when he came to write the two celebrated oratorios of his final creative decade. It was the faction of the ancients that remembered what had been splendid in the past achievements of Byrd, Gibbons, Weelkes and Purcell; but the manner in which they articulated this preference, as exemplified by their principal spokesman, the musical historian John Hawkins, was that of an obstinate and cranky antiquarianism. Burney's far more widely disseminated views represented an up-to-date internationalism that was consonant with professional music-making and concert-giving. It was the voice of the rapidly growing music market in which new forms of music - the symphony, the concerto, the keyboard sonata, the virtuoso string quartet - claimed autonomy for music instead of relying on its traditional functional relationship with words, dance, ceremony and drama. This autonomy was increasingly part of what some historians term the 'sacralisation' of culture in general and art in particular. The composer was on the verge of becoming, under the impulse of Beethoven's personal and artistic heroism, a prophet; the concert hall and, later in the nineteenth century, even the lyric theatre turned into a kind of temple.[3]

Open-mindedness towards the latest phenomena of musical art (especially when these can be imported as a revelation of new and hitherto unsuspected possibilities in a given genre) finds it relatively easy to co-exist with the denigration of the home-grown and the exaltation of the foreign. For whatever reason - among them, perhaps, influences from commerce, religion, education, society and sheer chance - musical creativity of an exceptional order had been in short supply among British musicians between the death of Purcell and the late-blooming career of Elgar. That in itself could be looked on as simply one phase in the cyclical changes in the proportions of artistic talent shared among leading European countries. The states constituting what is now Germany, for example, were of small account musically until the eighteenth century, when two masters summed up the scope of baroque music, and when an almost unprecedented dynasty of first-class creative talents, shared between Austria and other German-speaking lands, defined classical and romantic styles. It was Britain's misfortune, if you like, that its period of least creative distinction in the last six hundred years coincided with the decisive establishment of the standard repertories of concert and opera. The shortcomings of that period, in other words, are much more noticeable than they would have been in any other period.

Yet Britain's contribution to the concert industry, though creatively nondescript, was unique. England and, more particularly, London became, during the late eighteenth and early nineteenth centuries, the leading market for European music and musicians. Composers as diverse as Beethoven, Mendelssohn, Gounod and Dvorak benefited substantially from its unparalleled powers of patronage. Mozart, until death cut short his plans, had believed he might be on the verge of retrieving his fortunes in London. Haydn climaxed his pan-European fame there; and London helped to define for him what he had become, a creative figure independent of the system of patronage under which all his previous activities had taken place. That definition helped him, on his return to Austria, to reach a new relationship with his long-time Esterhazy patrons and to accept the elder statesman's role in music for which his London seasons had nominated him.

Britain (including and, most particularly, England) has been shown, in the course of developments in the last hundred years, to have misrepresented itself in a way that testified to its ignorance of its musical riches, rather than to false modesty. Its resources in traditional music, which Burney had other metropolitan figures thought to to be minuscule, have proved to be vast:

English traditional song and dance, when these were documented in a moderately systematic and sustained way from around the beginning of the twentieth century, have yielded more examples of striking and distinctive melody than can be accommodated in the experience of anyone but a specialist; the legacy of the English cathedral choir, sometimes regarded as limply complacent or effete, has turned out to be one of the few vocal traditions with any documented continuity going back to pre-classical times and has been the foundation on which English vocal ensembles have established a pan-European convention in the revival of pre-Romantic music. You can even hear British-style choral singing now in some churches in Rome. British, usually English, vocal ensembles have taught the rest of Europe - this includes the Italians and the French - a way of singing that has the merit of not being coloured by notions of expressiveness and tone quality inherited from the late nineteenth and early twentieth centuries. It is, in fact, the so-called inexpressiveness of English singing which has come into its own as a model for the all-conquering early music movement, with its prominence in modern record catalogues.

The male falsetto voice (often dubbed counter-tenor, though with little or no historical warrant) was first revived as a solo instrument in England under Arnold Dolmetsch's supervision in the 1890s (as Bernard Shaw's musical criticism of the time testifies) and was given its decisive professional re-introduction in post-World War II Europe by a former member of Canterbury Cathedral choir, the late Alfred Deller. This voice remained for almost a quarter of a century after that largely an English or at least English-speaking speciality: only in the last two decades has the English dominance in this voice been seriously eroded by individual German, French, Greek, Belgian and American singers, not to mention some conspicuously talented Australians.

Britain's composers, often at least the equal of their Continental colleagues up to the end of the seventeenth century, have given Britain once again an honourable creative rank in European music in recent times, though without surrendering their time-honoured liking for picking up or persisting with musical fashions after they have been dropped across the Channel. In time that may have no negative connotations: from our perspective today, it does not diminish the work of the early Tudor masters (active during the reigns of Henry VII and the first decades of Henry VIII) that they were working in gloriously irrational periods of long, looping melody at a time when an altogether more rational and economical system of imitation among the vocal entries had been well established by leading Continental polyphonists.

Official promotion of British music on the Continent has not always been blunted by tact. A 1951 Festival of Britain mounting of Britten's opera *Billy Budd* in Paris contained, as one of its most verbally intelligible moments, an episode in which British naval officers took up, in the manner of an impromptu round, the words 'Don't like the French, don't like their Frenchified ways'. Recently, on the other hand, I had the pleasure of witnessing a performance of the same composer's opera about the blighting tradition of a military caste, *Owen Wingrave*, in French translation at the Opéra Comique in Paris and of noting that it had considerably more insight and communicative power as a production and in its projection of the text than the most recent revival of that opera in Britain; and it is fair to say that Britten's *A Midsummer Night's Dream* has become even more of a repertory piece in France than in its native country. So there is nothing inherently present in British music which prevents it from communicating itself to the French or to other peoples of Continental Europe.

No one is likely to assert, for all that, that British music is or ever has been dominant on the Continent in recent times, not even when you take into account the popularity of the Beatles, the Rolling Stones and a few more recent rock and pop groups (not excluding the Spice Girls). All that is being claimed here is that the old gibes have lost their point: Brahms, were he alive today and supposing that the rumour about his diffidence in visiting a *Land ohne Musik* were true, could venture across the Channel to receive an honorary degree without feeling that he was entering intrinsically alien or unsympathetic territory. Britain has become a member of the European and international communities of musical nations, with standards of musical creation as well as performance that do not have to be apologised for, not even with the modest cough of the minor practitioner.

Mention of pop culture brings to mind a curious fact: Although Britain's production of punk fashions in some varieties of pop music as well as in personal appearance is far more radical than that of most of its counterparts in Continental Europe (perhaps only Berlin can offer rivalry in those departments), its latter-day composers for the concert-hall and in opera have tended to leave their island home for American or Continental bases whenever their path-finding has become too uncomfortable. Intransigent British serialists of the old school can still be found here and there comfortably marooned on American campuses; current path-breakers catering to the 'impossibilist' school of performance retain credibility with periods of residence at Californian universities or at IRCAM, the underground bunker of the musical avant-garde at the Centre Pompidou.

Even when their social views have been radical, British composers have been thought only rarely to disclose that radicalism in their music. They have not even been given credit for their bleaker visions of the society to which they belonged. It is part of the small change of musical comment to discern in the parodistic tramp and lilt of Mahler's music a portrait of a Viennese-centred imperial society in decline - going through the motions of ceremony but no longer believing in them; and it is equally common for some listeners to declare that they hear in the expressionistic phase of Schoenberg's creative development a metaphor for the disintegration and collapse of that society, a fin-de-siècle and post-fin-de-siècle phenomenon in which art seems to emulate the social fracture. In Vaughan Williams's *A London Symphony* from the same pre-World War I period, on the other hand, opinion has been conditioned to glimpse only the cheerful equivalent of double-decker buses, gracefully curtseying flower-sellers, the accents of Cockney perkiness, the solemnity of great civic occasions. This music takes on a somewhat different significance, however, when you know that Vaughan Williams was a socialist - a tweedy socialist perhaps, but certainly an idealist - and that he compared the enigmatic melancholy of the ending of the symphony with the close of *Tono-Bungay*, H.G. Wells's novel about capitalism run out of control, This significance is enlarged when you learn of the likelihood that many incidents in the symphony's final movement deal with the London of the unemployed, its stately but resigned processional section doing service, for example, as a kind of hunger march.[4] This is the same Vaughan Williams who has been presented consistently, not least by the British themselves, as a composer indulging solely in rural nostalgia and meandering daydreams. Yet where Schoenberg encouraged the disintegration of traditional tonality, Vaughan Williams brought even his starkest visions back to a tonal base. Without risking too many simple-minded correlations between the state of tonality and the state of society it is at least interesting to speculate whether that preference was related to some ultimate faith in the social cohesion of the nation or at least to the lack of an overwhelming, Viennese-type disharmony in the elements of society.

In seeking to estimate the prospects of British - more specifically, English - music in a European context of the future, it is obvious that even the most ardent advocate of national expansionism in the arts would hesitate to draw recommended procedures in too slavish or literal a way from the apparent lessons of history. A prolonged military invasion of the Continent as a means of promoting the currency of British music and other arts on the fifteenth-century model is not likely to be considered an option. Phenomenal success in trade could be the other most productive cause of enhanced awareness of British music beyond its natural boundaries. That might be wished for but its likelihood is hardly to be estimated at the moment except in the fanciful realms of economic prediction, realms too fanciful for the sober verities of art. Better prospects would seem to attach themselves to the idea of a Britain thoroughly involved in Europe and therefore able to take advantage of its channels of communication. The Chunnel may be regarded as rather rickety symbol of the beginning of a slow decline of insularity in art as in politics, though there will be persuasive arguments that insularity, despite its inherent time-lag, is not all bad.

The decisive factor in whether Britain retains and improves its current status as one fully paid-up member of a community of musical nations is almost certainly education. The deep-seated shift in British artistic capabilities in music brought about in recent times occurred in the wake of recognition of music as a fundamental part of the educational system and not as a matter best left to foreigners and metropolitan professionals or as a polite but undemanding accomplishment, this latter a habit that caused Chopin in the nineteenth century to take away an impression of Britain as a country in which, as he said, well-born amateurs played the wrong notes with feeling. Schubert's genius was a not a factor subject in itself to wise or prudent planning, but the context in which it was most likely to declare itself rested on the circumstance that one of the qualifications for being a village schoolmaster in the Austria that nurtured him was musical aptitude and training. Music as a regular and systematic educational subject, supported by county scholarships and a number of clearly defined paths for the development of talent, has transformed the resources of both professional and amateur music-making in present-day Britain. Will it last? Pessimists would see in the apparent determination of some elements of British politics and officialdom to destroy the BBCs World Service at the moment of its seeming apogee a reminder of the ease with which a nation can ready itself to discard the fabric within which excellence lives. If such a retrograde development is firmly banished from the musical agenda, British music is now in a good condition to enjoy the artistic benefits that Britain's deeper, less selective involvement in European affairs might bring.

Notes

[1] Tinctoris's opinion carries double weight as representing the view of a Franco-Flemish theorist and composer who had opportunities to take stock of Western European music and to recognise its characteristics.

[2] A. Peter Brown, 'The Sublime, the Beautiful, and the Ornamental: English Aesthetic Currents and Haydn's Symphonies,' in O. Biba, D. Wyn Jones

(eds), *Studies in Music History presented to H.C. Robbins Landon on his seventieth birthday*, London: Thames and Hudson, 1996, p. 45.

3 T.W.C. Blanning, 'The Commercialization and Sacralization of European Culture in the Nineteenth Century,' in T.W.C. Blanning (ed.), *The Oxford Illustrated History of Modern Europe*, Oxford/New York: OUP, 1996, pp. 130-132.

4 Alain Frogley, 'H.G. Wells and Vaughan Williams's A London Symphony: Politics and culture in fin-de-siècle England,' in C. Banks, A. Searle, M. Turner (eds), *Sundry sorts of music Books: Essays on The British Library Collections Presented to O.W. Neighbour on his 70th birthday*, London: The British Library, 1993, pp. 299-301.

II

PREVIOUS ENGAGEMENTS

5 Perceptions of Britain in Wilhelmine Social Democracy

DICK GEARY

The extent to which the German Social Democratic Party (SPD) shared national values and became integrated into the prevailing social and political order of the Wilhelmine Reich has been the subject of much controversy. Those who wish to identify such a process of integration - whether positive or 'negative' - stress the *revisionist* critique of Marxism mounted by Eduard Bernstein, Eduard David and Kurt Eisner amongst others; the growth of *reformism* in the social-democratic organisations of southern Germany, especially in Baden; the increasing role of cautious trade-union leaders, concerned with bread-and-butter questions rather than the prospect of distant revolution; the rejection of the general strike as a political weapon, which partly reflected the growing authority of these union leaders within German Social Democracy; and the party's first vote for the Imperial military budget in the Reichstag in 1913. Against this background, the SPD's declaration of support for the government's war credits on August 4 1914 is seen as the inevitable culmination of an irreversible process of deradicalisation, *embourgeoisement* and integration.[1]

Moreover, analysis of the SPD's massive cultural and leisure organisations has focused on the way in which they embodied or reflected 'bourgeois' cultural values. Thus workers' choral societies sang *Volkslieder* (traditional folk-songs); the workers' dramatic societies performed Schiller and Goethe; the workers' orchestras played Beethoven, Wagner, Lehar, and counted as increasingly important the professionalism of performance. Similarly the *Arbeiterturn- und Sportbund* (Workers' Gymnastics and Sports League) became penetrated by competitive values, which to some extent contradicted its original, participative values. Few workers borrowed books from union libraries; of those that did, few read the Marxist classics, many borrowed works on craft skills or evolutionary biology, and the most popular *genre* was historical fiction, especially as exemplified by the novels of Alexandre Dumas![2]

Yet this picture of *Verbürgerlichung* has been greatly qualified, if not actually destroyed, by a great deal of research in the last twenty years. We now know that the national party leadership and especially the SPD's Reichstag *Fraktion* were nothing like as radical as local organisations; that there were many party branches of a non-reformist hue (in Berlin, Brunswick, Düsseldorf, Esslingen, Göppingen, Remscheid, Solingen, Stuttgart), as well as some of admittedly non-radical hue, such as those in Göttingen, Hannover and Hamburg.[3] If anything, a 'syndicalist' undercurrent of rank-and-file dissatisfaction with bureaucratic caution on the part of trade-union and party leaders became marked in the years immediately before the outbreak of war;[4] whilst even the national leadership of the SPD was involved in the coordination of massive anti-militarist and anti-war demonstrations that brought hundreds of thousands of workers onto the streets of Germany's major cities in the last days of July 1914.[5] Before the First World War most of those expelled from the party stood on its right (e.g. the revisionist imperialists Richard Calwer and Max Schippel); it was the reformist South Germans who were out of tune with the largest SPD branches in Berlin and who contemplated leaving the party; and the largest single group within Social Democracy after 1905 was, as Dieter Groh has demonstrated, its centre left, which included prominent figures such as Hugo Haase, Georg Ledebour and, at this stage, Karl Liebknecht, rather than its right wing.[6] The party's agreement to vote for the military budget in 1913 was taken solely on the grounds that this provided for *direct* taxation, a long-standing SPD demand. Even Liebknecht, the great anti-war campaigner, thought the party had no choice in the matter for this reason. Furthermore, the vote for the war credits on 4 August 1914 did *not* denote a surrender of class identity to nationalist hysteria: that vote was no foregone conclusion, but took place in circumstances of utter confusion; the reasons for the 'yes' vote were many, but only a small section of the party welcomed the decision as betokening the final entry of Social Democracy into the nation, though this group did include the party *Fraktion* (parliamentary delegation); and the support was conditional upon a specific set of circumstances (national self-defence against Russia) and was not made from a long-term political perspective. Even the widely held belief in working-class enthusiasm for the war has to be qualified in the light of recent research.[7]

The view that SPD cultural organisations simply reproduced 'bourgeois' culture is also open to question. First of all, most members of these organisations were also members of the SPD; and such membership could spell trouble with employers and the police. Secondly, the very fact that they were *workers'* cultural organisations, described themselves as such and were separate from and often founded in opposition to middle-class cultural organisations, as in the case of the workers' sports and gymnastic organisation, speaks volumes about separate class identity.

Significantly, the prime value they embraced was very 'non-bourgeois': *solidarity*. The *Arbeiterradfahrerverein* (Worker-Cyclists' Club), for example, which described its members as the 'cavalry of the revolution', was even called *Solidarität*. Equally significant is the fact that there was not one but there were two *Schillerfeste* held in the Second Reich, one bourgeois, one social-democratic; and though workers might perform the classics of 'high culture', there is evidence that what workers took from Schiller was different to what middle-class readers and audiences took from the playwright. Workers' choral societies did sing labourist and revolutionary anthems (especially the *Arbeitermarseillaise*) as well as more traditional songs; and few SPD festivals were devoted exclusively to apolitical and leisure activities. These festivals further celebrated the martyrs of 1848, rather than German victory over France, and Lassalle's, not the Kaiser's, birthday. What the cultural activities of German Social Democracy did above all else was to sharpen the political and social awareness of the participants (*n.b.* this was a *participatory* culture). Such participation often meant emancipation for the individual worker, who learnt independence and self confidence through his (there were few women in these organisations) associational activities. Social-democratic subculture did offer an alternative view of work and recreation to Wilhelmine workers, just as the *Arbeiterpuppentheater*, which is preserved in the Fritz-Hüser-Institut in Dortmund, was designed as an alternative to the nationalist Punch and Judy shows of Imperial Germany.[8]

The predominant view of Britain in Wilhelmine Social Democracy reinforces this author's contention that social-democratic attitudes were not those of Imperial Germany's social and political establishment. The landowning aristocratic and military elites of Prusso-Germany had little time for bourgeois, free-trading, liberal Britain; but if anything their Anglophobia was eclipsed in the decades before the outbreak of war by that of sections of the German middle class, especially those who gave their support to the National Liberals. It was these, not the army-oriented, continentally pre-occupied Junker, who formed the backbone of support for the building of the German battle fleet, conceived by Admiral Tirpitz as a weapon against Social Democracy, who constituted the social basis of the naval officer corps, and who filled the ranks and the leadership of the most hysterical, anti-British *Nationalverbände*, such as the Navy League, with its one million members, and the smaller Colonial League.[9] Anti-British feelings were also incited quite deliberately by a regime which saw imperialism and *Weltpolitik* not only as a means to international greatness and a route to Germany's 'place-in-the-sun', but also as a way of distracting attention from domestic difficulties and mobilising the 'nationally-minded' masses behind the government and against the socialist threat.[10] Hostility to England and the idea that Britain stood in the way of German greatness was not only fuelled by a prevalent and rather crude social Darwinism, but also led to the appearance of works which saw war between the two nations as inevitable: General Bernhardi's *Deutschland und der nächste Krieg* and the Pan-Germanist Heinrich Class's *Wenn ich der Kaiser wär'*.

Such hysterical nationalism and Anglophobia was *not* shared by the bulk of the SPD membership, nor by its most prominent figures, as we will see. Working-class Germans had little to gain from colonial adventures, when only Togoland and Samoa amongst the German colonies were self-supporting, and when the building of the battle fleet and colonial entanglements were funded not by progressive, direct taxation but by increases in indirect taxes, which fell disproportionally on items of working-class consumption and were grist to the mill of socialist electoral propaganda. This helps to explain why only 26 working men were to be found amongst the 9,000 committee members of the Navy League and why pub conversations in Imperial Hamburg reveal scepticism about overseas involvement rather than a German counterpart to Victorian and Edwardian jingoism.[11] With Germany's China expedition of 1900 costing £10,000,000 and the repression of the Hereros revolt in South West Africa another £30,000,000, which again had to be funded primarily through indirect taxation, it is not surprising that the SPD attacked the Naval Bills in the Reichstag and that Wilhelm Liebknecht, who saw the colonialism of the Imperial regime as a mechanism for distracting attention from within Germany itself (a form of what Hans-Ulrich Wehler has more recently described as 'social-imperialism') denounced the '*Flottenschwindel*', as did the radical leftist Parvus.[12] Parvus, Bebel, Liebknecht, and above all Eduard Bernstein, of whom much more below, would all have preferred alliance with England to the actual trajectory of German policy; and from its beginnings until the outbreak of war in 1914, the key refrain in SPD foreign policy thinking was not hatred of Britain but *Russo*phobia, not least because the land of the Tsars was seen as the bastion of European reaction.[13] The reasons for the predominantly favourable attitude of the party to Britain will be discussed below.

It has to be admitted that there were some - though not that many - voices within the SPD which did identify with German navalism, colonial expansion, protectionism and Anglophobia. The 'revisionist imperialists', to use Roger Fletcher's phrase, wrote for the major revisionist monthly, the *Sozialistische Monatshefte*, and included its editor Joseph Bloch, Richard Calwer, Karl Leuthner, Max Schippel and Gerhard Hildebrand. The members of this group believed that Britain stood everywhere in the way of Germany and was the Fatherland's natural enemy, that British and German interests were necessarily contradictory and that British imperial policy constituted a 'peril' for the Reich. They further believed that protectionism and colonial expansion would benefit German workers by providing jobs in the dockyards, shipbuilding and the merchant marine, as they would also by keeping out foreign (primarily British) imports. To this way of thinking Manchesterism and free trade constituted an English fifth column in the German body politic and were to be resisted.[14]

These pragmatic/instrumental reasons for hostility to Britain were joined in the case of some of this group to a different kind of - cultural - prejudice. Stale 'old' England was contrasted with dynamic Germany; moves to replace French with English teaching in German schools denounced as 'barbaric'; and all because the English were bereft of a genuine *Kulturgut* (cultural heritage).[15] As Bloch wrote on 14 April 1909, 'I cannot summon up any warmth for this nation [Britain], possibly because of its inartistic nature. But even if I were infatuated with England, as is Bernstein for example, I would consider it absolutely necessary to oppose with the utmost vigour this pernicious and unqualified aping of all things English'.[16]

The protectionist and even pro-Prussian attitude of this group of 'revisionist imperialist' intellectuals on the right of the SPD, however, was far from typical of the party as a whole, as even Fletcher has to admit. In fact Schippel and Hildebrand were actually expelled from the party, whose commitment to low food prices and indirect taxes made both agricultural tariffs and navalism non-starters. Even as far as the revisionist intellectuals of the SPD were concerned, these imperialists were out on a limb. It was not to protectionism but Manchesterist free trade, not to Prussia but Britain, not to *Weltpolitik* but international understanding, that the important revisionists -Eduard Bernstein, Kurt Eisner and Eduard David - looked with approval. Indeed Bernstein, the high-priest of revisionism, was probably the most pro-British of all the SPD's one million members.[17]

It is well known that Eduard Bernstein was greatly influenced by the time he spent in England in the 1880s to avoid prosecution under Germany's anti-socialist legislation; and many in the SPD at the time, as well as numerous later commentators, attributed his revisionist critique of Marxism (rejection of the theory of surplus value, denial of the necessity or probablity of revolution, advocacy of collaboration with the bourgeoisie) to English contacts and conditions. So Bebel argued at the party conference in 1899; such was the opinion of Rosa Luxemburg; and so Karl Kautsky wrote to Bernstein at the time of the revisionist controversy: 'You have decided to be an Englishman - take the consequences and become an Englishman...And do not deceive yourself, you have lost touch with Germany'.[18] It is the case that Bernstein knew and admired the work of Cobden and Spencer, that he was conversant with British history, writing a book on the English Civil War (that country's 'bourgeois revolution') and that he followed British political developments closely, working as the London correspondent of *Vorwärts* for a time. It may also be that his many contacts with the British Fabians had an even more direct impact on his thinking.

This has been claimed not only by biographers of Bernstein, such as Peter Gay and Francis Carsten;[19] it was also a claim made by some of the leading members of the Fabian Society and other contemporaries. Both Max Beer and Edward Pease asserted that it was the revisionist who exported Fabian ideas to Germany;[20] and it is true that Bernstein was in close and frequent personal contact with several Fabians. In 1888 he visited Hubert Bland, a member of the Society's executive, and heard George Bernard Shaw lecture. In the following year he was present at several of Sidney Webb's talks and attended at least one Fabian meeting. He was on good terms with Ramsay MacDonald, Edward Pease and their respective wives; knew Headlam, Dearmer, Wallas and Massingham; and in 1895/96 wrote favourably of the Fabians and their eclecticism in Kautsky's *Die Neue Zeit*.[21]

Under these circumstances it is not surprising that some of the Marxists in the SPD smelled a Fabian/English rat; but this Bernstein himself expressly denied on more than one occasion. 'For a long time', he wrote, 'I had a prejudice against the Fabians' and he went on to claim that he avoided personal contact with them.[22] In 1898 he remonstrated with August Bebel that 'I haven't become *that* English'; and, even in summarising his intellectual development towards the end of his life in 1924, he stated that his English contacts were 'of small influence in my socialist thought'.[23] However, not only did Bernstein make some positive statements about Fabianism, as we have already seen; there are innumerable similarities between his political thinking and that of his English contemporaries. On a methodological level he rejected positivism, scientism and claims that socialism had a 'scientific' basis. Rather its legitimation was ethical. He emphasised the role of non-economic forces in recent historical development, criticised the theory of surplus value along lines not dissimilar to Shaw and Graham Wallas, believed that socialism could permeate capitalist society, especially through the municipalities, without some kind of revolutionary cataclysm, and advocated class cooperation (to its enemies 'collaboration') rather than the proletarian isolationism that chatacterised much of the SPD's theory and reality.[24] In all these ways Bernstein's thought was closer to that of his English contemporaries (the Webbs, for example) than that of his German party colleagues; and hence Kautsky claimed at the SPD congress in Dresden in 1903 that 'the practical starting point for revisionism is *not here* [*'nicht bei uns'*]. For that Germany is too backward'.[25] Finally, there were occasions when Bernstein did confess his debt to Fabianism. On 26 October 1895 he wrote to Karl Kautsky, pointing out that the Fabians had a 'good side', as they were not obsessed with slogans but with getting things done.[26] Even more revealingly, Bernstein wrote to Kautsky sixteen months later, saying: 'Bax is right, I am a Fabian; for these are the only socialists from whom one learns anything here'.[27]

Whatever the influence of English contemporaries and English conditions on Bernstein's outlook, there is no doubt that he had an extremely favourable view of England and the English. He admired 'Anglo-Saxon freedom' and the fact that 'the English worker was never under the thumb of a police state...'.[28] He saw Britain showing continental Europe the way to a more peaceful future and looked on British and French parliamentary practice as a model for Germany.[29] Bernstein pointed out that, even if British labour had failed to liberate itself from the coat-tails of bourgeois politics (a reference to the relatively poor showing of independent working-class and socialist groups in British elections at the time), it was militant in economic terms and it had managed to win for itself concessions which any German worker would envy: the extension of the franchise in 1867, improvements in the provision of elementary education and its administration, factory legislation and the replacement of indirect by direct taxation. Here was a case of 'the tail wagging the dog'; and, according to the German revisionist, it was significant that English workers realised their demands precisely because they did *not* adopt revolutionary slogans.[30]

Bernstein's admiration of things British also extended to a belief that British foreign policy was essentially peaceable and that there was a real difference between British colonialism and German imperialism, comparing the latter unfavourably with the former. The British Empire was to Bernstein peaceable, built on free trade and of benefit to the colonial peoples. In no way did it mirror the militarism that lay behind German colonial ambitions.[31] Moreover, where British imperialism did take on unpleasantly aggressive characteristics, these were, he thought, a *reaction* to the provocations of German policy, a 'most shortsighted and most foolish policy which makes the great English nation our enemy'.[32] In his 1911 polemic against the growing Anglophobia of the German right, *Die englische Gefahr und das deutsche Volk*, Bernstein pointed out that the British bourgeoisie was essentially peaceable, that the two countries were one another's best trading partners and that Britain did *not* constitute a threat to German interests.

He had been making similar points for some time, stressing that British imperialism was not reactionary; and that this in turn was linked to the fact that the British bourgeoisie was more liberal and had 'stronger nerves' than its German counterpart.[33] One might suspect that this stereotype of a peaceable, liberal England was one not shared by the Marxist 'Centre' (Kautsky) and 'Left' (Luxemburg) of German Social Democracy, who would rather tend to stress the similarities and realities of *capitalist/bourgeois* development in *all* industrial states. Indeed, Rosa Luxemburg made precisely this point in her critique of Bernstein and revisionism, even though she did believe that English conditions had influenced her fellow Social Democrat. As she stated in 1899, 'Bernstein constructed his theory on the basis of English conditions. He sees the world through "English spectacles"...'.[34]

This partial admission of British difference (from Imperial Germany) was then obviated, however, by Luxemburg's insistence that the decline of liberalism was a universal phenomenon in advanced capitalist states. In her very article entitled 'The English Spectacles' she saw Bernstein's warmth for the country's liberalism as *passé: even* in England liberal forces were in retreat.[35] Five years later, in 1904, the Polish revolutionary who had made her home in the SPD declared: 'For the past quarter of a century...the universal feature of political development in the capitalist countries has been a compromise between the bourgeoisie and feudalism', pointing to the obliteration of the differences between Whigs and Tories by way of example.[36] In this she was to some extent following Friedrich Engels, who wrote to August Bebel in 1892 that British big business had deserted to the Tories - though he also believed that this was in turn forcing British liberals to look to working-class voters.[37]

At the height of his influence in the first decade of this century, Karl Kautsky, the SPD's official theorist and editor of *Die Neue Zeit*, the most widely read Marxist journal of its day, also seemed to share Luxemburg's belief that the politics of imperialism and the increased threat from labour would push the bourgoisie increasingly into the arms of reaction. The bourgeoisie was making a common front with conservative landowners; still 'economically progressive', it was to Kautsky becoming 'politically reactionary'.[38] *Even in England*, these developments were to be seen when Joseph Chamberlain went over to the Conservative Party and espoused the ideology of imperialism. With the growth of socialism and the increasing political and economic organisation of workers, the bourgeoisie was becoming ever more disillusioned with parliamentarism.[39] In various articles about Britain and the Boer War Kautsky identified the decline of those classic bourgeois ideals, Manchesterism and free trade. In the wake of depression and concerned to protect markets and overseas investments, British high finance and heavy industry increasingly looked to the *state* to protect their interests, even in the classic land of liberalism. The forces of reaction in Britain were being strengthened by imperialism and its expression in the Boer War.[40]

This apparently uncompromising castigation of political developments across the North Sea on Kautsky's part was, however, qualified by the construction '*even in England*, which testified to a rather different view of that country and its politics. Luxemburg was of a generation that had not had to seek exile in Britain during the years of the anti-socialist laws (1878-1890), not only unlike Bernstein, but unlike Kautsky, who had met Marx and Engels in London in 1881 and lived there for most the time between 1885 and 1890, annoying Marx but engaging in mammoth, night-time claret-drinking sessions with Engels. Kautsky, Bernstein and the even older Wilhelm Liebknecht, who spent thirteen years in exile after the failure of the revolutions in Central Europe in 1848/49, could not but look with favour on the land that had sheltered them and refused to persecute the members of the Workers' International for their views. In his book on Thomas More (one in a series of works by Kautsky on *Communism from Plato to the Anabaptists!*), the Marxist 'Pope' not only delivered an interesting verdict on *The Merry Wives of Windsor* ('it typifies a bitter class struggle') but also spoke affectionately of the 'freedom loving sentiments of the people', which, according to him, had formed the only bulwark against Tudor despotism.[41] For Kautsky, England was the home of both the industrial revolution and the democratic movement, and as industrial capital became stronger, so 'British politics became more peaceable. Free trade and peace became the slogan of the leaders of industrial capital, of the Cobdens and the Brights'.[42] Since the end of the seventeenth century in Britain 'compromise has become the general form in which political and economic conflicts...are settled'.[43]

Kautsky did not believe that democracy removed class conflict; indeed he thought rather that it magnified it, but in ways that made possible the peaceful triumph of socialism. Where he disagreed with Bernstein was in thinking that peaceful victory was impossible in Germany's Second Reich, precisely because political institutions and traditions were so different to those in Britain. This point, which Kautsky repeated frequently, was *not* the fruit of increasing conservatism in Kautsky's old age, as Lenin sought to imagine. In a letter to Franz Mehring in 1893, Kautsky wrote: 'The struggle for a real parliamentary system will in my opinion become the decisive struggle of the social revolution in Germany, for in Germany a parliamentary regime means the political victory of the proletariat'.[44]

In Britain the situation was different, and peaceful revolution was a possibility, precisely because Britain was already a parliamentary state, which Imperial Germany, with its impotent Reichstag, most definitely was not. This was also true because the German bourgeoisie, unlike its English counterpart, had ceased to be liberal; and thus 'the English road is impossible for us'.[45] As Kautsky wrote to Bernstein on 15 February 1898, 'I completely agree with you that in England the road to the development of a socialist society is open without a revolution...Things are different in Germany'.[46] This admission of the singularity of British circumstances had been foreshadowed five years earlier in the same letter to Mehring cited above: 'For the dictatorship of the proletariat, I cannot imagine any other form than that of a powerful parliament on the British model'.[47]

In all of this appreciation of British democracy Kautsky believed that he was faithful to his mentor Marx; and with justification. Writing in the *New York Tribune* in 1852, Marx stated: 'universal suffrage is the equivalent of political power for the working class of England. The carrying of Universal Suffrage in

England would, therefore, be a far more socialistic measure than anything that has been honored with that name on the Continent. Its inevitable result, here, is *the political supremacy of the working class*'.[48] Speaking at a conference in Amsterdam twenty years later, Marx again highlighted the political differences between autocratic and democratic states when he said:

> We know of the allowances we must make for the institutions, customs and traditions of the various countries; and we do not deny that there are countries such as America, England, and I would add Holland if I knew your institutions better, where the working people may achieve their goal by peaceful means. If that is true, we must also recognize that in most continental countries it is force that will have to be the lever of our revolutions; it is force that we shall some day have to resort to in order to establish a reign of labour.[49]

To return to Kautsky, his favourable view of British political institutions was also matched by a far from unambiguously critical stance on the country's foreign policy. He frequently criticised British colonial rule, which he saw as exploitative. He even saw colonial revolts as a possible lever of revolution in the future, and, as we have already seen, he believed that the Boer War indicated a swing to the right in British politics.[50] In spite of all this, however, Kautsky to some extent shared Bernstein's belief that British foreign policy and colonialism were more peaceable than their German counterparts. Naturally British capital would incline to peace. The emergence of colonial and military reaction in Britain was essentially a *response* to the colonial ambitions of others. As he wrote in 1892, 'in so far as England is going along with it, it does so only under compulsion...'.[51] In India, Egypt and Cyprus, Britain was concerned to preserve the territories for free trade against Russian encroachments, whilst in Africa it was the French threat that led to the formalisation of British colonial domination.[52]

Such a view of Britain and British foreign policy was shared by many other leading figures in the SPD. In general, *Vorwärts* commented favourably on British domestic politics, always in comparison with reactionary Germany. Parvus' brochure *Naval Demands, Colonial Policy and Workers' Interests* called in 1898 for alliance with England, whilst Wilhelm Liebknecht, speaking in the Reichstag two years earlier, had claimed that Germany and Britain had common interests. Much as Bebel criticised English actions in the Boer War, he saw them as somehow atypical: Chamberlain did not represent the 'true England'.[53] The emergence of a tariff campaign and protectionism in Britain he blamed on German provocation in raising tariffs in 1879.[54] At times Bebel and Liebknecht came close to Bernstein's distinction between the peaceable colonialism of the British, which benefited colonies and mother country alike, and the brutalism and militarism of German colonial expansion.[55]

The impact of British experience on Bernstein and Kautsky has been described at some length, but many other leading figures also acknowledged influences and debts, some of a surprising nature. Friedrich Stampfer, editor of *Vorwärts*, confessed that it was Edward Bellamy's *Looking Backwards* which had turned him to socialism, and this despite the fact that its view of a technocratic, well-planned socialist society, where poverty had been abolished, was denounced by his party leader, August Bebel, who regarded its author as a 'moralistic bourgeois social reformer' who did not understand the realities of class war.[56] Perhaps even more surprisingly, Clara Zetkin, radical leader of the SPD's women's movement before the war, anti-war campaigner and founder-member of the German Communist Party in December 1918, actually translated Bellamy into German, despite the fact that she found his book 'unscientific', and issued a second edition in 1914.[57] Somewhat less surprisingly, Wilhelm Liebknecht wrote to William Morris as follows: 'the twelve years of exile I spent there [England] gave me my political education. And your working classes have been my teachers'.[58]

In truth, attitudes of German Social Democrats towards British labour and British socialists were somewhat schizophrenic. There were those like Bernstein who admired the pragmatism of British labour, though even he pointed out that *industrial* and *trade-union* militancy were not matched by *political* radicalism or independence.[59] Some, like Franz Mehring in the 1870s, admired the sheer size and determination of the British unions;[60] and Hermann Molkenbuhr, the party secretary, claimed that 'the workers of Germany have always looked to the English working class for example and inspiration';[61] but in general they saw in British labour a potential which was as yet unrealised. They, like Engels, despaired of the sectarianism of organisations like the Social Democratic Federation and the ideological deficiencies of individuals such as Hyndman and the Webbs. Engels complained repeatedly about the absence of independent working-class *politics* in Britain, about the sectionalism of British trade unions and their limited aims.[62] As he wrote to Kautsky, English workers viewed colonial policy in 'exactly the same way as they think about politics in general: the same as the bourgeois think'.[63] Marx too spoke of the 'apparent bourgeois infection' of the British working class.[64] In this sense at least, Engels thought British labour inferior to its German counterpart, organised in the SPD.[65] This point of view was expressed with great clarity by Max Beer, another *Vorwärts* London correspondent, who complained that Keir Hardie 'has no theories',[66] and repeated by a very non-socialist and bourgeois German:

Friedrich Naumann contrasted the 'intellectual poverty' of the British labour movement with the 'scientific quality' of SPD theory.[67]

Karl Kautsky summarised these positions by adopting a rather paternalistic (or patronising) attitude towards British labour organisations. He wanted the Labour Party to be admitted to the Second International, despite his reservations about its theoretical deficiencies, because at least it was an independent working-class party.[68] He also thought German Social Democracy should help its English colleagues overcome their disunity.[69] Most importantly, however, he believed that the absence of socialist revolution in Britain, where the objective preconditions of advanced industrialism and parliamentary democracy were already in existence, was primarily a consequence of the 'immaturity' (*Unreife*) of the British labour movement, and by this he meant the absence of a socialist consciousness, which could only be brought to the working class 'from outside' by bourgeois intellectuals. No amount of *trade-union* activity and organisation could generate such a united *class* consciousness, which had as its goal not limited and sectional material gains but the complete transformation of social relations.[70] For Kautsky, British workers, influenced by bourgeois liberalism and seduced by the material gains of colonialist domination of world markets, lagged behind their German comrades, at least in this regard.[71] German socialists such as Bebel believed that they, not the British, were the future.[72]

We arrive, therefore, at a rather strange conclusion. With the exception of a small group of 'revisionist imperialists' and an equally small number of radical Marxists who refused to acknowledge British exceptionalism, German Social Democrats were impressed by British liberalism, democracy and free trade, in a sense by the British bourgeoisie, but were far less impressed by British labour. This position, however, was quite enough to distinguish the SPD from the Anglophobia which prevailed in Germany in the years immediately before the First World War.

Notes

[1] There are many histories of the SPD, which incorporate at least some of this position: Roger Fletcher (ed.), *From Bernstein to Brandt* (London, 1987); Dieter Groh, *Negative Integration und Revolutionärer Attentismus* (Frankfurt/Main, 1973); W L Guttsman, *The German Social Democratic Party* (London, 1981); Susanne Miller and Heinrich Potthoff, *A History of German Social Democracy* (Leamington Spa, 1986); Gerhard A Ritter, *Die Arbeiterbewegung im Wilhelminischen Reich* (Berlin, 1959); Gerhard A Ritter (ed.), *Der Aufstieg der deutschen Sozialdemokratie* (Munich, 1991). On the increasing role of unions and reformism see especially Carl E Schorske, *German Social Democracy*

(Cambridge, Mass., 1955); on 'integration', Guenther Roth, *Social Democrats in Imperial Germany* (Totowa, N.J., 1963).

2   There is a growing literature on social-democratic culture. See, for example, Dick Geary, 'Arbeiterkultur in Deutschland und Großbritannien im Vergleich' in Dietmar Petzina (ed.), *Fahnen, Faüste, Körper* (Essen, 1986), pp. 91-101 and other contributions to the same volume. Also Horst Groschopp, *Zwischen Bierarbend und Bildungsverein* (2nd ed., Berlin, 1987); Helmut Fielhaber and Olaf Backhaus (eds), *Die andere Kultur* (Vienna, 1982); Wolfgang Hagen, *Die Schillerverehrung in der Sozialdemokratie* (Stuttgart, 1977); Gerhard Huck (ed.), *Sozialgeschichte der Freizeit* (Wuppertal, 1980); Dieter Langewiesche and Klaus Schönhoven, 'Arbeiterbibliotheken und Arbeiterlektüre im Wilhelminischen Deutschland' in *Archiv für Sozialgeschichte* XVI (1976), pp. 135-204; August Lehmann (ed.), *Studien zur Arbeiterkultur* (Munich, 1983); Vernon L Lidtke, *The Alternative Culture* (Oxford, 1985); Josef Moser, *Arbeiterleben in Deutschland 1900-1971* (Frankfurt/Main, 1984); Jurgen Reulecke and Wolfhard Weber (eds), *Fabrik, Familie, Feierabend* (Wuppertal, 1978); Gerhard A Ritter (ed.), *Workers' Culture in Imperial Germany*, a special issue of the *Journal of Contemporary History* 13 (1978) 2; Horst Überhorst, *Frisch, Frei, Stark und Treu* (Dusseldorf, 1973; Ulrich Wyrwa, *Branntwein und 'echtes' Bier* (Hamburg, 1990). Hartmann Wunderer, *Arbeitervereine und Arbeiterparteien* (Frankfurt/Main, 1980); Lynn Abrams, *Workers' Leisure in Imperial Germany* (London, 1989) stresses commercial aspects of popular leisure; whilst the 'integrationist thesis' is represented in particular in the works cited above by Langewiesche and Schönhoven, Ritter and Überhorst, as well as and especially by Roth, *Social Democrats*.

3   An extended version of this argument can be found in Dick Geary, 'The German Labour Movement, 1848-1918' in *European Studies Review* 3 (1976), pp. 297-330. See also Richard J Evans (ed.), *The German Working Class* (London, 1982); Friedhelm Boll, *Massenbewegungen in Niedersachsen* (Bonn, 1981); Mary Nolan, *Social Democracy and Society* (Cambridge, 1981). Erhard Lucas, *Zwei Formen von Arbeiterradikalismus* (Frankfurt/Main, 1976); Klaus Tenfelde, *Proletarische Provinz* (Munich, 1987); Adelheid von Saldern, *Von Einwohner zum Bürger* (Berlin, 1973); Adelheid von Saldern, *Auf dem Wege zum Arbeiterreformismus* (Frankfurt/Main, 1984); Volker Ullrich, *Die Hamburger Arbeiterbewegung vom Vorabend des Ersten Weltkriegs bis zur Revolution*, 2 vols (Hamburg, 1970).

4   Dick Geary, 'Radicalism and the German Worker' in Richard J Evans (ed.), *Politics and Society in Wilhelmine Germany* (London, 1978), pp. 267-86; Schorske, *German Social Democracy*, pp. 255-76; Hans Mommsen, 'Soziale und politische Konflikte an der Ruhr 1905 bis 1925' in Hans Mommsen (ed.), *Arbeiterbewegung und industrialler Wandel* (Wuppertal, 1980), p. 64; Klaus

5 Tenfelde, 'Linksradikale Strömungen in der Ruhrbergarbeiterschaft' in Mommsen, *Arbeiterbewegung*, pp. 202ff.

Georges Haupt, *Socialism and the Great War* (Oxford, 1972), pp. 233-39; Wolfgang Kruse, *Krieg und nationale Integration* (Essen, 1993); Dick Geary, 'German Social Democrats and the Outbreak of the First World War' in Dick Geary, *Hope and Impotence: Aspects of German Labour, 1870-1933* (London, forthcoming 1998).

6 Dieter Groh, *Negative Integration, passim*.

7 Geary, 'German Social Democrats'; Kruse, *Krieg* does see the SPD's parliamentary delegation as planning support for any (i.e. not just a 'defensive') war but also recognises that this did **not** represent general party attitudes. See also Susanne Miller, *Burgfrieden und Klassenkampf* (Düsseldorf, 1974).

8 The criticism of the concept of social-democratic cultural organisations as integrative mechanisms can be found in the works cited in note 2 by Geary, Lehmann and Lidtke. See also Guttsman, *Social Democratic Party*, pp. 176 and 198; Dick Geary, 'Working Class Culture in Imperial Germany' in Roger Fletcher (ed.), *Bernstein*, pp. 11-16; Vernon Lidtke, 'Recent Literature on Workers' Culture in Germany and England' in Klaus Tenfelde (ed.), *Arbeiter und Arbeiterbewegung im Vergleich* (Munich, 1986), pp. 336-362; Adelheid von Saldern, 'Wilhelminische Gesellschaft und Arbeiterklasse' in *IWK* 13 (1977), pp. 469-505.

9 Paul Kennedy, *The Rise of Anglo-German Antagonimsm, 1860-1914* (London, 1980), p. 68; Geoff Eley, *Reshaping the German Right* (New Haven, 1980), pp. 118-140; Jonathan Steinberg, *Tirpitz and the Birth of the German Battle Fleet* (London, 1965), p. 36.

10 Hans-Ulrich Wehler, *The German Empire, 1871-1918* (Leamington Spa, 1985), pp. 94-100 and pp. 163-215. A critique of Wehler, however, can be found in Geoff Eley, *From Unification to Nazism* (London, 1986), pp. 110-70.

11 Kennedy, p. 381.

12 *Reichstagsverhandlungen*, 9. Legislaturperiode, IV Session (1895-97), Sitting of 16.11.1896, p. 3279; Parvus, *Marineforderungen, Kolonialpolitik und Arbeiterinteressen* (Dresden, 1898).

13 *Reichstagsverhandlungen*, 11. Legislaturperiode, IV. Session (1905/6), Sitting of 7.12.1905; Eduard Bernstein, 'The naval race and German finance' in *The Nation*, 2 (1908), 22 February; Groh, *Negative Integration*, p. 724.

14 Roger Fletcher, *Revisionism and Empire* (London, 1984), pp. 40, 55, 57, 63, 85, 101, 110.

15 Joseph Bloch, 'Der Krieg und die Sozialdemokratie' in *Sozialistische Monatshefte* (1914), 2, pp. 1023-27; Bloch, quoted in Fletcher, *Revisionism*, p. 65 n. 5.

16 Quoted in Fletcher, *Revisionism*, p. 56.

17 Fletcher, *Revisionism*, p. 40; Nick Stargadt, *The German Idea of Militarism* (Cambridge, 1994), pp. 61f. For more on Bernstein see below.
18 Bebel to Kautsky, 10.10.1998, printed in Friedrich Adler (ed.) *Viktor Adlers Briefwechsel mit August Bebel und Karl Kautsky* (Vienna, 1954), pp. 256f; also to Kautsky 16.10.1898, reprinted in *Einheit* (1960), 2, p. 226; *Protokoll...Hannover (1899)*, p. 173. Rosa Luxemburg, 'Die englische Brille' in *Gesammelte Werke* III (Berlin, 1924), pp. 104-14; Kautsky to Bernstein, 30 Oct 1898 (IISG Amsterdam).
19 Peter Gay, *The Dilemma of Democratic Socialism* (London, 1962); Francis L Carsten, *Eduard Bernstein, 1850-1932* (Munich, 1993); Eduard Bernstein, *Sozialismus und Sozialdemokratie in der grossen englischen Revolution* (Stuttgart, 1898).
20 Max Beer, *Fifty Years of International Socialism* (London, 1935), p. 183; Edward Pease, *History of the Fabian Society* (New York, 1916), p. 239. Carsten, *Bernstein*, pp. 61f.; Herbert Frei, *Fabianismus und Bernsteinscher Revisionismus* (Frankfurt/Main, 1979), p. 182.
21 Various contacts are to be found in Eduard Bernstein, *Aus den Jahren meines Exils* (Berlin, 1917). Belfort Bax described Bernstein as a 'Fabian convert': *Justice* 7 (November, 1896). For Bernstein's favourable comments see *Die Neue Zeit* 14 (1895/6), pp. 80-85 and 15 (1896/7), p. 167.
22 *Aus den Jahren*, pp. 244f.
23 Bernstein to Bebel, 20 October 1898; also Eduard Bernstein, 'Entwicklungsgang eines Sozialisten' in *Die Volkswirtschaftslehre der Gegenwart* I (Leipzig, 1924, pp. 1-58.
24 Frei, *Fabianismus*, pp. 119f, 127f, 136f and 176ff.
25 *Protokoll...Dresden (1903)*, p. 179.
26 Bernstein to Kautsky, 26.10.1895.
27 Bernstein to Kautsky, 7.2.1897.
28 Bernstein, *The Preconditions of Socialism* (Cambridge, 1993), p. 105.
29 *Die Neue Zeit* 9 (1890/1), 1, p. 666; *Sozialistische Monatshefte* (1904), 2, pp. 888-95; *Parlamentarismus und Sozialdemokratie* (Berlin, 1906), pp. 57-59; *Sozialistische Monatshefte* (1912), 2, p. 656.
30 *Neue Zeit* 13 (1895), 2, p. 523f. and 571f.; *Neue Zeit* 14 (1896), 2, p. 650; *Die Voraussetzungen des Sozialismus* (Reinbek, 1969), p. 123; *Preconditions*, pp. 143f. and 188.
31 *Sozialistische Monatshefte* (1900), p. 244; *The Nation* 2 (1907), 7, 16 November. *Neue Zeit* 9 (1891), 1, pp. 25f.
32 *Die englische Gefahr und das deutsche Volk* (Berlin, 1911), p. 19.
33 Ibid., pp. 47f. Also *Reichstagsverhandlungen* 2. Legislaturperiode, Session 1, vol 1, p. 807.

34 Quoted in Fletcher, *Revisionism*, p. 124. See also Luxemburg, 'Die englische Brille', *passim*.
35 Luxemburg, 'Die englische Brille', *Leipziger Volkszeitung*, 9 May 1899.
36 *Sächsische Arbeiterzeitung*, 6 December 1904.
37 Engels to Bebel, 5 July 1892, reprinted in *Marx and Engels on Britain* (Moscow, 1962), p. 572.
38 *Neue Zeit* 18 (1900), 1, p. 593.
39 *Neue Zeit* 27 (1909), 1, p. 45.
40 *Neue Zeit* 18 (1900), 1, pp. 98, 197-200 and 587-97.
41 *Thomas More and his Utopia* (New York, 1959), pp. 33 and 123ff.
42 Ibid., p. 292.
43 Ibid., p. 368.
44 The letter to Mehring is quoted in Karl Renner, *Karl Kautsky* (Berlin, 1929), p. 86.
45 *Protokoll...Stuttgart (1898)*, p. 129.
46 Kautsky to Bernstein 15.2.1898.
47 As note 44.
48 Marx and Engels, *On Britain* (Moscow, 1962), p. 361.
49 Ibid., pp. 494f.
50 *Neue Zeit* 1 (1883), p. 393; 3 (1885), pp. 17-21 and 467-73; *VIIe Congrès Socialiste Internationale*, Stuttgart (1907), p. 314; *Neue Zeit* 25 (1907), 1, p. 491; 26 (1908), 1, p. 216. Also notes 43 and 45 above.
51 *Neue Zeit* 16 (1892), 1, p. 806.
52 *Neue Zeit* 16 (1892), 1, pp. 806-9 and 814f.
53 See note (12) and (13) above; Kennedy, p. 99; *Reichstagsverhandlungen* 10. Legislaturperiode, I Session (1898-1900), vol iv, sitting of 12.12.1899, pp. 3321f.
54 *Reichstagsverhandlungen* 11. Legislaturperiode, II Session (1905-6), sitting of 11.12.1905, p. 222.
55 Hans-Christoph Schröder, *Sozialdemokratie und Imperialismus* (Hanover, 1968), pp. 137ff.
56 Friedrich Stampfer, *Erfahrungen und Erkenntnisse* (Cologne, 1957), p. 12; August Bebel, *Die Frau und der Sozialismus* 10th ed (Stuttgart, 1891), pp. v-vi.
57 Edward Bellamy, *Ein Rückblick aus dem Jahre 2000* (transl. & ed. by Klara Zetkin, Stuttgart, 1914), pp. 3f.
58 Quoted in Kennedy, p. 329.
59 *Neue Zeit* 14 (1896), 2, p. 650.
60 Franz Mehring, *Zur Geschichte der deutschen Sozialdemokratie* (Magdeburg, 1877), pp. 83f.
61 Gay, *Dilemna*, p. 104.

62 Marx and Engels, *On Britain*, p. 33; *Labour Standard*, 23 July 1881.
63 Marx and Engels, *On Britain*, p. 560.
64 Ibid., p. 539.
65 Ibid., pp. 517f; *Labour Standard*, 23 July 1881.
66 *Neue Zeit* 17 (1900), 1, p. 434.
67 Friedrich Naumann, *Die Sozialdemokratie im Urteil ihrer Gegner* (Berlin, 1911), p. 12.
68 Moira Donald, *Marxism and Revolution* (London, 1985), p. 184.
69 *Neue Zeit* 32 (1914), 1, p. 465.
70 *Neue Zeit* 18 (1900), 2, p. 465; 19 (1901), 2, p. 80; 20 (1902), 1, p. 80.
71 *Neue Zeit* 18 (1900), 1, pp. 197-200.
72 Bebel, *Die Frau*, p. 379.

6 The Intellectual Connections between British and European Economists in the 1920s: Cambridge and Geneva on International Economic Policies*

GRANT FLEMING

This chapter focuses on British and European economists' proposals for world economic integration in the 1920s, with special reference to the work of J.M. Keynes and economists working at the League of Nations. The work of these researchers is placed in the broader context of economic and social policy debate emanating from Geneva. I examine League economists' contributions to international economic policy debate in the 1920s, and identify intellectual connections between British and European economic thought on integration.

Introduction

Historians of economic and social thought have recently turned attention to the organisation of economic research in Europe. Craver (1986) and de Marchi (1991) have mentioned the philanthropic function of the Rockefeller Foundation in providing seed and infrastructure funding for European social science research, and Morgan (1990, pp. 64-68) has analysed the functions of European business cycle institutes in the 1920s. Less attention has been directed to the intellectual connections between economic researchers working in Europe; in particular, the cross-fertilisation of ideas between the

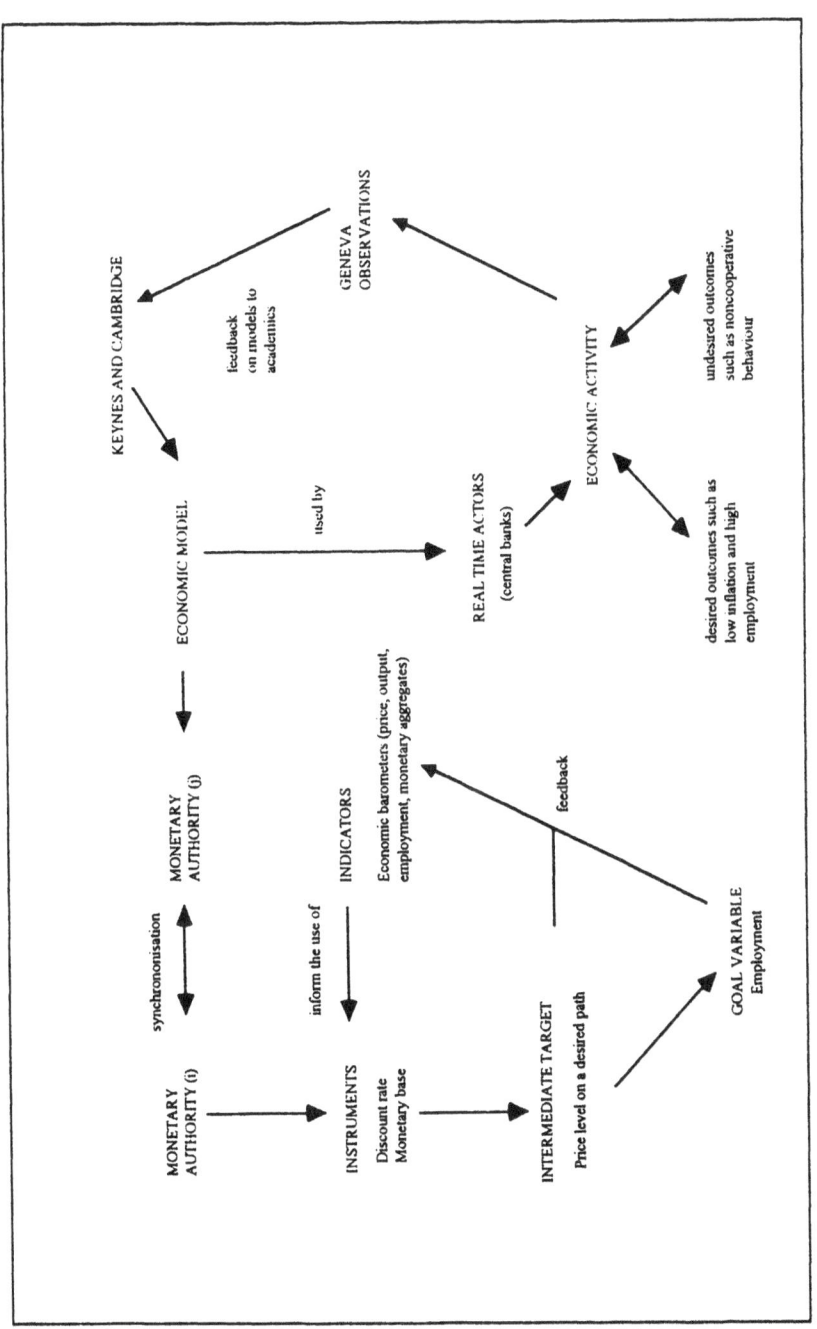

Fig. 1: The economic system and the process of economic inquiry

academic "hotbed" at Cambridge and other European centres. This dearth of analysis is even more striking for the case of economists working in international agencies. During the interwar period the League of Nations and the International Labour Organisation (ILO) developed research secretariats that disseminated information on economic and social issues, analysed postwar economic problems, and advocated policy prescriptions. These researchers were part of a larger European intellectual community, many of whom sought to apply the findings of social science research for the alleviation of social and economic problems.

The League and ILO economists were especially influenced by the work of British economist J.M. Keynes who sought to understand the economic-theoretic aspects of economic instability in postwar European economies and partook in contemporary policy debate. Like Keynes, much of the work of the League's economic secretariat was founded on a belief that international economic processes could be harnessed for the purposes of economic and social progress. In this chapter I describe the climate for interdisciplinary research in Geneva and examine the connections between Geneva and Keynes on the issue of economic integration. In doing so I focus on the economic secretariat of the ILO as an exemplar of the League's research institutions. I argue that the contribution of economists became engines of advocacy in the pursuit of a broad concept of economic and social justice. These researchers seized the opportunity to serve as "pragmatic intellectuals", sharing a belief that society would benefit from professional expertise.

My discussion begins in section II by outlining the establishment of the ILO's research programme. In Section III I describe the major aspects of ILO economic research which placed emphasis on cooperation in international economic policy, and examine connections between this work and that of J.M. Keynes in the 1920s. Section IV contains some conclusions.

The Establishment of the ILO Research Programme

The ILO was established as an office of the League of Nations through the Treaty of Versailles in 1919. The organisation was to report on conditions of labour "involving injustice, hardship and privation to large numbers of people as to produce unrest so great that the peace and harmony of the world [is] imperilled; and an improvement of those conditions is urgently required".[1] While the Treaty signatories envisaged the ILO to be solely an administrative body collecting information on labour issues, Albert Thomas, the ILO's founding director, soon won it greater independence and worked to make the Office an "instrument of action" - not only to study microeconomic and socio-legislative issues pertaining to labour in various countries, but to draw generalisations and recommend action from that research for the more lofty goals of world peace and harmony. Thomas's vision linked social problems associated with conditions of labour internationally with general economic problems. Thus it

> is no longer possible to separate [social problems] from the whole economic system...Nowadays during employment crises, it is not merely relief or employment that is demanded, but the whole system of organisation of industry, distribution of raw materials, and foreign exchange is called to account (Thomas 1921, p. 19).

Thomas's experience as Minister of Munitions in the French wartime government had shown him that the application of the techniques of scientific management could solve many problems associated with the "technical organisation of labour". Indeed, the war had been "a vast testing laboratory" that allowed him "to apply new ideas and methods in many areas of social and economic activity" (Fine 1977, pp. 549, 551).[2] The "reformist" attitude (especially a belief in modernisation) that Thomas brought to the ILO soon permeated the research culture of the institution: as the deputy director Harold Butler (1932, p. 4) was to later note, "it was not enough to bring the nations to Geneva,...it was equally necessary that the gospel of Geneva should be preached in the national capitals". Under Thomas the ILO sought to "act as an international arbitrator capable of harmonising conflicting interests and regulating social progress;...to *actively promote* the cause of social and economic reform throughout the world" (Fine 1977, p. 553, our emphasis). The quest for national security was intricately linked with economic stability. Without peace between countries there was no foundation for economic prosperity on which "to build a better social order". And for Thomas neither peace nor a better social order "could be attained except by conscious and coordinated international action, both in the economic and political spheres" (Butler 1932, p. 6).[3] Economic research was to play an integral part in achieving these goals by laying the theoretical foundations for economic reform.

The leadership of Thomas and the work emanating from Geneva fitted well with other European research programmes in the 1920s and 1930s, many of which were funded by the Rockefeller Foundation. This philanthropic organisation supported research on the "causes of fundamental human misery" and fostered "the growth of intellectually strong centres of interdisciplinary research where empirical methods of research were used" (Craver 1986, pp. 205, 207). This support extended to partially funding the Geneva School of International Studies in the 1920s and business cycle research undertaken by the League of Nations Financial Section and

Economic Intelligence Section during the 1930s (ibid, pp. 208, 213; de Marchi 1991, pp. 149-54). While it is unclear whether any Rockefeller funding found its way to the ILO, Thomas fostered links with other American philanthropists in order to gain money to support research on the social aspects of economic instability. The ILO and Edward Filene's Twentieth Century Fund jointly financed the Institute for the Scientific Organisation of Labour which encouraged the spread of cooperation and planning in industrial processes and economic policy: ideals that were close to the heart of ILO researchers (Fine 1977, p. 556).[4]

The research division provided a data collection service for the ILO, translated and published labour laws from various member countries, provided background papers for the ILO conferences and international meetings of delegates, and undertook independent research on all subjects relating to labour. By 1925 it comprised sections specialising in statistics, labour legislation, agriculture, unemployment, industrial health and safety, and social insurance and disablement. Investigations clearly straddled these pre-determined boundaries and the chiefs of sections acted as technical advisers on a variety of projects. Apart from reports on the above subjects, the division played out its role as an "instrument of action" when labour matters were due for discussion at the Assembly of the League of Nations. To fully inform their understanding of such matters the ILO's researchers considered broader economic and financial policies affecting industrial output, consumption, investment and business cycles on an international scale. It is this research that I examine in more detail below.

Intellectual Connections between Geneva and Cambridge

In July 1929 Keynes travelled to Geneva to give a series of lectures at the School of International Studies on foreign investment, World War I reparations, and a proposal for a world bank. The series attracted not only students and academics at the school, but intellectuals from various disciplines working in Geneva. Indeed, the subjects Keynes lectured on were familiar to ILO researchers, as several economists had drawn theoretical inspiration from his earlier work. J.R. Bellerby (one of the more prolific of the Geneva researchers) had close personal connections with Keynes and was to move regularly between Cambridge and Geneva.

From the early 1920s investigations at Geneva into the causes of unemployment focused on understanding the course of the business cycle. The League of Nations business cycle research programme was based at the ILO, which drew upon expertise of other League agencies when necessary. As noted above, the rationale for this programme was founded on the belief that economic stability was an important part of political stability. Cyclical downturns posed a real threat to international peace in that they caused human suffering and insecurity, and upset the system of finely balanced trade and financial linkages (de Marchi 1991, p. 144). The Fourth International Labour Conference of the League resolved that the ILO make "a special study of the problem of the crises of unemployment,...and to make known the measure taken with a view to sustaining economic activity" (ILO 1924, introductory note). Preliminary studies concentrated on country profiles and case studies, out of which general international conclusions were intended to be drawn. But soon ILO researchers realised that the conditions of labour could not be analysed in isolation from imposing macroeconomic trends associated with monetary forces and the macrodynamics of the business cycle in industrialised economies. Research turned to the causes of the business cycle and policy solutions.

Researchers set out a simple monetary theory of the business cycle, giving prominence to the linkages between the money supply and prices. As Fuss (1927, p. 603) noted, the "close relationship between movements in the general price level and the increase or decrease of unemployment is to be explained as the resultant of these changes in the ratio of money to goods". The view that variations in the price level was the major cause of unemployment reflected contemporary opinion but was also borne out be analysis of the postwar slump in economic activity. Researchers drew theoretical inspiration from American and British economists: Mitchell's (1913) business cycle project (continued at the National Bureau of Economic Research in the 1920s), Hawtrey's (1923) pure monetary theory and Fisher's (1911) equation of exchange. But this was inspiration tempered by a concern with application of those theories to recent economic downturns and a desire to formulate international economic policy designed to alleviate fluctuations in employment.[5] The Geneva researchers spent little time on the technical aspects of business cycle theory and directed attention to the policy implications of contemporary work, with particular emphasis on employment stability.[6] Indeed, it became a tenet of ILO research that the success of economic policy was to be judged by "the probable effect on social conditions, on the life and work of the great mass of the people" rather than with recourse to broad economic indicators such as public and foreign debt, and gold holdings (Martin and Riches 1933, p. 21).

By the late 1920s five major policy recommendations can be identified (see Endres and Fleming 1996a, p. 216) which focused on monetary reform and the prevention of unemployment. First, following arguments made as early as the Genoa conference in 1922, central banks should be strengthened so as to make private banks more dependent upon these institutions. Second, a greater amount of central bank power in the world's major money markets would permit the use of monetary instruments such as discount rates to achieve price level stability. Smaller countries could gain price stability by linking their currencies to one of the world's major countries (for example, the monetary connections developed between Britain and her Dominions). Third, in keeping with the adopted social criteria of economic policy, price level stabilisation must be contemplated and achieved in the light of the ultimate goals of output and employment stabilisation at high levels. The remaining two recommendations related to the conduct of monetary policy: international collaboration by the major central banks could bring about an "international policy of price stabilisation" and international economic stability; and monetary policies may guide the macroeconomy only if price, output and employment indices are used to inform discretionary actions.[7]

Much of the ILO work on business cycles and monetary reform was well known to British economists, in particular, J.M. Keynes. As mentioned above, Bellerby had spent some years with Keynes at Cambridge and had been described by the Cambridge don as being intimately involved in "the almost revolutionary improvement in our understanding of the mechanism of money and credit and of the analysis of the trade cycle".[8] Keynes's lectures in Geneva in 1929 (and his press interviews in the months before) wholeheartedly supported proposals for international cooperation as a means of achieving high and sustainable levels of employment. In particular, the ILO idea of a supra-national monetary authority to guide internationally-coordinated monetary policy (an early type of world bank), championed by members of the Young Committee, found favour with Keynes.[9] In an interview with American economist Irving Fisher, Keynes argued that "if we are to manage our monetary affairs in a rational manner in the years to come, unquestionably we shall need some supra-national authority of great influence which will provide an organisation for the collaboration of the central banks of the world". Such an institution would take its place alongside "the League of Nations and the International Court of Justice as one of the super-national institutions with which the world of the future will endeavour to keep its international arrangements in order".[10] Up to the late 1920s, then, the intellectual connections between Keynes and Geneva took place on the issues of world monetary reform and the possibility of designing international institutions to bring about world peace and economic security. Things were soon to change.

The worsening depression experience during 1930 and 1931 led Geneva researchers to greater involvement in debate over recovery policies and the role of international agencies in economic reconstruction. In this debate the intellectual connections were more complex with Geneva researchers drawing from but also informing their British academic contemporaries. The depression brought to the fore research on underconsumption as an explanation of cyclical instability - research that was motivated by the difficulties recognised in implementing an "international" monetary policy when the major central banks were apparently unwilling to cooperate. The research division embraced "demand-side" theories such as those by Americans Foster and Catchings (1925, 1928) which argued unemployment was caused by a decrease in consumption expenditures - a decrease in aggregate demand which occurs when "the community uses part of its buying power, not to pay for goods, but instead lends it to industry to enable industry to take on more workers" (Martin 1926, p. 42). Policy solutions to this type of unemployment focused on the use of public works to boost purchasing power in the economy. A 1931 ILO survey of the theory and practice of public works identified positive downstream effects from government works activity during cyclical downturns (ILO 1931, pp. 4-5, 25-26), but recommendations were confined to works at a national level on a relatively small scale. The international-cooperative possibilities of public works were recognised a year later during the April 1932 ILO Conference, and drew upon Thomas's founding vision that planning and cooperation could alleviate social problems. It was now felt that "Government delegates...should as soon as possible be given instructions to draw up a list of big international works on a large scale calculated to encourage the general development of the economic situation of the countries concerned" (ILO 1932, p. 221).

The development of Keynes's ideas on the use of public works expenditure to increase national purchasing power during economic depressions has been well documented. By the early 1930s Keynes had worked through many of the theoretical implications of public works and had provided key advice to the British MacMillan Committee. Keynes's arguments on public works (otherwise termed home investment) concentrated on the immediate effects of an increase in government expenditures on the British economy, although he does rather opaquely mention that at the international level the "world-wide encouragement of investment and of capital development generally would help" (quoted in Flanders 1989, p. 116). The ILO investigatory work on an internationally based large scale public works policy went well beyond Keynes's prescriptions for Britain. Of course, like Keynes, they were concerned about the speed of adjustment of private sector investment intentions following introduction of easier monetary policy (for example, Martin and Riches 1933, p. 50). In such a climate public works expenditure would not act to deter private investment; employment would not simply be diverted from so-called more productive private employment to public sector employment, and inflation was not inevitable.[11] But the Geneva researchers linked *international* monetary policy coordination with *large scale investment schemes.* Provided central banks in surplus countries pursued expansionary monetary policies and provided public authorities carefully planned public works schemes, the activity in one country would have demonstration effects for others and lead to a revival of employment internationally (Woytinsky 1932). Moreover, the revival would be enduring if public works schemes ceased to be regarded as temporary measures. The ILO would assist authorities in ILO member countries with planning, given that the Office had collected much detailed information on suitable schemes. Carefully planned public works not only helped revive economic activity but they also had a long term place in economic development by maintaining investment and purchasing power at high levels. As the ILO Director noted, "public enterprise is an indispensable method of stimulating industrial activity". The role of the ILO was to be a world observatory of economic conditions, facilitating economic cooperation in terms of public expenditure in major European countries. That the Geneva researchers were innovative in these "internationalist" policies was acknowledged by Keynes himself in his *magnum opus The General Theory,* where he described the ILO's "consistent appreciation" of the need for active public investment programmes involving concerted international initiatives (Keynes 1936, p. 349 n.1).

Concluding Remarks

Economic cooperation and concern with the social effects of economic policy were central themes in Geneva research in the 1920s and in Keynes's policy prescriptions. Geneva researchers and Keynes disseminated the idea in Europe and Britain that governments could play a major role in the restoration and maintenance of employment levels; international coordination of monetary and public works policies would yield a new social order in which economic stability would play a major role in the maintenance of world peace.

During the 1920s Geneva researchers drew upon contemporary models to explain the workings of the economic system. In many instances, however, researchers went beyond mere adoption of pre-existing theory to offer modifications if that theory was at odds with economic reality. For example, the goal of price stability was set by academic economists such as Keynes during the 1920s on the assumption that the attainment of price stability was necessary for the private sector to operate at its full potential - and full employment was a result of this. Price stability was to be achieved through central bank manipulation of the domestic money supply; either by changing the discount rate or by open market operations. The information -

or signals from the economy - necessary for success of this system was encapsulated in price level data (see left hand side of Figure 1 above). Geneva economists adopted this model from contemporary academic research in order to explain trade cycles and to dictate policy. However, these researchers found that the world acted differently to the basic precepts of their model in two areas: the use of price level data to signal deteriorating economic conditions (and thus guide monetary policy), and the non-cooperative strategies adopted by national governments in times of "necessary" international payments adjustment. Thus, Geneva economists performed the role of economic practitioners, using the economic model to determine the actions policymakers could and could not pursue. The traditional single country approach, as outlined in contemporary models of the economy, of undertaking monetary policy on the basis of the movement of gold reserves - movements responding to international trade and payments flows - should be replaced by a continuous system of credit regulation at the international level, based on the observation of industrial conditions assessed by reference to a wide range of quantitative variables. For the practitioners in the ILO it was crucial that the *effects* of price movements, that is, effects on production and employment, be understood and monitored in tandem with price indices. The Geneva economists, users of economic models and monitors of the behaviour of real-time economic actors (central banks), provided feedback to academics regarding the empirical validity or explanatory power of their models (see right hand side of Figure 1 above). Academics such as Keynes clearly drew upon the extensive empirical work of the League and the ILO in forming opinions about the usefulness of their conceptual frameworks. Apart from Keynes's several acknowledgments of ILO and League work in his theoretical writings, we find him adopting League of Nations' classification systems, and keeping up-to-date with major League and ILO inquiries and reports.[12] The intellectual connections between Cambridge and Geneva were therefore reinforcing rather than one-way derivative. European practitioners at the international agency level played an important role in informing British academics of the workings of the complex post World War I economic world.

References

Butler, H.B. (1932) "Albert Thomas, the First Director", *International Labour Review* vol. 26 (1), pp. 1-7.
Craver, E. (1986) "Patronage and the Directions of Research in Economics: The Rockefeller Foundation in Europe, 1924-1938", *Minerva* vol. 24 (2-3), pp. 205-22.
De Marchi, N. (1991) "League of Nations economists and the ideal of peaceful change in the decade of the 'thirties", *History of Political Economy* vol. 23 (supplement), pp. 143-78.
Endres, A.M. and Fleming, G.A. (1996a) "International Economic Policy in the Interwar Years: The Special Contribution of ILO Economists", *International Labour Review* vol. 135 (2), pp. 207-26.
Endres, A.M. and Fleming, G.A. (1996b) "Monetary Policy and the Business Cycle: The View from Geneva in the 1920s", *Australian National University Working Paper in Economics and Econometrics*, No. 311, September.
Fine, M. (1977) "Albert Thomas: A Reformer's Vision of Modernization, 1914-32", *Journal of Contemporary History* vol. 12, pp. 545-64.
Fisher, I. (1911) *The Purchasing Power of Money* (New York, MacMillan).
Flanders, M. June, (1989) *International Monetary Economics, 1870-1960: Between the Classical and the New Classical* (Cambridge: Cambridge University Press).
Foster, W.F. and Catchings, W. (1925) *Profits* (Boston: Houghton Mifflin).
Foster, W.F. and Catchings, W. (1928) *The Road To Plenty* (London, Pitman and Sons).
Fuss, H. (1927) "Money and Unemployment", *International Labour Review* vol. 16 (5), pp. 601-17.
Hancock, K.J. (1960) "Unemployment and the Economists in the 1920s", *Economica* vol. 27, pp. 305-21.
Hawtrey, R.G. (1923) *Monetary Reconstruction* (London, Longmans).
International Labour Organisation (1924) *Economic Barometers* (Geneva, ILO Studies and Reports Series N No. 5).
International Labour Organisation (1931) *Unemployment and Public Works* (Geneva, ILO Studies and Reports Series C No. 15).
International Labour Organisation (1932) "Resolution Adopted by the Sixteenth Session of the International Labour Conference Concerning Action to be Taken to Remedy the Crisis", *International Labour Review* vol. 26 (2), pp. 220-21.
Keynes, J.M. (1936) *The General Theory of Employment, Interest and Money* (London: MacMillan).
Martin, P.W. (1926) "Overproduction and Underconsumption: A Remedy", *International Labour Review* vol. 14 (1), pp. 37-54.
Martin, P.W. and Riches, E.J. (1933) "The Social Consequences of a Return to Gold", *International Labour Review* vol. 27 (1), pp. 25-50.

Mitchell, W.C. (1913) *Business Cycles* (California, University of California Press).
Morgan, M. (1990) *A History of Econometric Ideas* (Cambridge, Cambridge University Press).
Perry, L. (1986) *Intellectual Life in America: A History* (Chicago, Chicago University Press).
Stromberg, R.N. (1981) *European Intellectual History since 1789* (New Jersey, Prentice Hall).
Thomas, A. (1921) "The International Labour Organisation: Its Origins, Development and Future", *International Labour Review* vol. 1, pp. 5-22.
Wohl, R. (1986) "The Generation of 1914 and Modernism", in M. Chefdor, R. Quinones and A. Wachtel (eds) *Modernism: Challenges and Perspectives* (Urbana, University of Illinois Press), pp. 66-78.
Woytinsky, V. (1932) "International Measures to Create Employment: A Remedy for the Depression", *International Labour Review* vol. 25 (1), pp. 1-22.

Notes

*   This paper is part of a larger project entitled "Economic Thought and Policy Advice at the International Labour Organisation: The First 50 Years 1919-1969" in collaboration with A.M. Endres (University of Auckland). All errors and omissions in this paper, however, remain mine.
1   Preamble to the Charter of the International Labour Organisation, Treaty of Versailles, Part XIII quoted in *International Labour Directory*, 1925, p. 1.
2   We should note the similarity between Thomas's experience in France and that of American planners. Wartime experience in America "strengthened a conviction...that intellectuals had a special non-partisan role to play in service of an expanded national government." Amongst American economists impressed by wartime planning were Wesley C. Mitchell, Thorstein Veblen and Rexford Tugwell (Perry 1989, pp. 349-50).
3   Thomas's belief in the ability of the social scientist to solve the economic and social problems of a modernising society stands in contrast to the post-World War I "modernist" views of European artistic circles. There "[s]cientific analysis was considered a mental instrument of severely limited validity; intuition into the multiplicity of human realities was recommended in its place; and action rather than contemplation was valued as a source of knowledge. The new culture was subjectivist and relativistic; truth was both pastoral and temporary" (Wohl 1986, p. 73; see also Stromberg 1981, pp. 249-59). On such views in America see Perry (1989, pp. 324-44).
4   This Institute was to later receive funds from the Rockefeller Foundation (ibid).
5   By contrast, many orthodox economists at the time recognised the economic and social problems associated with unemployment but refused to subjugate

the goals of fiscal balance, debt reduction and price level stability for maintenance of high employment levels. As Gregory noted, it was "useless to allow working-class sentiment to govern monetary policy" and that "the question of deflation is not to be disposed of by showing that it will lead to unemployment. For it may be worth while to pay this price, not merely to 'do justice to the rentier' but e.g., to get back to a sound currency" quoted in Hancock 1960, p. 306.

6 An exception was their work on the design of practical goals, rules and methods for the conduct of monetary policy which deserves acknowledgment in the history of the rules versus discretion debate (Endres and Fleming 1996b, p. 27).

7 The nuances of ILO recommendations on monetary policy and the business cycle are discussed in Endres and Fleming (1996b).

8 See Keynes in *The Collected Writings of John Maynard Keynes*, vol. XI (London, MacMillan, 1983), p. 419 and p. 419n.

9 The Young Committee was established in 1928 to review Germany's payment of reparations after the First World War.

10 Interview with I. Fisher for the *New York's Evening World* reprinted in *The Collected Writings of John Maynard Keynes*, vol. XVIII (London, MacMillan, 1978), p. 345.

11 It should be noted that research of public works also drew upon ILO and League investigations into economic planning at the micro and macro levels. Since its inception the ILO research division had maintained a Russian service to monitor the operation of socialist economic planning, and there was interest from the League in the Italian fascist economy (for example, see studies in the 1931 and 1932 conferences on *The State and Economic Life*).

12 See, for example, Keynes in *The Collected Writings of John Maynard Keynes*, vol. XI, p. 447; vol. XIX, p. 775-81; and vol. XIII, p. 347.

7 The British in the Rhineland

HEIDI ZOGBAUM

Historically, the Rhineland is more strongly associated with France than Britain, since it is a disputed border province which successive French governments between the 17th and the 20th century coveted and wished to annex to France in order to have a strong Eastern border defence in the form of Europe's mightiest river. The short period when large parts of the Rhineland did indeed belong to Napoleon's expanding empire is still locally known as *die Franzosenzeit,* and few Rhinelanders believe that it was a good time.

After the French defeat and German unification in 1871, most of the Rhineland became a Prussian province and France, honoured in blood-curdling speeches as the *Erbfeind* every *Sedanstag*, no longer constituted a threat to the Rhineland. Britain, isolated and far away, speaking a language few Germans mastered and most found rather ridiculous, never greatly impinged on the consciousness of Rhinelanders until WW1. However, throughout much of the 19th century Britain began to exert a strong influence in the whole of Germany in an unexpected quarter: namely sport, and more particularly soccer. The most important centre from which this influence grew was a small town on the Eastern bank of the Rhine, Neuwied, about 20 km upstream from Coblenz.

Founded in 1653 by the Princes of Wied, Neuwied is a typical product of the Enlightenment. The new town quickly became known as a place of great religious tolerance where craftsmen of all denominations were welcome if they helped to build the prosperity of the town. By the early 19th century almost every denomination -including a large Jewish community- had settled there. The single most important religious group was the *Herrnhuter Brüdergemeine*, the Moravian Brethren, a Protestant sect which had been driven out of Moravia in the middle of the 18th century.[1] The Count von Zinzendorf, the founder of the Moravian Brethren, had lived in London for several years and exerted great influence on John Wesley. The Moravian Brethren and their school put Neuwied on the international map.²

During the 19th century Neuwied became known as the City of Schools. The Moravian Boys' School educated a total of 4,573 students, 2,720 of which came from England, Scotland and Ireland. British students began to arrive in increasing numbers from about 1820 onwards and in 1838 the school built an indoor swimming pool, something quite unknown in Germany at the time. This was followed in 1845 by a gymnasium which was rather exceptional as well. In 1871 an impressive three storey building made from local black lava stone was built to house the ever increasing numbers of British students and English was now the official teaching language. In 1873, the year of its greatest prosperity, the school had 113 pupils, 100 of which were British. Henry Morley, a close collaborator of Charles Dickens, and the novelist George Meredith were "Old Neuwieders," so were Lucas Pigott and Arthur Chamberlain. By 1883 the school had only British students.³

During the 1880s the girls' school had an average of 80 English borders a year. This was at a time when there was no proper secondary education for girls in England. In 1878 the school had to turn down 150 applicants. Among them was the King of Siam who wished to see ten of his sons educated at Neuwied. But his application was rejected on religious grounds. The importance of Neuwied was such that the London-Chatham-Dover-Railway Company issued tickets London-Neuwied in 1891 and special carriages from Harwich via Rotterdam stopped at Weissenturm, opposite Neuwied, from whence passengers took the boat ferry.⁴

An important part of the school curriculum was open air activity, including extensive walks through the surrounding hills and forests of the Westerwald. But the British students also brought tennis and football with them, both sports quite unknown in Germany. The Moravian Boys' School is credited with having organised the first international soccer match in Germany in 1886. "*Geheimrat* Professor Dr. Dr. Ferdinand Hueppe", a local of Neuwied and former pupil of the school, one of the founders of bacteriology in Germany and a close collaborator of Prof. Robert Koch, first came in contact with soccer through the English students during a teaching spell at his old school.⁵ Being a promoter of open air sports, he asked a group of Neuwied boys from the local school's rowing club for a match against the English team. The local newspaper reported that "the English from the Herrnhut School, clad in carnival costumes, ran after an inflated bladder and tried to drive it through two posts by way of kicking it."⁶ However, the first "international soccer match" was so amateurish that no score was recorded and the reporter of the local paper obviously had no idea what he was dealing with. But the British game was quickly adopted by working-class boys and a number of football clubs came into existence, the last of which was founded in 1899.[7] Prof. Hueppe himself became the founding president of the German Football League in 1900.[8]

Although neither football nor tennis were adopted by the sons of the respectable Neuwied middle class, the British influence was strong. In 1838, the year when the Moravian Boys' School opened its indoor swimming pool, the director of the local secondary boys' school made *Turnen*, gymnastics, a regular part of the school curriculum, long before this became the rule throughout Germany. In 1877 rowing was added and Neuwied was the first town in Germany to have a rowing club attached to its secondary school.[9] It was from this club that Prof. Hueppe invited some boys to play soccer. But it does not look as if the boys took away a lasting impression. On the contrary, soccer quickly fell under a double spell: by being adopted by the working class, it was not seen fit to be played by the sons of the middle class. More damning still, soccer was clearly identified as a British sport which made it impossible for nationalist middle class lads to engage in. Soccer only received some grudging acceptance when the Crown Prince introduced it in the Army during WW1.

In September 1913 the Moravian School was forced to close. The deteriorating political climate between Germany and Britain had made it inadvisable for British parents to send their children to Germany for education. The British students were so isolated after the turn of the century and the start of the anti-British propaganda campaign in about 1903 that the son of the *Landrat*, the highest Prussian county administrator or district magistrate, did not know until I told him in 1994, and he was 93 years of age then, that such a school had ever existed in his home town.[10]

But the Rhinelanders were soon to change their minds about the British, even though they were to come as military occupiers rather than guests. The occupation of the Western side of the Rhineland was part of the Armistice conditions of November 1918 to ensure clearance of Alsace and Lorraine and demilitarisation of the Rhineland. Three bridgeheads of a 30 km radius reaching across the Rhine were established. The British occupied the northern bridgehead around Cologne. The official British report of the Military Occupation stated that

> word had gone forth from Berlin that the French Army of Occupation should be given as much trouble as possible and that all should go smoothly in the American and British areas with the specific purpose of separating the English-speaking contingents

from their Gallic ally and creating prejudice against her, if, as she did, she rose to the fly.[11]

This charge was always denied in Germany for good reasons. There was no need for Berlin to put out any such word; the Rhinelanders knew from experience whom they had to fear: namely the French.[12]

Neuwied lay inside the U.S. occupied Coblenz bridgehead and the Neuwieders were lucky. Many of them came to think that the American occupation was the best thing that ever happened to them after 1914. Just south of Coblenz started the French occupation zone whose inhabitants were considered the unluckiest and hatred of the *Erbfeind* and his colonial troops grew into serious warfare between the local population and French troops. One of the most popular songs of the time was a new version of the old drinking song *Warum ist es am Rhein so schön?* Anyone caught singing *Warum ist es am Rhein nicht schön? Weil der Franzmann, der Drecksack, das Rheinland besetzt hat*, was clapped into jail forthwith.[13] Considering the brutality with which the Germans had invaded and ransacked their country, the French occupiers were rather restrained, but no matter: they were hated even before they arrived.

In contrast, the British were eagerly awaited, especially by Konrad Adenauer, the mayor of Cologne. In the Eastern industrial suburbs of the city red flags had gone up in the course of the Spartakist uprisings. The first British cavalry troops to cross the Rhine on a grey and rainy 6 December 1918 described the locals as "friendly, curious and socialistic."[14] The Cologne business community, led by the mayor, looked to the British to rid their city of the red plague.

The British military commander, General Lawson, and later Sir Charles Fergusson, tried to make short shrift with the local soviets: they were dissolved and martial law imposed. Then the bridgehead was sealed: nobody could travel in or out without a passport issued by the British. What was particularly alarming to the British commander was the fact that Spartakists circulated pamphlets among British soldiers, causing strikes in the transport and catering corps.[15] A number of bloody street battles between military and Spartakists ensued but only when the British commander decided to placate German workers in the heavy metal industry with extra food rations was some form of peace established. Ironically, the tables turned quickly. When the Socialist Berlin government sent out *Freikorps* to crush uprisings, especially in the Ruhr, many Spartakists took refuge in Cologne and were not bothered unless they started trouble inside the bridgehead.

It soon became apparent that the strict enforcement of martial law brought more problems than it solved. The Cologne district had a population of 2,145,000 and contained some of Germany's most important industries such as Bayer Leverkusen and the Solingen steel industry. Without raw materials industry after industry slowed production and workers were out of work. Starvation was rife in the city of Cologne, not least because of the continuing British blockade of German ports. Instead of the normal 2,700 calories a day, people in Cologne received about 1,500.[16]

Members of the occupation force were forbidden to purchase food from Germans. Instead, the British lived off their own rations so as not to be a burden on German food reserves. The food situation became so desperate in 1919 that the British commander decided to violate his own orders and army emergency supplies were issued to the locals.[17]

Until the ratification of the Treaty of Versailles in January 1920 Cologne, Düsseldorf, Bonn, Solingen and Leverkusen were ruled with all the bureaucratic rigour of martial law. No private telephones, curfew, heavy censorship on press and mail and no free movement. Particularly vexing to Germans was the duty to greet British military personnel by doffing one's hat. The rules were enforced by summary courts which imposed heavy fines and jail terms. Complaints were rejected with the argument that these were exactly the same conditions which the German army had imposed in Belgium.[18]

Until January 1920, some 250,000 British and Dominion troops had to be accommodated in and around Cologne. This put enormous strain on already restricted housing and forced occupiers and occupied to live closely together which often led to frictions.[19] The Cologne city council opened an Occupation Bureau where complaints could be lodged. They ranged from flying practice over cemeteries -a No-No in Germany- to turning trucks ripping up the pavement. Requisitioning brought most complaints. At the same time, a good deal of strictly forbidden fraternisation was going on and some 500 British soldiers found themselves German brides.[20] There was also a good deal of philandering and a large crop of illegitimate children was born.

The biggest problem for the British troops was boredom. After the reds had been contained, soldiers had to be kept busy with what was known as spit and polish routines and sport, from polo to football, also helped a great deal. In that situation drinking was rife, particularly, since German wineshops and pubs know no drinking hours. In the course of drunken routs all manner of mostly harmless pranks were perpetrated. Two drunken officers placed chamber pots on the heads of the statues of Kaiser Wilhelm and his wife Auguste Victoria, much to the consternation and outrage of nationalistic citizens of Cologne.[21] In July 1919, after the signing of the Treaty of Versailles, the British Army allowed wives to join their husbands in Germany. Then strife took on new dimensions. Not only did the wives have to be accommodated and households fitted up by requisitioning, they had also gone through years and years of anti-German propaganda, and unlike their husbands who had very quickly seen that no German eats Belgian or any other babies, the wives were suspicious of Germans. Houseproud German housewives decided that the English women were dirty. Educated Germans, in turn, saw them as unspeakable, brash and tasteless. The English wives sat in the opera occupying the boxes set aside for military personnel, eating chocolates and beating time with their feet. The ultimate outrage was that they regularly violated the German opera dress code. As one German put it: "They sat there in all the glory of golfing jumpers and studded brogues."[22]

Apart from such minor vexations the British military occupation forces came to be trusted by the Rhinelanders because throughout they had proved to make balanced and fair decisions. In 1922 Lloyd George decided against any further policy of weakening German industrial strength and when the French occupied the Ruhr in 1923 Americans, Germans and British cooperated openly against the French who threatened to blockade the British occupation zone.[23] The victors had fallen out with each other over French attempts to convert their occupation zone into a French province and to bleed Germany white.[24] It was from this situation that British military personnel suspected that it had all been a well laid plot by Berlin. In 1924 the Dawes Plan which finally regulated reparations payments on a sustainable level, was set up by Britain and provided a rational solution to a problem which threatened to lead to further warfare.

The British occupation of Cologne ended on 31 January 1926 when protection against the French was no longer required. Considering that one British soldier in Germany cost 14 shillings a day to maintain and the Berlin government was expected to foot the bill, it was a relief for both. The local press only had praise and called the British "most conciliatory occupiers." Konrad Adenauer always maintained that the British had been scrupulously fair in all their dealings with Germans and they were seen off by grateful Cologne citizens who had observed their boredom. They nicknamed the parting British "The Army of No Occupation."[25]

However, the British never achieved what the Americans did. When they vacated their Coblenz bridgehead, they received the biggest send-off ever given an occupying army. That the U.S. intervention had caused the disastrous German defeat in the first place, was never really acknowledged in Germany;[26] in fact, it had already been forgotten when the fully motorised U.S. Army crossed the Rhine at Neuwied and stunned the local boys, my father among them.[27] The Americans were fully redeemed in German eyes when they refused to sign the Treaty of Versailles which was considered an act of French villainy. People stood in the streets crying that "their" Americans had to leave. Families had adopted individual soldiers and some 1,500 German girls went along as the wives of American soldiers.[28] This was the beginning of a German love affair with all things American which lasted well into the 1980s. The British had merely gained respect.

After the defeat of 1945, all of Germany was divided into occupation zones and the British returned to Cologne. People who did not end up under Soviet occupation considered theslevles lucky and the British, on the whole, lived up to their reputation of fairness. However, the British officer corps was now staffed by somewhat different personnel. One of the more memorable incidents in Cologne was caused by two enterprising officers who went to the house of the heiress of the 4711 factory. The formula for 4711 was a family secret, handed down from generation to generation and had now come into the hands of a rather old but plucky lady. The officers came to bully her in order to extract the formula from her and set up shop in Britain. But the old lady remembered the days of the first occupation and went to complain to the city commander who quickly took care of the situation.[29]

But Cologne was also a very different town from what it had been in December 1918. Massive British and American bombing raids had reduced the city to rubble and the only building still standing tall, although seriously damaged, was the Dome. Food aid for the starving civilians had to be provided, and the British now had an occupation zone which stretched all the way north to the Danish border. It was imperative to get Germany working again in order to form a bulwark against Stalin's sinister plans. But the British army had few industrial specialists to spare.

Most of German heavy industry had been destroyed or severely damaged. But there was still the odd steel mill in the country such as Georgsmarienhütte near Osnabrück. When a British military delegation entered they were in for a shock. They were greeted by a tall, lanky, red-headed young man, dressed impeccably in British tweeds, speaking fluent English. He gave them a tour of the steel mill and it turned out that he was a trainee, but no ordinary trainee. He was the oldest son of an old Düsseldorf family who owned extensive steel works and who, along with the Krupps and the Thyssens, had actively supported Hitler's war effort. His father had been present when Hitler came to negotiate the end of trade unions at the *Industrie-Klub* at the Düsseldorf Parkhotel.

The British officer now made a completely pragmatic decision: he put the English-speaking scion of a Hitler-supporting industrial clan in charge of the entire steel mill of Georgsmarienhütte. He did well. Production started immediately because communication was so easy. A few years later the young man went on to become a high German official at the European Coal and Steel Community in Luxemburg.[30]

British soldiers with their white plastic spats and officers with their swagger sticks were a common sight in the cities of the Rhineland. They now had much less difficulties with civilians because thanks to Hitler, English had been taught in secondary schools since the 1930s. To us children, the British soldiers were a source of unending curiosity, especially, since they persistently ignored us. Just around the corner from where we lived at Düsseldorf, there was the British Forces HQ, a drab, angular building knocked together from inferior materials on the site of two ruined villas. A strange smell hung around the building and the soldiers going in and out. My mother, who had spent much of her youth in England, explained to me that in England this was the typical smell of poverty. I have since identified the smell as being a mixture of Velvet soap and stale lamb fat.

Officers and their families stayed in requisitioned houses in the best parts of town. One of my school mates had befriended two English girls living around the corner from her. One day she was invited into the house and came back quite shocked. "The house is awful," she said, "cold, dark, with dreadful, cheap furniture." For afternoon tea she was offered soggy white bread with bitter *Orangenmarmelade*, the marmalade so peculiar to the British. And there was a fusty smell everywhere. "They have no flowers," she complained, "instead, they have this bowl of stinking old rose leaves sitting in the entrance hall!" My friend suddenly reached a surprising conclusion and whispered to me: "You know, they are poor people."

Although we were not quite ten years old and it was the second half of the 1950s with the German Economic Miracle quickly gathering momentum, we began to perceive dimly that something extraordinary had happened after 1945: the difference between victors and vanquished had become strangely muddled.

Notes

1. Joseph Gregor Lang, "Alle wohnen in Eintracht beisammen," in Willy Leson (ed.), *So lebten sie am Rhein zwischen Mainz und Düsseldorf: Texte und Bilder von Zeitgenossen*, Bachem, Cologne, 1976, 68-9.
2. One of them gained international fame shortly after settling in Neuwied. David Roentgen, the founder of the *Neuwieder Werkstatt* (manufacture) and his son after him supplied the courts of Europe with prized pieces of marquetry furniture of exquisite workmanship.
3. [No author], *1653-1953: 300 Jahre Neuwied: Ein Stadt- und Heimatbuch*, Neuwieder Verlagsgesellschaft, Neuwied, 1953, 411.
4. Dr. M. Doerfel, "Die Engländer in Neuwied," *Evangelische Brüdergemeine Neuwied. 1785-1985*, Festschrift on the occasion of 200 Jahre Kirchensaal Friedrichstrasse, no publisher, Neuwied, 1985, 79.
5. For details on Prof. Hueppe see "Zum 50-jährigen Doktorjubiläum des Bakteriologen und Sportführers," *Neuwieder Zeitung*, no. 35, 11 February, 1926.
6. See "In Fastnachtskostümen einem aufgeblasenen Ball nach," *Neuwieder Zeitung*, 13 September 1953.
7. ibid.
8. "Vor 99 Jahren wurde Prof. Hueppe in Neuwied geboren," *Neuwieder Zeitung*, 24 August 1951.
9. Erich Pfund, "Sport und Leibesübungen in Neuwied: die Anfänge," *300 Jahre Neuwied*, 494.
10. Personal interview with Joachim von Elbe, Bonn, May 1994.
11. Imperial War Museum, *The Occupation of the Rhineland*, Her Majesty's Stationery Office, London, 1987, 109.
12. Personal interview with E.A. Zogbaum (born 1901), Gräffrath, May 1994. This was also confirmed by Joachim von Elbe (born 1902) and Dr. Julius Dilger (born 1904), personal interview, Neuwied, May 1994.
13. "Why isn't it nice on the Rhine? Because the Frenchie, the scumbag, has occupied the Rhineland." Werner Krämer, "Siegreich welle mer... Ich derf's net sage..." in Rudolf Pörtner (ed.), *Alltag in der Weimarer Republik*, Econ Verlag, Düsseldorf, 1990, 552.
14. IWM, *The Occupation of the Rhineland*, 99.
15. D.G. Williamson, "Cologne and the British," *History Today*, vol.27, November 1977, 695.
16. ibid, 697.
17. The Americans in the U.S. occupation zone did the same. They also eventually fed the civilian population out of Army rations. Only the French

army insisted that the Germans feed the occupiers. Hence much of the ensuing strife.
18 D.G. Williamson, *The British in Germany, 1918-1930. The Reluctant Occupiers*, Berg, London, 1991, 17.
19 Dieter Höroldt (ed.), *Geschichte der Stadt Bonn: von einer französischen Bezirksstadt zur Bundeshauptstadt*, Dümmler, Bonn, 1989, vol. 4, 476.
20 J. Garston, "Armies of Occupation II," *History Today*, vol. 2, July 1961, 485.
21 Personal interview with Mrs. M. Baumgarten (born 1901), Bonn, May 1994. This incident is also mentioned in D.G. Williamson, "Cologne and the British," 700.
22 ibid, 701.
23 J. Garston, 486.
24 For the Americans see K.L. Nelson, *Victors Divided*, University of California Press, Berkeley, 1975. For the French see W. McDougall, *France's Rhineland Diplomacy 1914-1924: the Last Bid for a Balance of Power in Europe*, University of Princeton Press, Princeton, c1978. For the British see Sara Moore, *Peace without Victory for the Allies, 1918-1932*, Berg, Providence, 1994.
25 *Geschichte der Stadt Bonn*, 477.
26 Ernst Fraenkel, "Das deutsche Wilsonbild," *Jahrbuch für Amerikastudien*, vol. 5, 1960, 66.
27 Personal interview with E.A. Zogbaum.
28 For details see Major General Henry T. Allen, *My Rhineland Journal*, Boston, 1923.
29 Personal interview with Mrs. M. Baumgarten.
30 Personal interview with Aletta Schmidt-Lueg, Düsseldorf, June 1994.

III

A NEW BRITAIN
IN A NEW EUROPE?

8 Britain, the European Union and National Identity

PETER SHEARMAN

It is interesting to note that while the question of Britain's place in Europe has not been a salient issue for the general population of voters, it has been the single most important issue determining the fortune and fate of Britain's party political elites. The debate on European integration has been élite driven, and, although inter- and intra-party squabbles over Europe have often resulted in saturation coverage in the media, mass opinion surveys have consistently shown that the wider public have relatively little knowledge or interest in these matters. The general election in May 1997 demonstrates this clearly. Many individual candidates for the Conservative Party stood on an anti-EU platform, the result of which was simply to convince voters just how seriously split the party was, hence undermining further the already poor confidence people had in the ability of the Conservatives to govern effectively. As a 'policy' issue, Europe ranked eighth in people's voting priorities and was not therefore a significant factor in the election result.[1] But as a 'perception' issue it seems that Europe further eroded faith in the Tory leadership.[2] Europe has been an emotive and critical issue for political élites, but a peripheral issue in the British electorate's voting intentions. It is interesting also to note that Margaret Thatcher, widely considered a staunch antagonist to European integration during her years as Prime Minister, had little impact on general attitudes on Europe. A study has shown that levels of satisfaction with Thatcher had little effect on public opinion on the EC; in fact the more positively Thatcher was viewed, the more positively people viewed the EC![3]

The reason for this discrepancy - Europe as a key issue in élite politics and a peripheral issue in mass opinion - is tied into the question of national identity and Britain's place in the world, a question most often limited to and conducted by political and cultural élites. Questions of national identity can of course be utilised, especially in times of economic and social crisis, to mobilise the masses for instrumental political purposes. This was the case in and helps to explain the collapse of communist regimes in East/Central Europe and the ensuing violence in the Balkans and the Caucasus. Although Britain cannot be said to have experienced the same level of 'national identity crisis' as the former communist states, nevertheless the élite political debate over Europe during the second half of the twentieth century is linked to this issue of national identity.

Conservatism and Britain as a Great Power

National identity is linked to the past - to a common history and traditions. Yet it is linked also to a common destiny. Issues of national identity are determined not so much by tangible elements such as language, but subjective, psychological factors based upon a sense of group belonging. British élites during the post-1945 period have tended to see Britain's destiny through a rose-tinted view of its past which failed to recognise or accept its radically changing position in world politics. It is remarkable, yet something many take great pride in, that in a century that has seen revolution, the end of imperialism, the spread of democracy, increasing interdependency and economic globalisation that Britain's political institutions have remained intact, with radical political reform, when it has sneaked onto the agenda, dead at birth. Britain has been an inherently conservative society, reluctant to endorse any change that would effect its traditions and self-perceived superior form of parliamentary democracy.[4] These perceptions of Britishness have been reflected in political attitudes towards Europe, often bringing the far right and the far left together in opposing the European integration process. Yet, tracing the question of Europe in British politics over the past fifty years it becomes clear that élite attitudes are changing (even if surveys show more scepticism among the wider public), and that finally Britain is coming to take on a more positive and constructive role in the EU, reflecting new realities in a number of areas, geographical, economic, political and social.

For many, especially on the left of the (old) Labour Party, the post-war Attlee government was the most progressive and radical this century - and in a number of social policy areas this has to be acknowledged. Yet the Attlee Labour government was also remarkably conservative, especially given its large electoral mandate at a time perhaps most conducive, in the aftermath of war, to breaking down social barriers through political reform.[5]

Britain under Attlee seemed incapable of recognising Britain's decline, and did very little indeed to adjust Britain to the changing international circumstances. Defence spending in 1947 stood at 18 per cent of gross national product and British Foreign Minister Ernest Bevin was as reluctant as Winston Churchill to even countenance the idea that Britain should give up its Great Power status.[6] It was Churchill who gave us the concept of the 'iron curtain', and who defined British foreign interests in terms of three circles: Europe, the United States, and the Commonwealth. There was a good neighbourly aspect to relations with Europe, a 'special' relationship with the United States, and an emotional attachment to the Commonwealth. The European circle was seen as the less important one. Britain's perceived strategic interests, its economic interests, and its traditional foreign policy orientation combined to ensure that Britain's engagement with Europe from the outset of the integration process would be difficult. As Anthony King put it: "Its preoccupations, its national interests, and its self-image...combined to keep Britain *apart* from Europe". Psychologically "the countries of Europe were "over there", foreign, alien".[7] The Iron Curtain and the perceived threat of Soviet communism gave added impetus for British political élites to develop close relations with the United States, then clearly the dominant military power. Britain, reflecting its perceived great power status, played a leading role in the establishment of the North Atlantic Treaty Organisation and in the development of the security architecture in Europe, whilst remaining aloof from the early moves at economic integration.[8] Britain's 'greatness' became tied up with its close relationship with the United States, resting chiefly on its military status and self-perceived global diplomatic interests and skills at a time when geography and economics were pulling the other way, towards Europe. But early post-war governments, both Conservative and Labour, failed to acknowledge these changing realities.[9]

The Reluctant European

Yet, by the 1960s, the relatively high levels of economic growth being achieved by France, Germany and Italy - twice those of Britain - led to a reevaluation of the European project. These economic imperatives were reinforced by a political momentum, as Britain's political relationship with both the United States and the Commonwealth was changing rapidly. The emblems of greatness were determined by the empire, but now the former colonies were conducting independent policies that were not always in the interests of Britain, whilst the demise of sterling, the dominance of U.S. power, the economic rise of Japan and Germany and the humiliation of Suez together undermined Britain's ability to maintain its foreign policy priority in the two non-European circles. Emotively, British élites still clung to the Commonwealth, and in trying to keep a special relationship with the U.S. attempts were made to portray Britain as a bridge between Washington and Europe. But in practical terms it was recognised that economic imperatives demanded a more positive approach to Europe, with the Conservative government of Edward Heath eventually leading Britain into the EC in 1972.

Yet once the Tories took Britain into Europe all subsequent government policies relating to Europe reestablished the negative trend: internal divisions within the Labour party forced a referendum on Britain's continued membership of the EC under Wilson and a 'renegotiation' of the terms of entry. Although Harold Wilson ultimately called upon voters to support continued membership, his heart, and his energies, were directed elsewhere. In renegotiating the terms of entry Wilson made a special plea for New Zealand butter, telling his counterparts in the EC that this was one of the "most emotive issues in Britain", whilst two key considerations were always in Wilson's mind: "the need to keep the Commonwealth united and the vital importance of the Anglo-American alliance".[10] In government, Wilson would spend up to half of his time dealing with Commonwealth issues, and his love for the Commonwealth was "romantic and traditional" - he believed that Britain's role in Africa and Asia was "essential for world peace".[11] The negative, antagonistic approach to the EC continued under Thatcher with the re-negotiation of Britain's contribution to the budget and her warnings about the EC undermining British parliamentary sovereignty.[12] These arguments were being made just as forcefully on the left of the political spectrum, with, Tony Benn, for example, warning that EC integration risked the "permanent surrender to the common market of democratic self-government" and giving away "for ever, the independence of our country and the liberties of the people".[13] During the Thatcher years the "special relationship" with the United States became the dominant approach in foreign policy, but with Britain reasserting a distinctive identity that was often portrayed as being threatened by the European project.

It is somewhat ironic that, at the same time that élites were holding on to the idea of Britain as a great power with a superior form of governance to that of other European states, there existed simultaneously a deep sense of decline. Part of Britain's unsure attitude to Europe has been based upon a self-perception of "exceptionalism". Lord Beloff refers to Britain's specific historical experience, its unwritten constitution, and its identity which is contrasted to that of the "continental" Europeans. Unlike *them* the British are not suitable for full and devoted membership of the Union.[14] Yet this superiority complex was accompanied by a realisation that Britain had long been suffering from relative decline and a decreasing faith amongst some sections of the élite in Britain's political institutions. As Andrew Marr in his critique of British democracy states: "Let us admit it. Most of us have been, for some time, ashamed of what our country has become, even when that shame is tempered by defiant patriotism".[15]

The Changing Role of the Monarchy

As Britain lost its empire and searched for a new focus of identity which would bind the population to a new common sense of belonging, the monarchy took on increasing symbolic and functional importance in the second half of the twentieth century. The reinforcement of national identity was tied in to royal celebrations such as the 1953 coronation, the investiture of Charles as Prince of Wales in 1967, the Queen's silver jubilee in 1977, and the royal wedding between Charles and Diana in 1981. This focus upon the monarchy served to reinforce traditional British conservatism, perpetuating, as Stephen Haseler puts it, "a culture of deference, obsequiousness, patronage and class privilege" which is hardly conducive to a nation in need of modernisation.[16] Robert Harrison has argued that the survival of the monarchy was used as a convenient symbol of identity for a hybrid nation, pointing out that: "The existence of the monarchy defines the British not as citizens, but as subjects, and from that flow the socially binding British virtues of discipline and deference to authority - of which the corresponding *vices* are conformism, snobbery, and obsession with class".[17]

Relatively few authoritative books have been written on the British Constitution, but one of the most influential was Walter Bagehot's *The English Constitution*, in which the monarchy is portrayed as an important institution used by the political establishment to dupe the masses of ignorant voters into accepting and hence legitimising the workings of government. The term 'establishment' actually only came into use later, following a 1953 article in the *Spectator* where the term was employed to describe an interlocking élite (the "Establishment") that was said to exercise power socially through its own networking. The establishment incorporated prime and other ministers, Archbishops, Earl Marshalls, Chairpersons of Arts Councils, Director Generals of the BBC, etc. It can be argued that no other country has such a small elitist base as Britain. Much has also been made of the narrow social base from which the establishment stems: a small number of public schools and the two ancient universities of Oxford and Cambridge. Walter Ellis has produced the latest detailed empirical assessment of how these two institutions so fully dominate government, parliament, the civil service, the foreign office, the law, church, banking, high arts, publishing, media, science and technology.[18] The dominance of these two institutions, given the fact that they represent a mere two percent of British university graduates and that this two percent is highly unrepresentative of the graduate pool, let alone British society as a whole, has inhibited or at least restricted how far Britain has been able to move away from its old traditions. But as Martin Harrop has noted, the House of Commons elected in 1997 has seen a new balancing of its composition: "...from the private to the public sector, from public school to state school, and from Oxbridge to the other universities".[19] A new, younger breed of politicians with less deference to traditional political institutions and more reflective of society at large sit on the New Labour benches in parliament.

Bagehot saw the monarchy as representing dignity, reverence, and, most importantly, stability. He warned that if the political élite allowed the mystery of the monarchy to be broken - or, as he put it, if the daylight was let in upon its magic - then it would hold dangers for the stability of the political system. Although the magic was put to effective use with grand royal celebrations from the 1950s through to the 1970s, with no controversy within the British political establishment about the importance of this magic, the daylight was gradually seeping in. The more ferocious and intrusive media, combined with changing values in British mass society, served to undermine the place of the monarchy as a symbol of British national identity. A sense of decline among British élites and decreasing faith in British political institutions combined with a crisis in the monarchy to produce a stark recognition of Britain's exaggerated view of itself and its real diminished place in the modern world. These developments together undermined the traditional deferential nature of British society and produced an identity crisis that is now playing itself out in terms of Britain's role in Europe.

Changing Social Attitudes

It is an irony that two of the most influential individuals in undermining Britain's sense of identity and the class-based nature that was an integral part of it came from the same British élite that had previously so effectively nurtured it. It is also perhaps instructive to note that the two individuals in question were not men. Margaret Thatcher may not have changed British political institutions, but she is widely regarded as having radically changed political attitudes. Princess Diana may not herself have taken on an overt political role, yet she can be seen as having had a significant impact on people's attitudes to the monarchy and hence the symbols central to the British sense of identity. Together, the very different roles of these two women can be said to have impacted profoundly on the cultural and social mores at the heart of what was previously considered to be 'Britishness'. Although neither was an ardent supporter of the European idea (indeed one was adamantly opposed to any such idea, whilst the other was part of what made Britain unique), they nevertheless both unwittingly paved the way for a more positive approach to European integration.

The Thatcher years marked a decisive shift away from old Tory traditions of paternalism, statism, and deference. Encapsulated in the term 'enterprise culture', Thatcherism took on the old political establishment. Not only were the BBC and public services forced to undergo audits and efficiency tests, the Royal List was also subject to scrutiny. The Queen was persuaded ('voluntarily') to pay taxes, whilst tax payers were loath to use the public purse to pay for fire damage to Windsor Castle - or to fund a new Royal Yacht.

Charles became the first prince to divorce the mother of his heirs, raising difficult issues pertaining to succession and relations between the monarchy and church and state. During and following her difficult marriage to Charles, Diana became a focus for the media; through a series of interviews, articles and books a spotlight was placed on the previously closed world of the Royal House of Windsor.[20] The national outpouring of grief following Diana's sudden death in August 1998 and the subsequent open criticism of the response from the Royal Family demonstrated clearly just how much British social attitudes had changed. A pre-modern institution, long the symbol of the British nation, was now widely perceived to be wanting as a focus for national identity. If the monarchy was to survive, it became manifestly clear at that moment that it would need to modernise itself. In the early 1980s Anthony Sampson had said of the monarchy that it was the one institution that was not only unscathed, but one which had even "increased its prestige".[21] By the 1990s this was no longer the case.[22]

Modernisation and New Labour

It is the term 'modernisation', as used by Tony Blair and New Labour, that best describes changes in how the British are coming to perceive themselves. Whereas the Thatcherite right moved away from traditional notions of Toryism, New Labour also marks a profound shift in the politics of the Left, as it has renounced old conceptions of socialist working class solidarity based in the trade union movement. Both Tory and old Labour reflect pre-modern value systems based upon old notions of class solidarity.[23] Many in the old Labour Party considered that achieving socialism would be hampered by economic integration into a fundamentally capitalist European Community and held firm to the idea of retaining British 'parliamentary sovereignty'. Tony Benn, who came within a whisker of gaining the deputy leadership of the party in 1981, has accused Tony Blair of systematically repudiating Labour's core beliefs. In the 16th annual Attlee lecture at the Royal Overseas League in London in February 1998, Benn argued that Blair would do well to re-examine the contemporary relevance of what Attlee did in the post-War Labour government. Benn, who was the key architect of the 1983 Labour Party manifesto (Gerald Kaufman called it the 'longest suicide note in history'), referred to him as labour's 'greatest leader'.[24]

Yet the idea that Blair somehow represents a new brand of conservatism or even a continuation of Thatcherism seriously misrepresent what New Labour stands for. Whereas Thatcher did challenge the establishment, trade union power, the labour left, and helped to break down sterile and dangerous notions of class warfare, she left intact the political institutions that grew up around them. Whilst accepting some of the changes made by Thatcher, especially in the realms of individual responsibility and economic efficiency, Blair's modernisation programme is fundamental and radical and promises to alter profoundly the workings of power and governance, which will have a further impact on perceptions of identity. Professor Hugh Trevor-Roper stated that whatever qualities the British have as a people come not from "blood or from race" but "from the historic continuity of our institutions, which themselves form our identity as long as we remember them".[25] Devolving powers to Scottish and Welsh assemblies, seeking a political settlement to the Northern Ireland problem, instituting proportional representation for elections to the European Parliament, abolishing hereditary peerages, establishing the office of elected Mayors for Britain's cities - this will all inevitably impact not only the workings of government, but also upon the sense of group identity.

Conclusion

As an island nation, separate from 'continental Europe', and as a great empire with a unique set of political institutions, British élites came to see their country as distinct from Europe, and British identity came to be linked to its Great Power status and world role. Even as modern communications and technologies made distance less significant (especially the small amount of water separating Britain and the 'continent') and Britain's empire (and its relative power) was evaporating after 1945, the élites nevertheless clung to status and (now) Commonwealth as the main components of self-definition. The monarchy became the central component that symbolised uniqueness, institutional and social continuity, and the pomp, circumstance and glory that surrounded the aura of the monarchy were employed to foster a continued sense of national identity and solidarity. Strategic and power considerations were further strengthened due to the threat from the Soviet Union, with the constraints of bipolarity determining to a great degree issues of identity and nationhood. This led to a focus on the so-called 'special relationship' with the United States.

Britain's entry into the EC was late, and was followed by divisions within both major parties and a difficult and sometimes hostile relationship with Europe. By the 1980s and 1990s, however, a number of economic and political factors combined to produce a more realistic appraisal of where British interests lay. Whereas, for example, the EC accounted for 25 percent of British foreign trade in the mid 1950s, by the mid 1990s this figure had reached 51 percent. As Will Hutton has pointed out, British exports to Holland exceed those to the whole of South-East Asia.[26] Britain's future, it was recognised by most serious politicians in both major parties, must be closely tied to Europe. British society has also become less deferential, the old class divisions of left and right have disappeared, and there is a general acceptance of the need for institutional political change, as reflected in the referendums in Scotland and Wales in 1997. The sense of decline also seems to be giving way to a greater sense of optimism for the future. As Prime Minister Blair put it in a speech in the Hague in January 1998 "There is a confidence in Britain, a sense of dynamism and adventure and, as a result, people are not frightened of Europe".[27] Those that remain frightened of Europe are now a rump in what is left of a divided Conservative Party that is now largely limited to the English home counties. Although much is made of the similarities between Blair and President Clinton, and the development of a new 'special relationship' between Britain and the United States, New Labour's political philosophy is much closer to European social democracy than it is to Clinton's liberalism, and Blair's government is taking a much more pro-active, positive, leading role within the councils of the EU than any previous British government. There will surely continue to be intense debates and disagreements about various aspects and policies relating to Europe, not least as to whether Britain should adopt the Euro. But the days when Britain was the spoiler are gone. Previously, the logic of arguments in favour of Britain in Europe has been driven by economic considerations. That is now changing, as social and political factors are now seen by many élites in a positive light. The Blair government's signing up to the Social Chapter immediately on coming to power is indicative.

This chapter in no way suggests that Britain's identity is going to give way to a 'European' one. Rather it argues that Europe will no longer be used as a negative in debates about what it means to be British. Changes in British society have led to a situation in which it is no longer useful, in terms of garnering votes or in devising conceptions of Britain's role in the world, to constantly criticise the European Union. The British political establishment is changing, and as it changes it recognises that, as Defence Secretary George Robertson noted whilst in opposition, that Europe is "the only real arena where British influence can be exercised".[28]

Notes

[1] The most salient issues in the general election related to unemployment, crime, and the domestic economy. See *The Weekend Australian*, April 19-20, 1997, p. 14.

[2] Although British opinion during the election campaign was moving in a Eurosceptic direction it was not a key issue determining voter preferences. But the issue did reinforce perceptions of divisions in the Conservative Party. See on this Martin Harrop, "The Pendulum Swings: The British General Election of 1997", *Government and Opposition*, 1997, pp. 305-319, p. 316.

3   Jorges Rasmussen, "What Kind of Vision is That? British Public Attitudes Towards the European Community During the Thatcher Era", *British Journal of Political Science*, vol. 27, no. 1, 1997, pp. 111-155.

4   An American specialist on British politics has noted just how resistant to change and inherently conservative British institutions are, and what little impact Thatcher's so-called 'revolution' had on the fundamentals of British politics. See Dudley T. Studlar, *Great Britain: Decline or Renewal*, Boulder, Westview, 1996.

5   Indeed according to Anthony Howard the Labour victory in the general election of 1945 did not herald a social revolution but rather the "greatest restoration of traditional values since 1660". Cited in D.J. Taylor, *After the War: The Novel and England Since 1945*, London, Flamingo, 1994, p. 26.

6   See Peter Clarke, *Hope and Glory: Britain 1900-1990*, London, Penguin, 1996, p. 252. Clarke makes the point that foreigners were "naturally quicker to recognise the reality of Britain's changed world status that were most Britons", (p. 319).

7   Anthony King, *Britain Says Yes. The 1975 Referendum on the Common Market*, Washington D.C., American Enterprise Institute, 1977, p. 6.

8   As Helen Wallace has put it only a small minority of British élites felt a strong "symbolic attachment" to European integration whilst NATO and Atlanticism attracted "positive symbolic resonance", see her "At Odds With Europe", *Political Studies*, vol. XLV 1997, pp. 677-688, p. 686.

9   Christopher Coker has argued with regard to the so-called "special relationship" with the United States that it was a "consolation for a country that had "lost its way" which allowed it to "legitimise its detachment from Europe". See his "Britain and the New World Order: The Special Relationship", *International Affairs*, vol. 68, no. 3, 1992, pp. 407-421, p. 416.

10 Philip Ziegler, *Wilson: The Authorised Life*, London, Harper Collins, 1993, p. 219 & p. 425.

11 Ziegler, *Wilson*, p.219.

12 On her battles with the EC on the budget see Margaret Thatcher, *The Downing Street Years*, pp. 536-545.

13 Tony Benn, *Arguments for Socialism*, London, Penguin, 1979, p. 99.

14 Lord Beloff, *Britain and European union: dialogue of the Deaf*, London, Macmillan, 1996.

15 Andrew Marr, *Ruling Britannia: The Failure and Future of British Democracy*, London, Michael Joseph, 1995, p. 9.

16 Stephen Haseler, *The End of the House of Windsor*, London, Tauras, 1993, p. 6.

17 Robert Harrison, *Culture and Consensus: England, Art and Politics Since 1940*, London, Methuen, 1995, p. 7.

18 Walter Ellis, *The Oxbridge Conspiracy*, London, Penguin, 1995. Ellis shows, for example, that out of the 1,186 members of the House of Lords in 1991 fully 510 went to either Oxford or Cambridge. And the score for the top 8 ambassadorships (Washington, the EU, the UN, Moscow, Bonn, Paris, Tokyo and Rome) was Cambridge: 5, Oxford: 3, the rest: 0! p. 38.

19 Martin Harrop, "The Pendulum Swings: The British General Election of 1997", p. 307.

20 The most damaging was the publication in 1992 of Andrew Morton's book *Diana: Her True Story*, London, Michael O'Mara Books.

21 Anthony Sampson, *The Changing Anatomy of Britain*, London, Hodder and Stoughton, 1982, p. 5.

22 A poll taken for *The Guardian* in August 1997 showed that, for the first time, support for the monarchy fell below 50% (it was 48%), with only one-third of those under 25 years of age supporting the monarchy. As reported by Derek Draper, "No Old Monarchy for New Labour", *The Spectator*, September 17, 1997, pp. 10-11. Another poll found that fewer than one in five in Britain still believes the Commonwealth is more important to Britain than Europe - see *The Weekly Telegraph*, no. 320, 1997.

23 Samuel Beer has referred to this as 'pre-modern solidarities'. See his "The Roots of New Labour", *The Economist*, February 8, 1998, pp. 19-23.

24 *The Guardian*, February 10, 1998. Dennis Kavanagh has stated that Tony Benn is only of interest now because he is "so out of date". He also notes that the old Labour left's anti-Europeanism is no longer a strong force, and rather: "The European Union has taken the place of loony left local government councillors and trade union barons as the new dragon for the Conservative right in the 1990s". Dennis Kavanagh, "British Party Conferences and the Political Rhetoric of the 1990s", *Government and Opposition*, vol. 31, no. 1, Winter 1996, pp. 27-44, p. 32.

25 Quoted in Sampson, *The Changing Anatomy of Britain*, p. xi.

26 Will Hutton, *The State to Come*, London, Vintage, 1997, p. 101.

27 *The Weekly Telegraph*, no. 340, January 28-February 3, 1998.

28 George Robertson, "Britain in the New Europe", *International Affairs*, vol. 64, no. 4, 1990, pp. 697-702, p. 699.

9 New Europe, New Labour: British European Policy Reconsidered

HELEN WALLACE

1997 marked a moment of political change in the United Kingdom. A new government took office in May 1997 with an extraordinarily large parliamentary mandate. The new government was self-described as 'new Labour' - differentiating itself thus from both the previous Conservative regime and from earlier incarnations of the Labour Party. The sense of anticipation about what might follow from the victory of 'new Labour' linked from the outset domestic and foreign policy. The main electoral platform had been built around domestic issues, reflecting, among other things, the knowledge that the electorate's priority concerns were about economic and social preferences. The careful testing of electoral opinion carried out by Labour Party strategists (in itself a fascinating innovation) had led Tony Blair and his campaign team to focus on a prudently crafted domestic agenda.

New Labour was pitting itself against a Conservative Government that had found itself increasingly mired on European issues. The severe unpopularity of the Conservatives reflected many points of recoil from the heavy and dogmatic agenda of the long period of Thatcherism. But the fortunes of both the government and the party had been further eroded by the deep difficulties of establishing a coherent and sustainable European policy. John Major had entered office determined to 'put Britain at the heart of Europe', yet over the five years of his premiership he found himself more and more isolated from his European partners and beleaguered within the Cabinet, the parliamentary party and with public opinion. European integration had repeatedly been among the trickiest and most contentious of issues for successive British governments. By 1996/7 European policy had become an open battle ground.

It followed that one key test that the Labour team had to pass was the search for electoral credibility on European issues. Their analysis of previous electoral defeats had indicated that the party's stance on foreign policy and European issues was relevant to its overall credibility. An apparently 'unrealistic' stance during the 1980s on both defence and European integration had contributed to defeat. As party leaders, Neil Kinnock and John Smith had worked hard to reverse the negative image, efforts on which Tony Blair and his team had sought to build an image of positive engagement and party unity. But in the 1997 general election they faced an additional challenge vis-à-vis a Conservative Government that had become deeply divided on European policy. The 'Eurosceptical' wing of the party had been fighting to establish for itself a populist position based on national, even nationalist, independence. Nervous of this as a factor of potential vulnerability, the Labour Party leadership opted for united prudence on European policy so as to avoid being accused of lack of patriotism.

The net result was that 'new Labour' adopted a European stance which sought to balance positive rhetoric with imprecise commitments on substance. In electoral terms, the stance served the party well by sidelining European policy in the election campaign. As a basis for government policy it was less useful, precisely because it left so many points of detail unspecified. in particular, it left the new government with two key European issues demanding immediate attention, on which the core of policy had not been clearly defined: first, whether or not to aim for early membership of economic and monetary union (EMU); and second, what stance to take in the Intergovernmental Conference (IGC) on treaty reform.

On the other hand, the new government also had an extraordinary window of opportunity. It succeeded a Conservative government that had tied itself in knots on European policy, with the collapse into factionalism that had marked the post-Thatcher and post-Maastricht period. The deterioration of British relations with EU partners was marked, and the endgame in the IGC itself had been deferred pending the outcome of the UK general election. Both for the new British government and for the rest of the EU, the election offered scope for a reorientation. Other EU leaders and practitioners felt encouragingly sympathetic to the Blair government and especially to Blair himself. Blair and his advisers were keenly aware that there were prizes to be won.

An assessment of how these opportunities were approached has, of course, to include an appraisal of the substance of policy that emerged in the subsequent months. But it also requires an understanding of how the new government team was composed and of its internal dynamics. A primary feature of the new government was just how much it came to be a 'Blairite' team. It rapidly became clear that Tony Blair intended to take firm control of government strategy, with a close circle of advisers around him. The 'No. 10' team was one crucial element; another was the key role of Peter Mandelson, who had strong European credentials, as a Minister without Portfolio. Both factors were to play into the way policy developed. Also of crucial relevance was the appointment of Gordon Brown as a Chancellor of the Exchequer who was inclined to accept the goal of EMU as reasonable and attainable.

Another signal was transmitted by the inclusion in the government team (as Minister responsible for competitiveness issues) of David Simon, former Chairman of BP and a leading Europeanist. He had close experience of the EU, including as a member of the Ciampi group on European competitiveness. This appointment reflected the wider ambition of the new government to build a partnership between government and business. The choice of the ministerial team for the Foreign and Commonwealth Office was more ambiguous in its implications. Robin Cook, the new Foreign Secretary, was not an enthusiastic European, and indeed his own indicated priority was the goal of an 'ethical foreign policy', as announced in the new mission statement on 12 May. It was to prove difficult for Cook to focus squarely on the European agenda. Curiously, the awarding to Douglas Henderson of the second-rank post of Minister for Europe in the FCO was decided less by considerations of European policy than by the endeavour to balance the appointment of Cook, a party left-winger, with someone close to Gordon Brown's views. It was to prove quite difficult for the new team to develop a coherent overall European policy, in spite of the immediate pressure of preparing a Council presidency approach.

Amsterdam

The most immediate test for the new government was to determine its approach to the IGC, the forum within the EU through which treaty reforms are periodically negotiated on both institutional and core policy issues. Preparations in opposition had familiarised incoming ministers with the broad shape of the issues. They were helped by the fact that the IGC had achieved only modest progress in sketching a reform agenda. On policy substance they were not faced with too many difficult choices. The British opt-out on the Maastricht Social Protocol was to be removed, a signal of closer and more relaxed involvement that won enthusiastic commendation from EU partners. It should, however, be noted that the Labour Government made it clear that it would not support a large extension of European social legislation. The new government was also willing to go along with efforts to 'green' the treaties. The second pillar debate, dealing with efforts to build a common foreign and security policy, might have proved difficult for a very 'Nato-minded' government, had it not been that the IGC had in effect already abandoned notions of grand design as regards the CFSP.

The main problem concerned the discussion of Schengen and the third pillar. The third pillar had emerged from the 1992 Maastricht Treaty on European Union to encourage EU governments to cooperate on justice and home affairs. The Schengen Agreements, originally between France, Germany and the three Benelux governments, had a different origin as an attempt to reduce border controls between these adjacent countries. British ministers had been reluctant to engage with Schengen and nervous about the development of the third pillar. There were two explicit reasons for this: first, the nervousness about any erosion of national sovereignty on such sensitive issues; and, second, the confidence in the efficacy of Britain's border controls at ports of entry, a consequence of island geography. A third, less clearly stated reason, was that the British believed themselves to have established a kind of equilibrium in their immigration and race relations policies, in sharp contrast to the increasing contention in continental Europe about immigration and asylum-seekers.

By the time of Amsterdam, it had become clear that most other EU governments were keen to incorporate the Schengen Agreements into the EU. British efforts were therefore concentrated on retaining national controls over borders, a direct if less strident echo of the previous Conservative Government's position. The device adopted was a special protocol to permit a long-term British exclusion from the emerging EU regime, thus a reassuring British opt-out. This seemed straightforward, though it left much to be clarified later. The new arrangements envisaged that Britain (and Ireland, tied by the Anglo-Irish Free Travel Area) might adopt particular items from the Schengen *acquis* that was to be incorporated under the EU treaties. We should note, however, that a note of British-Spanish tension crept in, resulting from the persistent bilateral difficulty over Gibraltar; late in the night the Spanish somehow inserted into the treaty text an insistence that the UK could not join the 'communitarised' Schengen regime *except with the unanimous consent of existing EU members*. A more experienced government might have achieved softer terms that would allow more room for manoeuvre as they came to establish those areas of cooperation in which they wanted to be more closely involved.

On the institutional issues, the British were helped by the modest character of what had emerged earlier in the IGC. The Labour Party had already moved towards accepting a rather pragmatic approach to institutional questions, thus being willing to endorse some extension of qualified majority voting in the Council and of the European Parliament's powers of legislation. On what came to be called 'the institutional problem' to be resolved in advance of further enlargement, i.e. weighting of Council votes and the composition of the college of commissioners, the new government more or less echoed its predecessor's position. Thus it argued for giving more Council votes to the 'bigger' member states and accepted the loss of one British commissioner. This fashionable (if misleading) orthodoxy had become and remains British policy. No new proposals came from the British at Amsterdam; it was too early for innovation.

Instead, effort was concentrated on seeking to mitigate the impact of the proposals on 'flexibility'. In the months of deliberations in the IGC, flexibility had become something of a bandwagon concept. It had become code for finding ways of allowing the more integration-minded EU governments to proceed more rapidly and more extensively with integration, without being encumbered by the reluctant. Among the origins of the concept was a keen desire of some EU governments to find ways of evading the British awkwardness and negativism which had become such a hallmark of the Conservative Government. Conveniently, devices to permit flexibility, or to facilitate 'closer cooperation' seemed also to promise at least a partial remedy for the risks of further enlargement. But it was a poisoned chalice for a Labour Government, keen to bring Britain back into the mainstream, and still unsure as to which the areas of EU activity were in which it might want a fuller involvement. In the event, Tony Blair and his team were, along with some other worried governments, able to reduce considerably the potential scope of the flexibility clauses in the text.

The net result at Amsterdam was that Tony Blair had a good European Council. He struck up positive relations with his opposite numbers, winning quick respect and establishing a position strong enough to be asked to play an important part in the drafting of key sections of the text. It was a promising starting position for a different approach to European policy.

Economic and Monetary Union

The most tricky issue by far was not the IGC but how to deal with EMU. Over the months of tense debate in the UK over EMU, the Labour Party had adopted a cautious and bifurcated approach. It had sought to avoid getting trapped into opposition in principle, albeit at the high price of conceding that British entry to EMU would, if advocated, have to be put to a referendum.

But the leadership team had given a number of signals of sympathy for the notion of EMU. Blair, Brown and Simon were all thought to be in favour of taking sterling into the eventual single currency, although no clear collective commitment had been announced. Two different arguments played into their approach. One was political and rested essentially on a judgement about whether and when joining EMU could be sold at home. The other was economic and related to the timing of a possible British entry into EMU, given that it was argued that the British economic cycle was in a different phase from that of the continental economies. Interestingly, one of Gordon Brown's first acts as Chancellor of the Exchequer was to announce that the Bank of England would become independent, thus fulfilling one of the necessary admission criteria for EMU.

On 17 July 1997, Gordon Brown sought to structure the debate by announcing five conditions to be satisfied for the UK to join EMU: a positive environment for investment in the UK; good prospects for the British financial services sector; a compatible business cycle; an EMU able to withstand economic shocks; and an EMU that would promote economic growth and employment. In the autumn it became clear that the government was nervous of making an early announcement about joining EMU, not least because of continuing evidence of hostile public opinion on this issue. On 27 October, after a series of speculative leaks in the press, Gordon Brown announced in the House of Commons that the UK might well be ready to join in 2002 or 2003, thus clearly after the next general election. It was hoped that a debate would follow, in which EMU would be seen less as a test of political judgement and rather as a more practical question of what made best sense for the British economy.

The Government was not, however, out of the woods. Plans were continuing for the detailed arrangements for the introduction of EMU, including the composition of the executive board of the European Central Bank (ECB) and the prospect of a special club emerging of finance ministers from only those EU member states that were fully within EMU. Gordon Brown fought a hard, and in the end unsuccessful, battle in December to engineer a British seat in the ECB and to prevent the emergence of the 'Euro-X' group of finance ministers, which would include only the ministers from the governments which had accepted the single currency. EMU remained the toughest test of the government's European policy, and thus the clearest obstacle to the UK finding a place for itself at the heart of the EU political process.

Changing Policy Priorities

Two examples illustrate some new policy directions: first, the response to the BSE problems; and, second, the environmental agenda. On BSE, Jack Cunningham, the Secretary of State for Agriculture, and his team set about repairing the damage both at home and abroad that had flowed from the BSE crisis. Within the relevant European forums the team began to rebuild trust with European counterparts and the European Commission, both in order to make it possible for British beef-producers to recover their international trade and to reassure European partners that the British government was to be cooperative and constructive. Patiently efforts were continued to produce technical arrangements that would satisfy the concerns expressed through the EU's various committees. These efforts were aided by two announcements: first, that the Government would establish a new food agency; and, second, the establishment of an independent enquiry into what had gone wrong in the earlier handling of the issue. Nonetheless it should be noted that the frustrations of British farmers had led to an outburst of militancy, with scenes of Welsh farmers blocking ports at which Irish beef was imported into the UK, images more reminiscent of French agricultural politics. Another signal of persistent difficulty was the announcement in December that 'beef-on-the bone' was no longer to be sold in the UK, a decision taken very rapidly and nervously on the basis of rather slender scientific evidence.

On the environment, the new government quickly signalled a preference for much more stringent and greener policies, including efforts to strengthen both European and international agreements. Thus within the EU, the government switched to much more positive advocacy of European controls than its predecessor had entertained. John Prescott, Deputy Prime Minister and Secretary of State for Environment and Transport, went to the Kyoto conference on climate change in autumn 1998 as a strong advocate of tough measures to reduce emissions. He was active and vociferous among the Europeans engaged in a fierce effort to put pressure on the US government to reduce its emissions.

Preparing for the Council Presidency

Every six months the presidency of the council of the EU rotates among member governments, with the British turn falling due in January/June 1998. Preparations for this council Presidency had to be made before the new government had really had time to develop a European strategy. Instead, ministers opted for a change of style and for rather broad policy objectives.

The style consisted of both positive language and symbols and a new emphasis on trying to create a 'people's Europe'. Quite what this latter point meant was not clear, except in so far as it signalled a commitment to European policies that would resonate with the ordinary citizen. The new style was reflected in a flurry of efforts to bring colourful imagery to the presidency, not least in the logo designed by children from EU member states. The broad policy objectives were: to facilitate from the Council chair a successful launch of EMU; to pursue economic-reforms aimed at enhancing competitiveness and employment; to give a firm impetus to further enlargements and the EU policy reforms that this implied; to strengthen EU efforts to fight organised crime and to promote a cleaner environment; and to develop the common foreign and security policy, including a firmer emphasis on human rights and a code of conduct on arms exports.

In the event, the new government did not find it easy to make its mark on the presidency or to exploit it domestically. Policy had not crystallised in a coherent way. Robin Cook as foreign secretary found himself distracted by other issues, including personal matters. The predominance of EMU on the EU agenda meant that the still uncommitted British were necessarily on the sidelines of the main discussion. The legacy of years of ambivalent European policy could not easily be eradicated.

Factors of Political Change

Among the more important factors of political change signalled by the new government was its strong commitment to constitutional reform. The Labour and Liberal Democrat parties had agreed, in advance of the May election, on a package of constitutional changes. These included: devolution to Scotland and Wales; electoral reform, in the first instance for the European Parliament and the Scottish and Welsh assemblies, even in due course perhaps for Westminster; a reconfigured House of Lords; and freedom of information legislation. Taken as a whole, these intended measures would make an enormous difference to the workings of government and to the character of British politics. Necessarily they would have an impact at the European level, perhaps most importantly by giving the UK a far less centralised political system and by opening up a broader discussion on domestic constitutional issues that might make it easier to have a more open discussion on issues of European constitutional and institutional reform.

Interestingly, the devolution proposals would give Scotland, and to a lesser extent Wales, a real area of engagement and potential autonomy in the development of European policy. While this was 'normal' in some other EU countries (Germany, Spain, and Austria), it was a real revolution for the UK. It will take time to see how devolution works in practice, but it is to be expected that there will be tensions, whether creative or acrimonious, between London and the new organs of government in Scotland and Wales. Similarly, the other parts of the new constitutional package - electoral reform, a reformed second chamber, a form of freedom of information - will have a potentially large impact on the conduct of European policy. One possible outcome is that the British may become more open to constructive discussion related isssues within the EU.

The Conservative Party Regroups

John Major announced his resignation as Conservative Party leader immediately after the election defeat. In the ensuing party election European issues loomed large, with Kenneth Clark and Stephen Dorrell as candidates from the pro-European wing. Several Eurosceptical candidates stood: Michael Howard, Peter Lilley and John Redwood. In the event a young, and rather untested, William Hague emerged in June as the victor of the run-off against Kenneth Clark, with an enormous task: to rebuild the base of support for the party and to find a *modus vivendi* on European policy. In the months that followed, the European issue continued to haunt the Conservatives, with policy drifting towards the camp of the more Eurosceptic wing.

Towards a New and Sustainable European policy?

During 1998, elements were set in place to give the UK a transformed profile on European issues. Many of the lines of concrete policy continued, with changes mainly of nuance, especially as regards the management of the economy, where the new government was committed to keeping a steady hand on the tiller. But in political terms the mood and atmospherics had altered, as had the scope for fundamental constitutional reforms. Yet the precise consequences for European policy remained to be addressed. More positive tones of voice and of imagery began to shift the terms of the public debate and to rebuild relationships with opposite numbers in the EU. But it was too early to be sure that a clearly articulated and sustainable policy was in place. In May 1998, Tony Blair began to engage more explicitly with European policy and to kick-start a wide-ranging review of policy. With broader changes under way in Europe, including the prospective eastern enlargement and potentially important changes in Germany, there was a window of opportunity for a differently configured British policy.

References

Hughes, Kirsty and Edward Smith (1998), 'New Labour - new Europe', *International Affairs*, 74/1, January.
Scottish Office, *Scotland's Parliament*, Edinburgh, Cm 3658, July.
Wallace, Helen (1997), 'At Odds with Europe', *Political Studies*, 45/4, September, 677-688.
Welsh Office, *A Voice for Wales*, Cardiff, Cm 3718, July.
Wilkes, George, ed. (1997), *Britain's Failure to enter the European Community, 1961-63*, London: Frank Cass.

This article was prepared with research support from Ulrich Sedelmeier.

10 The Sources of New Labour

RODNEY SMITH

For some time before their election success earlier this year, everything about New Labour and Tony Blair seemed to have a distant or not so distant Australian connection. Blair maintained several friendships with Australian Labor Party politicians, including West Australians Geoff Gallop and Kim Beazley, dating from his Oxford days. He had an Australian spiritual mentor in Anglican minister Peter Thomson, another university friend who was given credit for introducing Blair to the works of Scottish philosopher John Macmurray, Blair's intellectual hero. At the other end of the divine order, the Labour leader made a much reported 1995 trip to Hayman Island in Australia's tropical north to sup with Rupert Murdoch. Paul Keating, also at Hayman Island, offered Blair friendly advice and reportedly continued to do so at least until the end of the British election. The British Labour Party even reportedly used a former Australian Broadcasting Corporation journalist and Labor government staffer to dig the dirt on Tory parliamentarians prior to the British election campaign (*Electronic Telegraph*, 17 July 1995, 5 October 1996; *New Statesman and Society*, 31 May 1996: 18-19; *Sydney Morning Herald*, 15 January 1997, 3 May 1997).

More systematically, it has been argued in some quarters that the ALP of Bob Hawke and Keating provided the model for New Labour. Hawke, Keating and Blair (along with his sometimes forgotten predecessors Neil Kinnock and John Smith) were all labour party modernisers; all embraced the market with an enthusiasm not found in past labour leaders; all showed a willingness to at least selectively roll back the public sector. Aside from these broad parallels, New Labour seemed directly to borrow specific ALP policies, such as its cultural policy. In a recent philippic against the Hawke and Keating legacy published in *New Left Review*, the Australian sociologist Boris Frankel pushes this argument further by claiming that Australian Labor forged a new type of government British Labour was somehow bound to follow:

> ... recent Australian experience represents not only the demise of traditional labourism, but prefigures a new political model not yet fully seen in European social democratic and labour parties. ... Casting around for suitable strategies, it is now the turn of the Australian model to be imported by parties such as British Labour (Frankel 1997: 3-4)

How seriously should such claims be taken? The argument in this chapter is that they are generally unpersuasive. Not only do they lack substantial empirical evidence, they ignore or underplay differences between the specific economic, social and political circumstances confronting the British Labour Party and those confronting the ALP or other parties. These differences make borrowings in anything other than an ad hoc way unlikely. The organisational, policy and rhetorical shifts in the BLP from Old to New Labour can best be read as responses to Labour's domestic political fortunes since 1979 and to deeper facets of British political history. One of the consequences of debates within British Labour about how to respond to these domestic circumstances was the creation of the rather peculiar conception of 'Britain' around which Labour fought the 1997 general election. The second half of this chapter analyses this idea of 'Britain' in the collected speeches of Tony Blair (1996) and New Labour's election manifesto *New Labour: Because Britain Deserves Better* (British Labour Party 1997).

Brother, Can You Spare a Policy?

One major difficulty with the notion of New Labour borrowing Australian Labor's model is empirical: it lacks evidence for its position and ignores abundant evidence for the contrary view. Frankel's article is remarkable for its inability to provide cases where New Labour has borrowed Australian Labor's policy clothes, let alone a full 'model'. Equally importantly, since Frankel's argument at times is that Australian Labor took the elements of its own model from overseas, including Thatcher's Britain, he substantiates few cases of ALP borrowings. Instead, the argument almost completely proceeds on a mixture of assertions ('But there is no doubt that the vigorous example set by Thatcher helped bolster all those who sought to implement similar policies in Australia' Frankel 1997; 8) and the identification of global economic forces as a theoretical driving force behind broadly similar policy changes across different countries (Frankel 1997: 29). At this level, parties often appear to move in the same directions, but such a broad scale view conceals important differences (see, for example, *The Economist*, 10 May 1997: 43-44).

A more rigorous search for Australian model and policy borrowing by New Labour soon runs up against insurmountable problems. Take, for example, the centrepiece of the Hawke-Keating model, the incomes policy Accord between government and unions (Beilharz 1994: chs 5 and 6). New Labour has an incomes policy, but it looks nothing like any of the versions of the Accord pursued by Labor governments in Australia (BLP 1997). In fact, the British Labour Party had been retreating from its flirtation with centralised, corporatist-style incomes policy since the early 1980s, recognising that it suited neither the decentralisation of British unions nor their traditions of wage bargaining (Wintour and Hughes 1990: 129; Shaw 1994: 43-45, 95-7). Moreover, an Accord approach would have tied New Labour policy making and the unions more strongly at a time when the party leadership has been moving to progressively weaken such ties (Wintour and Hughes 1990: ch. 14; *New Statesman and Society*, 5 May 1995: 14-15; Coates 1996: 71-2). Blair himself (1996: 39) has repudiated the logic of corporatism as a way of pursuing public policy. To the extent that New Labour does see government building institutional links with economic interests in the pursuit of policy agreements, these are envisaged with business rather than unions (Shaw 1994: 98-99; Thompson 1996: 44; *New Statesman*, 22 November 1996: 24-25, 31 January 1997: 12-13).

In other policy areas, unambiguous cases of borrowings from Australia, or indeed any single source, are equally hard to find. New Labour's cultural policy was said by some to be taken from the Keating government's *Creative Nation* policy paper. Certainly, elements such as the emphasis on new electronic media seem to be drawn from *Creative Nation* (Blair 1996: 100). Nonetheless, New Labour's policy also draws on at least French, United States and Irish cultural policies and on the extensive experiences of Labour councils in devising and implementing local cultural policies (see *New Statesman*, 28 June 1996: 30-31; *Electronic Telegraph*, 4 January 1997).

The same difficulties arise when New Labour's ideological or rhetorical borrowings from Australian Labor are sought. Hawke and Keating both pursued policies couched in ideological terms, the former largely via ideas of internal national reconciliation, the latter via a more externally grounded construction of Australia's place in the world (see, for example, Hawke 1984; Keating 1995). While both of these bear vague resemblances to New Labour's emphases on the stakeholder society and a modern, outward-looking nation, the resemblances are only vague. Blair's communitarian notions of the stakeholder society cannot be found in the rhetoric of Hawke or Keating, or of any of their ministers. In terms of external influences, communitarian notions have far greater resonance with recent North American ideas, particularly those of the sociologist Amitai Etzioni, who visited the United Kingdom in 1995 to publicise his ideas and discuss them with Labour figures (Etzioni 1993; *New Statesman and Society*, 10 March 1995: 20-22, 12 May 1995: 24-5; *The Guardian*, 13 March 1995). Equally, however, New Labour's emphasis on community can be seen to derive from Blair's reworking of the ideas of earlier British thinkers such as Macmurray,[1] or to David Blunkett's persistent arguments about the importance of community in party forums in the mid-1980s (Hughes and Wintour 1990: ch. 5).

Blair's dramatic reworking of British Labour's Clause IV is another case in point (*The Guardian*, 13, 14 March 1995). While Australian Labor undertook a similar exercise a decade and a half before (O'Meagher 1983), there is no evidence that this stood as a particular inspiration for British Labour's modernisers. Indeed, the externally-inspired elements in New Labour's reformulation of the relationship between state, ownership and market drew primarily on the experiences of West European left parties as far back as the German Social Democratic Party's 1959 Bad Godesberg declaration (see, for example, Radice 1989: 5-9; Hughes and Wintour 1990: 60-1; Shaw 1994: 89-94). Nonetheless, Labour's new Clause IV was not borrowed wholesale from any of its European cousins.

The temptation to see more straight borrowing by parties of policies and ideas than actually exists is obvious. Instant and pervasive communications between countries have given parties easy access to an enormously expanded range of lessons from their cousins abroad. While this makes the possibility of policy borrowing easier, it also makes taking ideas wholesale from single sources less likely, since parties can be more promiscuous in searching out ideas. In many cases, such borrowings have simply become part of contemporary political ritual. Acknowledging that leaders have seriously considered another's ideas and policies, for example, often appears to be little more than a form of politeness to political hosts or guests. Blair's claimed consideration of Singaporean social policy and the lessons of John Howard's election campaign both seem to fit this category (Blair 1996: 294; *Australian*, 21-22 June 1997). In other cases, borrowing of ideas or the sources of those ideas seems to be a totemic symbol of association with powerful and successful politicians and parties elsewhere. The rumour that the Labour Party would have Clinton electoral strategist George Stephanopoulos working on its 1997 campaign seems a clear example of this, as did the claims immediately after Blair's victory that the Australian Labor Party would borrow (back?) New Labour ideas (*New Statesman*, 24 January 1997: 14-15; *Sydney Morning Herald*, 3 May 1997).

In any case, to be effective, borrowed ideas and policies have to be brought home and fitted to the domestic political context. As Blair notes in a number of speeches, differences in political contexts effectively kill off any serious idea of the wholesale importing of political models or even central policies (1996: 92, 94, 110, 169, 187, 294, 305). The differences between Australia and the United Kingdom are obvious in this context. They include, in no particular order, different external constraints imposed by Britain's membership of NATO and the EU, its unitary system versus federalism, first past the post ballots versus preferential voting, the powers of the House of Lords versus those of the Senate, and the respective labour parties' different constitutional structures.[2] Moreover, the culture and traditions of countries and of the parties themselves make parties wary of drawing heavily on international models. Many British Labour politicians, for example, were for years resistant to rhetoric, policies and campaign techniques that smacked of the 'Americanisation' of their party or of British electoral contests (Ellison 1994: 217; Shaw 1994: 26, 53-4)

A better way of understanding political parties is to see them as primarily responding to domestic political constraints and opportunities. Thus, rather than New Labour being a borrowing of the ALP's own borrowing of Thatcherism, as Frankel suggests, it makes much more sense to see it as a direct response to the domestic electoral and cultural success of Thatcherism in Britain. While some dismissed Labour's 1983 election loss simply as the folly of the Labour Left or the luck of the Falklands; for Kinnock and other key Labour figures the defeat sparked a widespread and lengthy period of reconstruction of Labour Party ideology, policy and organisation.

This modernising project, viewed by the leadership as increasingly urgent following the subsequent 1987 and 1992 losses, finally produced New Labour. The driving force in this reconstruction was a desire to win elections (Shaw 1994: 166). In turn, from around 1985 the Labour leadership relied much more heavily than previously on quantitative and qualitative research to gauge voter preferences and on a commercial marketing strategy to position itself and its policies in line with these preferences. In order to present the party as a marketable package, dissenting voices were formally and informally constrained. These developments have been extensively discussed elsewhere (see, for example, Hughes and Wintour 1990; Shaw 1994). British Labour's about face on unilateralism, its gradual scaling down of expectations of tax reform to its 1997 position of no change to income tax progressivity, its caution on public spending, its reconstruction of Clause IV, its shift away from protecting the power of unions and its relative neglect of environmental issues after 1990 all represented deliberate reactions to these perceptions of voter attitudes (Hughes and Wintour 1990: 14-17, 28-9, 31-4, 127, 136-42, 144-5; Shaw 1994: 44-45, 72-4, 130-4, 136-40; Heath and Jowell 1994; *Electronic Telegraph*, 31 October 1996, 5, 9, 21 January 1997, 8 March 1997). As Blair explains, the importance of changing Clause IV, rather than letting sleeping ideological dogs lie, was to make New Labour invulnerable to scare campaigns directed at British voters: 'This ... modern party ... requires a modern constitution that says what we are in terms the public cannot misunderstand and the Tories cannot misrepresent' (Blair 1996: 49; see also *The Independent*, 11 March 1995).[3]

A party in this mode - testing every policy against public perceptions, packaging all aspects of its presentation around electoral viability and intolerant of maverick voices - is particularly unlikely to be able to borrow external models or policy ideas in any straightforward way. While the British Labour Party certainly looked outside Britain for some of its inspiration, any external ideas were refracted through the powerful prisms of British conditions and public opinion.

In recrafting its ideology, policies and structure in the late 1980s and early 1990s, the British Labour Party was responding to an image of Britain, and particularly the British electorate. Such a response simultaneously constructed an image of Britain, one that was rather different to the images held by the Labour Party in previous decades. This new image of Britain can be found in a number of recent British Labour texts, but it is given its fullest expression in the speeches of Tony Blair and Labour's 1997 manifesto *New Labour: Because Britain Deserves Better*.

Blair's Britain: Values without History

An examination of Blair's speeches and 1997 manifesto reveals a rather curious 'Britain' defined repeatedly and almost entirely by a set of qualities such as 'tolerance', 'openness', 'sticking up for the underdog', 'social justice', 'innovation', 'creativity', 'ingenuity', 'inventiveness', 'adaptability', 'willingness and vigour ... to improve [the] local environment', 'extraordinary talent in science, research and innovation', 'fair play', 'decency', 'responsibility', 'mutuality', 'an outward-looking spirit of adventure and discovery', patriotism and defence of others (Blair 1996: ix, 49, 111, 233, 294, 297, 308).

These values are particularly British, or particularly found among Britain's people: '... our people, by their intelligence, grit and creativity, are still a people unrivalled anywhere in the world' (Blair 1996: 291). Blair takes such values to have been uniform and unchanging across British history. They are its 'traditions', or 'basic instincts' (Blair 1996: ix, 308). They were not produced by identifiable historical circumstances. The 'people's vision' for Britain during and after World War Two, for example, embodies exactly those qualities found across its history - 'a generous, brave, forward-looking bastion of decency and social justice' (Blair 1996: 9). For Blair, such traditions define Britain's important place in the world, uniting its past, present and future: 'I want a Britain that is true to itself - true to its history, true to its character and gifts, and above all true to its future. That is the only way to regain our sense of direction and fulfil the historic destiny of our country' (Blair 1996: 287).

There is nothing strange about Blair's construction of such a list of national virtues or about his assertion of their timelessness. Many people, including many British citizens, would no doubt argue against the accuracy of Blair's list, pointing to omissions and contradictions or to an alternative, less celebratory list.[4] Others would question the notion of 'British' values, arguing for the distinctiveness of English, Welsh, Scottish and Ulster values, or for even finer regional distinctions. Yet others would question the timelessness and uniqueness of such values, insisting on their historically specific roots. To take these approaches would merely be to acknowledge that Blair's is a project of nationalist myth-making (see Anderson 1991).

What does seem more distinctive, and indeed curious, about Blair's Britain is that he almost entirely divorces what he takes to be distinctive British qualities from discussion of the events, experiences, achievements, institutions or practices that they might have helped produce or been developed through. His is a Britain recognisable by the value psychologist but not the anthropologist or cultural historian. Or, in the sense that he does refer to 'history' in his speeches, his is a British history largely without dates, events, institutions or characters. This is odd, because when a group of people define themselves and their values, they tend to confirm the truth of those values by telling and retelling stories that embody them, stories with the logic 'We are this sort of people, and this is shown by ...'.[5] Such stories are virtually absent in Blair's speeches.

There are rare exceptions. Interestingly, they do not occur in Blair's obviously political speeches—to the party faithful, or electors, or interest group audiences. They occur in texts that, while they are public, have an ostensibly more intimate, personal audience. In a 'Dear Kathryn' letter to his daughter published in the *Daily Express*, Blair initially links a range of experiences, artefacts and products with the values of Britain:

> Britain is a great nation. A country where we can watch the most exciting sport - Wimbledon, the FA Cup, Test cricket. Where you can listen to the best pop music - the Beatles, Blur, Oasis and Simply Red. A nation that leads the world in fashion, animation, computer software. A country of stunning beauty - the Lakes district, the Yorkshire Dales and Moors, the Highlands of Scotland, Snowdonia, the Cotswolds, seaside towns. A nation blessed with a rich language, fine literature, art and architecture - and a unique sense of humour (Blair 1996: 251)

In an even more explicit link between values and the experiences of many Britons, Blair began a 1995 speech honouring Stanley Matthews on his eightieth birthday at the Football Writers Association by identifying the man with a British culture of fair play and generosity:

> Sir Stanley Matthews is a culture, and it is one that in all too many areas of the game has been eroded. He was never booked, let alone sent off, and was always able to find time for the children crowding around the players' entrance, for he knew that without them and their enthusiasm the game's future is [sic] bleak.
>
> People talk of the game's crowd-pullers today, and set them alongside their earnings and transfer fees, but did anyone ever pull them like Sir Stan? (Blair 1996: 254)

In both cases, however, Blair attempts quickly to cut off any nostalgic response to his description of British cultural achievements. He urges Kathryn:

> Never let anyone say that there is a better place to live than Britain. But never let others tell you that Britain cannot be better. We are a country of talent, but a country that often does not let that talent flourish. At times we seem to be a nation that has become old, tired, resentful. Relying on our past as a great nation long before you were born, rather than working to make us a great nation in the future. Reluctant to face new ideas. Reluctant to take risks. ... Yet our history is all about being outward-looking, imaginative, clever.' (Blair 1996: 251)

Similarly, questioning the increased commercialisation of football since Matthews' playing days, Blair argues that his '... is not some Corinthian cry for a return to amateurism ...' What, then, is it? It is '... a belief that basic decent values should not be compromised whatever the commercial pressures ....' (1996: 255).

Both of Blair's strategies here break the link between values and powerful past experiences as soon as it is made. In his Kathryn letter, the past is presented as seductive but ultimately debilitating and destructive, its only useful message to encourage people to look away by looking forward. Blair often repeats the bones of this message elsewhere, particularly in the context of his vision for Britain as 'a young country': 'We are a country with a great past but too often we seem to live in it rather than learn from it'; 'We are proud of our history but its weight hangs heavy upon us'; 'A young country should be proud of its identity and its place in the world, not living in its history but grasping the opportunities of the future' (Blair 1996: x; 65, 70).

The logic of turning away from past experience is presented most succinctly in Blair's constant use of 'new' (Britain, Labour, purpose, direction, leadership, relationship, industrial world, vision, politics, economy, nation-state). It is also found in his common deployment of 're-' words like renewal, reborn, rebuilding and recreating to mark breaks with the past rather than its recapturing.[6] Blair is, of course, not the first Labour leader to emphasise the 'newness' of Labour's Britain. Harold Wilson's collected 1964 speeches bear the title *The New Britain* (Wilson 1964) and a number of Labour policy documents from the 1980s and early 1990s utilise 'new' in their titles.[7] The difference is in the comprehensiveness of Blair's use of new and the radicalness with which he severs connections between the values of new Britain and experiences of the past.[8]

In the case of Stanley Matthews, Blair divorces values from experience by firmly separating individuals from their social and cultural locations. Blair's criticism of commercialisation of sport strongly implies that Matthews' values and behaviour have to be understood as supported, enforced and at least partly produced by class and other socio-economic forces and relations of 1940s and 1950s Britain. Instead, Blair undercuts such a position by asserting that contemporary players could exhibit the same values as Matthews, an assertion that disregards the huge shifts in football from working class experience to mass consumer spectacle since Matthews' era.[9] For Blair, Stanley Matthews *is* a culture not because he belonged to a culture rooted in specific social relations and experiences but because as an individual he displayed particular values. Other individual players could do the same today. The values are timeless, the context unimportant and unconstraining.

Where he does recount stories of specific British experiences, then, Blair characterises them as either unnecessary to or destructive of the values they might otherwise be taken to support and explain. The result is a curiously insubstantial and abstract depiction of Britain, populated by people apparently unable to make safe connections between their values and their present and past collective experiences. This might be seen as paradoxical coming from a political leader who has contrasted his vision of individuals thriving within communities so sharply with the raw individualism of Margaret ('There is no such thing as society') Thatcher and the Conservative Party. The paradox is solved when the details of Blair's communitarianism are analysed.

Communitarianism without Communities

Blair's much vaunted communitarianism rests on a very thin conception of communities: the values they embody are those of every community but no specific community in Britain (or elsewhere). As with other concepts, what Blair means by communitarianism is left somewhat hazy.[10] Nonetheless, in both his main ways of discussing communities, Blair presents them as means to ends. The most familiar version is often repeated by Blair and other Labour modernisers (see, for example, Radice 1989: ch 5), and echoes older arguments in the right-wing parties of Anglo-democracies.[11] In this version, communities provide a means to balance individuals' existing rights with new responsibilities (Blair 1996: xii). The right of the unemployed and lone parents to social payments, for example, must be balanced by their responsibility to contribute work to society in return (*New Statesman and Society*, 21 March 1997: 13; BLP 1997). While the conservative eroding of rights in this version worries English liberals (see, for example, Russell 1996), Blair's second version of communitarianism sits closer to much twentieth century British liberalism. Here, communities are prerequisites for the expansion of individual freedoms and capacities.[12] Many of the specific benefits of community that Blair highlights can be restated simply as an individual's rights to enjoy education, health, property, personal safety and so on (see, for example, Blair 1996: 30, 31). More generally, Blair sees community as the mechanism for solving the liberal problem of selfish interest:

> The word 'community' ... for me ... expresses the mutuality of both interest and obligation that rises above a narrow view of self-

interest. It allows a more enlightened and actually a more rational idea of self-interest, and by placing the individual within society, rather than apart from it, recognises that people need to cooperate as well as compete (Blair 1996: 218).

Community provides individuals with equal opportunity to develop their capacities:

> ... individuals prosper only when supported by a strong community. Individual and family are not the antithesis of community, as Mrs Thatcher said, but dependent on it. And the great power of community - of what we do together - is to make more equal our opportunity and ability to develop our talents to the full (Blair 1996: 156; see also 38-39).

In Blair's second version, then, communities make up deficits in liberal individualism rather than directly challenging it.

Given the weight he puts on community in both versions, it might be expected that Blair would point to specific examples of the capacities of actually existing British communities to produce either type of benefit. This is particularly so given that many existing communities by their racism, sexism, feuding, localism and so on appear to limit rather than extend many individuals' rights and opportunities (see *New Statesman and Society*, 10 March 1995: 20-22; Russell 1996: 82;).[13] Failure to provide examples of existing communities also leaves Blair open to the flip-side of his own criticism of new Right individualism: 'Increasingly, the intellectual inadequacy of an analysis based on the theoretical rights of individuals without reference to *the specific family and community structures in which they live* has been recognised' (Blair 1996: 245, my emphasis). Despite these dangers, aside from vague claims - 'Across Britain, and perhaps especially in some of its most deprived neighbourhoods, people give selflessly of themselves to help each other ....' (Blair 1996: 307) - Blair ventures no examples of real communities achieving the values and outcomes he supports.[14]

In fact, Blair diverts people from looking for community in two places where they might expect to find it. First, community is overwhelmingly missing in contemporary British society, destroyed by crime, drugs, greed, family breakdown and the like. One of the only specific experiences of social life that Blair draws on relates this negative vision of thwarted community:

> At a party meeting I spoke to in Glasgow, a woman describing herself as 'just a ordinary housewife, mother and grandmother'

stood up and spoke of the grim reality of her life raising a family in an estate ruined by drugs, crime and poor health (Blair 1996: 249).

These anti-communities are not limited to depressed housing estates, but are ubiquitous: 'the consequences of social breakdown in society [*sic*] lie all around us' (Blair 1996: 244). The end point of existing trends in British society, Blair warns, is a *Blade Runner* society (Blair 1996: 308; *Electronic Telegraph*, 30 January 1996).

Second, community cannot be regained from the past. One obvious response that Blair's depiction of contemporary society would clearly elicit from audiences is a desire to revive earlier British communities centred on work, the patriarchal family and neighbourhood (*New Statesman and Society*, 10 March 1995: 20-22). Perhaps Blair avoids discussing actually existing communities partly because he wants to block the romantic path from those communities to remembered or imagined stronger, safer communities of the past. That he is aware of this danger seems clear in passages like the following:

> Look at the balance between family and work. Women are working in ever greater numbers. We welcome that. But we are living in a world where the assumptions of the forty-hour work week are a thing of the past. There is no going back to the world of full-time jobs paying men a family wage, with lifetime security, a guaranteed pension and a carriage clock at the end of it (Blair 1996: 157. See also 189, 237).

Elsewhere, he is blunter: 'Community is not some piece of nostalgia' (Blair 1996: 37).

In ways paralleling his treatment of values and history, Blair dislocates his idea of community from most of the concrete and imagined experiences that would give it content for his audiences. If Blair is convinced that they want the attractive balance of rights and responsibilities produced by community (just as they all share British values), he is equally insistent that they must look to the future for them. The present is a wasteland, the past unrecoverable.

Explaining Blair's Britain

Why does Blair construct this abstract and ahistorical kind of Britain, a Britain with values but few experiences, a desire for community but no knowledge of it? Part of the answer is that, speaking directly or indirectly to the country as a whole, Blair does not and cannot know his audience. Paradoxically, the assumption that political leaders can know their audiences has become less tenable the more party pollsters and other researchers learn about those audiences, since the main lesson is one of diversity. Despite the assumption of one 'Britain' in his speeches, Blair must have been aware from Labour research and his own observations that members of his British audience vary enormously in their experiences, knowledge and interests. Raising specific examples of experiences and community is therefore dangerous, since what might appeal to parts of his audience would repel others. The danger is presumably heightened for a Labour leader who knows from recent elections that to win government he must extend his party's electoral appeal to new types of voters without losing old supporters (Radice 1992; Shaw 1994: 133-4, 138). Blair's rhetorical response is *amphiboly*— casting his net as widely as possible to catch all the fish he can.[15] His references to Britain as tolerant, inventive, decent and so on are a key part of this strategy, since everyone in his audience can attach (different) meanings to these positive but vague qualities. Specific experiences that might reduce their possible meanings, trapping fewer fish in the net, are omitted (see *New Statesman*, 4 April 1997: 7).

Uncertainty about his audience and *amphiboly* are not full explanations for Blair's abstract Britain, however. Blair is not content for people to attach any and all meanings or experiences to British values. New Labour is necessarily pitted against two types of connections British citizens might make between their values and specific political institutions, policies, practices and experiences - those between fair play, social justice, decency and the like and Old Labour and those between fair play, patriotism, adventure and the like and the Conservative regime. Either type of connection would weaken the case for New Labour. In his speeches, Blair explicitly suggests that neither connection really existed.

Arguments from a Labour leader or manifesto that the Conservative Party does not represent British values are unsurprising. Blair certainly makes such arguments, blaming the Conservatives for Britain's malaise, accusing them of false patriotism and distancing Conservative values from those of the British people. Blair's speech to the 1995 Labour Conference, in which he recalled VJ celebrations earlier that year, combines all three themes:

> As the Tories wave their Union Jacks I know what so many people will be thinking. I know what the people want to say to those Tories: It is no good waving the fabric of our flag when you have spent 16

years tearing apart the fabric of our nation, tearing apart the bonds that tie communities together and make us a united Kingdom, tearing apart the security of those people [at the celebrations], clutching their Union Jacks, swelling with pride at their victory over tyranny, and yelling at me to 'get those Tories out', because they want security, because they want to leave a better world for their children and their grandchildren than they created for themselves and because they know the Tories cannot supply it (Blair 1996: 71-72).

Labour's 1997 manifesto introduces every policy area by reinforcing this message ('Education has been the Tories' biggest failure'; 'The Conservatives have in 18 years created the two longest, deepest recessions of this century' etc.).

According to Blair, however, not everything the Conservatives did was mistaken. Thatcher 'got certain things right' (Blair 1996: 206. See also *Electronic Telegraph*, 11 January 1996). Blair does not have specific policies in mind here as much as the Conservatives' removing the rationale and capacity for the state to pursue interventionist, large spending economic and social strategies. Their strengths comprised:

... a greater emphasis on enterprise; rewarding not punishing success; breaking up some of the vested interests associated with state bureaucracy. ... But I want to suggest that in the end it was a project more successful at taking on and destroying some outdated attitudes and prescriptions than it was at building and creating (Blair 1996: 206; see also 216-217).

Whose attitudes and prescriptions? The second and potentially trickier target of Blair's attempt to sever the connections between British values and political experience is the pre-1990s British Labour Party, or 'Old Labour'.

Blair attempts this by constructing a history of the Labour Party in which at some point it lost contact with the values of the country. In some versions, this happened as recently as the 1970s and 1980s, in others the 1960s or 1950s, and in yet others 'early Left thinking'. The first causes of this lost contact were the Old Labour policies of 'statist socialism', 'rigid economic planning', 'powerful collectivist institutions' and 'state control', later supplemented by 'indifferen[ce] to the family and individual responsibility' (Blair 1996: 6, 22, 206, 216, 221). If Labour's 'timeless values' remained those of the British people, its policy approaches until the 1990s did not match those values (Blair 1996: 18, 22, 23, 62, 107). In this sense, Blair presents the Labour Party as a party lacking experiences that are unequivocally true to its values.

The extent to which Blair pursues this theme is evident in his appraisal of the Attlee Government, a government that espoused and undertook the kind of Old Labour policies Blair rejects. Attlee's Labour certainly embodied the values of British society, Blair argues, but this was despite its policies rather than because of them: '... its prospectus at the [1945] election was strongest in the new direction it offered, not in the minutiae of policy detail' (Blair 1996: 5). Blair later expands on this point, suggesting various reasons why Labour's policies were unimportant to its election:

It was not a raft of detailed policies that took that government to power, but the clear sense of purpose and direction. There was, of course, Beveridge, and the Labour plans for social security developed during the war. And the coalition government had passed the 1944 Education Act. But in the 1930s the debate on economic policy and the role of planning, though long, was rather confused. Other things were done on the hoof—for example, Aneurin Bevan and the structure of the health service. What the 1945 government did have, however, was a very strong sense of direction based on core Labour values—fairness, freedom from want, social equality (Blair 1996: 8, 9).

In 1945, Labour was elected on its values, not its policies. It lost government and subsequently failed to establish itself as the 'natural party of government' because it mistakenly took those policies to be more important than they were (Blair 1996: 13; Coates 1996: 69).

Any suspicion that Labour's values in the post-war period were understood in the electorate to be fairness, freedom from want and social equality in large part because these values were demonstrably consistent with Labour's policies of state welfare, education expansion, economic planning and the like is thus rebutted. Blair elsewhere denies even the argument that Labour's core working class voters were ever attracted to collectivist politics:

> There is a myth that at some point the nature of the people themselves then changed: they were collectively minded and became selfish. In fact, if you speak even to miners in County Durham about voting Labour in 1945, never mind the south of England, they weren't voting for everyone else or for some abstract notion of the public good: they were voting for a collectivist government because that government was going to do good by them. They would get on in life as a result, and their hope was that their children would not

spend their lives underground in the way that they were forced to (Blair 1996: 216).

Then as now, people just wanted government to make things better for them, without particular regard for how this was done.

It is not clear whether Blair really believes this account of the connections between Labour's voters, Labour values and Labour policy since the 1940s. The extent to which it distances people's political behaviour and values from their broader values, socio-economic circumstances and specific community settings is quite implausible. This very implausibility suggests the way Blair's account should be understood. His attempt to cut every connection between the specifics of people's lives and their political values suggests that he is all too aware of the very power of those connections—the fact that people's everyday experiences and understandings often spill over into political meanings. To awaken any but the most trite and general values or senses of community is to risk awakening in people connections with the politics that helped to sustain those values and communities and gave them meaning. In the case of Durham miners, and indeed many of their non-mining neighbours, these meanings included strengthened working class consciousness, local collective self-help and support for union struggles, nationalisation of mines and state intervention (Butler and Stokes 1969: 182-4; Bulmer 1978, especially chs. 6-9; Douglass and Krieger 1983, especially ch. 9). With the exception of collective self-help, these are precisely the sorts of political approaches New Labour rejects.

With this in mind, Blair's general severing of the connections between British values and specific institutions and practices analysed earlier in this chapter becomes more comprehensible. This general severing makes it easier for Blair to cut off political nostalgia based on lived experiences of the connections between values and past Old Left and Right policies. Since many experiences contain the potential for such political connections, it makes perfect strategic sense for Blair to deny the importance of all of them.

Blair's picture of political Britain is one of enduring and important values unfulfilled by the policies of the Right and Old Left. Each was elected due to their temporarily matching values, not policies, with those of the British electorate. Their subsequent failures lay in their policies. Neither became 'the natural party of government', a concept that suggests the possibility of a long-term match between the values of people and party. This is indeed Blair's aim (1996: 20). A major strategic implication of Blair's analysis is that his party should play down policies and focus as much as possible on values. Many of Blair's critics would argue this is exactly the logic he has followed; however, it is not the conclusion Blair himself draws. Instead, he sees New Labour as for the first time providing the policies and programme that fit British values. An early section of the 1997 manifesto, for example, summarises this approach:

> In each area of policy a new and distinctive approach has been mapped out, one that differs both from the solutions of the old left and those of the Conservative right. This is why new Labour is new. We believe in the strength of our values, but we recognise also that the policies of 1997 cannot be those of 1947 or 1967. More detailed policy has been produced by us than by any opposition in history. Our direction and destination are clear.
>
> The old left would have sought state control of industry. The Conservative right is content to leave all to the market. We reject both approaches. Government and industry must work together .... (BLP 1997)

Despite its softer than usual reference to past Labour governments, the message of the manifesto is clear enough—until May 1997, Britain was a set of values looking for its perfect political match.

Blair's Britain in Europe—Leading and Using, Not Belonging

New Labour's construction of Britain in this way has implications for its construction of Britain's 'other', Europe. Much has been made about the change in attitudes toward Europe between the 'little Englander' Conservatives and New Labour. It is a recurring theme in Blair's speeches and the 1997 manifesto (see, for example, Blair 1996: 210). On closer inspection, the differences between New Labour and the Conservatives are not as stark as they first appear. Many Tories saw a strong Britain outside or against Europe; New Labour's policies are built around the idea of a strong Britain leading the European Union (see, for example, Blair 1996: xiii, 24, 71, 128, 210, 285). New Labour almost always presents the possible relationships between Britain and Europe as dichotomous - a choice between leadership and exclusion. Other alternatives, such as a cooperative membership among equals,[16] let alone 'a federal superstate' (Blair 1996: 264), are not countenanced:

> I want Britain to be leading in Europe, so that we can shape Europe to suit Britain's interests rather than being sidelined and humiliated as the decisions get taken elsewhere (Blair 1996: 252).

The importance of the leadership-exclusion dichotomy is that it confronts one way of preserving national autonomy (isolation) with another (leadership). Neither alternative suggests Europe should or will affect what it means to be British. Blair further emphasises this conclusion by constantly stressing the need for widespread reform to central European Union policies (see, for example, Blair 1996: 24, 32, 70, 29, 285). Britain will reform Europe rather than vice versa.

For New Labor, the question of Europe is reduced to an instrumental one about whether its approach or Conservative isolationism will best advance an already defined set of British interests. Europe is important only to the extent that it is a historically specific vehicle for Britain to continue realising its timeless national qualities on the world stage:

> Historically, while being a European power, Britain has been special in having an empire and a global role. This has led us to think of ourselves as apart from Europe. But if we want to maintain that global role now we must be a leading player in Europe. We no longer have an empire, and although the Commonwealth gives us valuable links around the world it is not an alternative to Europe. ...
>
> Our road to maximum influence leads through Europe ...
>
> The real patriotic case, therefore, for those who want Britain to maintain its traditional global role, is for leadership in Europe (Blair 1996: 210. See also 283).

This instrumental approach to Europe is reflected in New Labour's equivocal support for specific EU policies such as the Social Chapter, which might have been expected to find a comfortable home in the Labour Party. While Blair promises that New Labour will sign the Chapter (1996: 45, 53), he is careful to demonstrate that this will not bind British governments in specific ways:

> The Social Chapter is not detailed legislation. It is a set of principles. The real fear is that by being part of it we may in future agree to the import of inefficient practices to Britain. A Labour government will not pursue such a course (Blair 1996: 108).

Britain's identity and values will shape the Social Chapter, not the other way around.

The Social Chapter presents in microcosm the challenges of Europe more generally for Blair's conception of Britain. Europe's policies and institutions reflect its specific history and experiences. A New Labour government buying into a more active role in European policies and institutions would inevitably seem to be validating these. If New Labour wants to avoid the British public understanding domestic politics by delving into its own experiences, it also wants to avoid the appearance that it is buying into politics that reflect the experiences of others. New Labour's way of containing such fears is to set up a solid, hard Britain of settled values taking only what suits it from Europe and leading a Europe in need of reform. A conception of British membership of Europe that went beyond leadership would present challenges to New Labour's abstract construction of 'Britain' similar to the challenges presented by richer conceptions of British community and national identity.

Conclusion: A Sustainable Image?

This chapter has argued that in response to a series of election defeats, the British Labour Party leadership has reconceptualised Britain as a country of values but one without the history and experiences by which people would normally confirm these. Similarly, New Labour's image of Britain is one yearning for community but lacking reliable experiences of it. Such a radical separating of people and their values from their experiences and history recognised, although it could not directly admit, the potential power of experience and history to prevent people from accepting the case for New Labour's new Britain. Labour's strategy is, however, one with inevitable limits. It remained plausible only while New Labour was in opposition. While the only alternative to the past remained a future (and therefore unexperienced) New Labour, a radical denial of past experiences in favour of that glittering future could be confidently asserted. New Labour has, however, now won office and is implementing a programme that will increasingly form part of British people's stock of experiences. As this implementation proceeds, the New Labour leadership will be unable to resist drawing on those experiences of its policies to legitimise and defend them. Once the importance of some experiences is admitted, it will be impossible for New Labour to deny comparisons with other, older experiences under Conservative and Old Labour governments. New Labour's struggle with old Britain is far from over.

References

Anderson, B. (1991) *Imagined Communities*, London, Verso.
Beilharz, P. (1994) *Transforming Labor*, Cambridge, Cambridge University Press.
Blair, T. (1996) *New Britain: My Vision of a Young Country*, London, Fourth Estate.
British Labour Party (BLP) (1997) *New Labour: Because Britain Deserves Better*, http://www.labourwin97.org.uk/olp/
Bulmer, M. (ed.) (1978) *Mining and Social Change: Durham County in the Twentieth Century*, London, Croom Helm.
Butler, D. and Stokes, D. (1969) *Political Change in Britain*, Harmondsworth, Penguin.
Coates, D. (1996) 'Labour governments: Old constraints and New Parameters', *New Left Review*, 219, September/October, 62-77.
Committee of Review (1983) *Facing the Facts*, Canberra, Liberal Party of Australia.
Condren, C. (1985) *The Status and Appraisal of Classic Texts*, Princeton, Princeton University Press.
Critcher, C. (1979) 'Football Since the War', in J. Clarke, C. Critcher and R. Rohnson (eds), *Working-Class Culture*, London, Hutchinson.
Douglass, D. and Krieger, J. (1983) *A Miner's Life*, London, Routledge and Kegan Paul.
Ellison, N. (1994) *Egalitarian Thought and Labour Politics*, London, Routledge.
Etzioni, A. (1993) *The Spirit of Community: Rights, Responsibilities and the Communitarian Agenda*, New York: Crown.
Frankel, B. (1997) 'Beyond Labourism and Socialism: How the Australian Labor Party Developed the Model of "New Labour"', *New Left Review*, 221, January/February, 3-33.
Hawke, R. (1984) *National Reconciliation: The Speeches of Bob Hawke*, Melbourne, Fontana.
Heath, A. and Jowell, R. (1994) 'Labour's Policy Review', in A. Heath, R. Jowell and J. Curtice with B. Taylor (eds), *Labour's Last Chance?*, Aldershot, Dartmouth.
Hughes, C. and Wintour, P. (1990) *Labour Rebuilt*, London, Fourth Estate.
Keating, P. (1995) *Advancing Australia: The Speeches of Paul Keating, Prime Minister*, Sydney, Big Picture Publications.
O'Meagher, B. (ed.) (1983) *The Socialist Objective*, Sydney, Hale and Iremonger.
Radice, G. (1989) *Labour's Path to Power: The New Revisionism*, Houndsmills, Macmillan.
—— (1992) *Southern Discomfort*, Fabian Pamphlet 555, London, Fabian Society.
Russell, C. (1996) 'New Labour: Old Tory Writ Large?', *New Left Review*, 219, September/October, 78-88.
Shaw, E. (1994) *The Labour Party Since 1979*, London, Routledge.

Teles, S. (1997) 'Can New Labour Dance the Clinton?', *The American Prospect,* 31, March-April, 49-56.
Thompson, N. (1996) 'Supply-side Socialism: The Political Economy of New Labour', *New Left Review,* 216, March/April, 37-54.
Tönnies, F. (1955) *Community and Association,* London, Routledge and Kegan Paul.
Tudor, H. (1972) *Political Myth,* London, Pall Mall.
Wilson, H. (1964) *The New Britain,* Harmondsworth, Penguin.

Notes

1 Even here, it is important to recognise that Blair's is an interpretation of Macmurray, rather than a straight borrowing. See *New Statesman,* 7 February 1997: 18-20.
2 Interestingly, Frankel is aware of these differences (see 1997: 6, 15 and 17 for examples), but they do not alter his insistence that parties in some meaningful sense borrow models from each other. For a similar argument to mine, this time focusing on the difficulties of Blair borrowing from Clinton, see Teles (1997).
3 Contrary to common belief, public ownership rated but one sentence in Labour's leftist 1983 manifesto and even by then was far more peripheral to the Labour Left's economic strategy than it had been to mainstream Labour policy a decade earlier. In the 1980s, soft left and right wing Labour figures like David Blunkett and John Smith saw the old Clause IV as still relevant not because of any belief in widespread public ownership but because of its suggestion of the role of the state in guiding enterprise. By the late 1980s, the Party Conference had diluted the Party's commitment to public ownership and Party economic debates focused on the best modes of public control, not public ownership. See Wintour and Hughes (1990: 130-3); Shaw (1994: 13-14, 47-9, 85-9). On the success of the Conservative's 'fear-arousal strategy' against Labour in 1992, see Shaw (1994: 144-5).
4 Blair himself suggests some of these contradictions and alternatives in his speeches. Adventurousness and innovation sit oddly beside British stoic inertia: 'If we have a fault, it is that, unless roused, we tend to let things be. We say, "Things could be worse" rather than "Things should be better"' (Blair 1996: 49, 50). Egalitarianism and adaptability confront elitism and passivity: 'Today the old attitudes live on. Too many people at the top say that the search for more excellence will lead to less of it—"More means worse" in the appalling phrase. Too many at the bottom say education is "not for me"' (Blair 1996: 162).
5 For analysis of one form of such stories, see Tudor (1972).
6 Blair sometimes contrasts 're-' words that indicate others' desire to go back with his own forward-looking vision, as in the following (Blair 1996: 218, my emphases): 'There is therefore a desire [among British people] to *regain*

our identity as a society, to advocate and use social action once again - *but only in a way that learns from the excesses and failings of the past and does not repeat them. What, then, should the new relationship between society and individual consist of?'*

7   For example, the 1985 TUC-Labour Party Liaison Committee's *A New Partnership. A New Britain*, and Labour's 1987 policy papers *New Jobs for Britain, New Skills for Britain, New Industrial Strength for Britain* (Hughes and Wintour 1990: 129; Shaw 1994: 43).

8   Coates (1996: 65) has noted the parallel with Wilson's use of 'New Britain', but overlooks the important difference that Wilson's speeches often tie his ideas and vision in detailed ways to past Labour achievements and policies, whereas Blair does as much as he can to separate his ideas from Labour's past.

9   For a persuasive analysis of the impact of such shifts on footballers' values in England in the post-war period, see Critcher (1979).

10 For a discussion of the haziness of Blair's other big idea, the 'stakeholder economy', see Thompson (1996) and *New Statesman and Society*, 29 March 1996, pp.18-20.

11 For an Australian example, see Committee of Review (1983).

12 In the traditional sociological sense, of course, social groups that are understood by their members to exist because they serve individual ends of this sort are not really communities at all but associations. See, for example, Tonnies (1955).

13 The criticism applies equally to Blair's claim that we can understand the benefits of community by looking at families (Blair 1996: 37, 247).

14 Anna Coote suggests that part of Blair's problem here is that, as a politician, he has little personal experience of community (*The Guardian*, 24 March 1995).

15 Thanks to Conal Condren for suggesting this term. For discussion and examples from a range of political texts, see Condren (1985: 242-52).

16 For an exception, see Blair (1996: 20).

11 Public Opinion, Sovereignty and the European Union

ELIM PAPADAKIS

Among the challenges facing the European Union is how to persuade public opinion about the advantages of monetary union and further expansion of the association. Recent national elections (for instance, in France in 1997) have highlighted the strains between government and opinion associated with efforts to meet the criteria for monetary union.

Two of the aims of this chapter are to consider both arguments about and evidence of convergence and divergence between the views of political élites and the mass public on questions of European union. Research has shown that support for and opposition to European integration (both in Britain and in other European nations) depend, among other factors, on the commitment and capacity of national political élites (that control political parties) to mobilise public opinion on questions of national sovereignty and identity, on socio-demographic factors and political orientations and on levels of knowledge, information and trust with respect to the objectives of European unity.

Sovereignty and the Democratic Deficit

The question of convergence or divergence between the opinions of political élites and of the mass public is particularly important in the context of arguments about the 'democratic deficit' of the European Union (as perceived by citizens in Britain and in other European nations). The notion of a democratic deficit has been defined as 'the gap between the powers transferred to the Community level and the control of the elected [domestic] Parliament over them, a gap filled by national civil servants operating as European experts or as members of regulation and management committees, and to some extent by organised lobbies, mainly representing business' (Shirley Williams, cited by Newman, 1996, 190). The concept of a democratic deficit is therefore linked to considerations like legitimacy and the division of power between the nation state and transnational organisations.

Before considering more fully some of the concerns about a democratic deficit, it may be useful to reflect on the notion of sovereignty, an idea that implies the power assigned to one or more agents 'entitled to make decisions and settle disputes within a political hierarchy with some degree of finality' (King, 1991, 492). The concept of sovereign power, of a supreme authority, originates from the work of the French philosopher, Jean Bodin, and it underpins the work of the most influential writer on this topic, Thomas Hobbes: 'For Hobbes, once the members of the commonwealth have come together and agree to constitute a sovereign power to rule over them, the powers of that sovereign are almost unlimited. The terms of the contract are irrevocable and, since members of the commonwealth have mutually willed the creation of the sovereign, they are deemed to have vicariously willed all of its actions' (Pierson, 1996, 14-15).

Like any concept, the notion of a sovereign power can also be modified in numerous ways, as in the idea of a 'sovereign people' suggested by Jean Jacques Rousseau. This radical democratic interpretation posits that the ultimate arbiters are the people. This is of course not the standard view. The more conventional view is that power in western democracies either is or ought to be divided up. The principle of the separation of powers refers to the division of power between executive, the legislature and the judiciary.

There are many other ways of conceiving sovereign (like state sovereignty, legal sovereignty and popular sovereignty) and there are some significant challenges to the notion (centred on arguments about sovereignty as a myth, divided sovereignty, sovereignty as a danger) (Newman, 1996). Some of these concerns can be expressed as a 'counter-movement' against the idea of sovereignty (Pierson, 1996, 16). This reflects the idea that centres of power emerge outside the official channels of authority - and that these alternative sources of power constrain and limit the power exercised in the official channels. Among the dispersed sources of power are interest groups and social movements as well as prominent individuals who challenge the authorities.

Given the wide range of interpretations of the concept of sovereignty - and it is worth bearing in mind that sovereign power has been exercised not just by leaders of nation states but by emperors - it is not surprising that the question of a democratic deficit has preoccupied both supporters and opponents of the European Union. Moreover, they have interpreted the democratic deficit in ways that reflect a wide range of conceptions of government including ideas about popular sovereignty, about representative government and about direct participatory government.

The democratic deficit is said to be a problem affecting a range of institutions within the European Union. For instance, though elected by popular franchise in the member states, the European Parliament is said to have insufficient powers. Even less accountable is the European Commission. It is not elected but is comprised of members appointed by member state governments. The Council of Ministers and the European Council have also come under scrutiny because of a perceived lack of controls and of processes of accountability.

The opponents of the European Union, though critical of the lack of accountability of the organisation, are none the less not interested in the introduction of more controls and improved processes. This may be a paradox. Yet it is understable given that from the point of view of the opponents, the nation states remain the most desirable base for political decisions.

However, from the perspective adopted by many proponents of European integration, notably the parliamentarians, the problem lies in their lack of powers in the European Parliament. The argument is that the European Parliament should serve as the vehicle for reclaiming the powers which have been lost by the parliaments within the member states.

To achieve this they have proposed changes to institutional practices like: the introduction of a mechanism for 'co-decision' (which would meant, for example, that the Council could not enact measures which had been rejected by the European Parliament), the assignment to the parliament of more control over the budget and over decisions by the Commission on the implementation of policy, the formal right for parliament to initiate legislation; as well as more radical measures like the right of parliament to elect either/both the President of the Commission or/and the entire Commission (Newman, 1996, 180).

What are the problems in implementing this 'more democratic' model? The most obvious are that it would be strenuously opposed by political élites within the member states and that it would be unlikely to attract the support of most citizens in the member states - at least initially. There are also many other considerations, like the difficulty of creating appropriate and effective institutional structures at the transnational level. However, the primary focus in the remainder of this chapter will be on what it means to secure consent and on the actual problem of securing popular support for transnational initiatives by government.

Perceptions of a Democratic Deficit

Before exploring more fully the question of what it means to achieve consent and to bridge the gap between political élites and citizens and in anticipation of a more detailed analysis of the constituents of support for different aspects of European Union, I want to summarise some recent findings which appear to back the argument about the problem of a democratic deficit.

Opinion surveys have provided considerable support for the view that citizens perceive a democratic deficit in the European Union. For instance when asked, in 1993, about whether they were satisfied with the way democracy worked in the EC only 3 per cent of the total sample (of 12,043 people) indicated that they were very satisfied and 38 per cent that they were fairly satisfied with it (Niedermayer and Sinnott, 1995, Table 12.1).

However, this question needs to be placed in a broader context. For example, the same question, when related to the respondents' own countries elicited, in aggregate, a similar response: only 5 per cent were very satisfied and 37 per cent fairly satisfied with the way democracy worked at the national level. These are again aggregate figures across all European Union countries, and there were some interesting variations between nation states. Of particular interest is the variation in the United Kingdom. The number of respondents in the United Kingdom who were very satisfied with democracy the European Community was only 2 per cent. By contrast those who very satisfied with democracy in their own country accounted for 7 per cent of the sample. Similarly, the figures for those who were fairly satisfied with democracy in the European Union was 36 per cent. The figure for those who satisfied with democracy in their own country was 42 per cent.

When asked about levels 'to what extent do you think the way the EC works is democratic' only 6 per cent in the United Kingdom responded 'completely democratic' whereas the average, across twelve member states was 12 per cent. Finally, in response to a question about whether or not citizens had 'sufficient influence in decision-making in the European Community' 84 per cent in the United Kingdom answered in the negative. This contrasted with an average of 71 per cent across the member of states (Niedermayer and Sinnott, 1995, Table 12.1).

The Context for Challenges to Élitist Views of a European Project

The focus on survey data and on statistical averages may or may not tell us much about what constitutes Europe and about the process of gathering support for or mobilising opposition to European unity. The successful efforts to promote European integration in the 1950s were élite-driven. This may partly explain why concern about mass opinion was usually peripheral to efforts to understand and predict the process of European integration. In the 1950s one of the most influential writers, Ernst Haas (1958), explicitly rejected the notion that surveys of opinion play a significant part in efforts to understand the process of political integration. As Sinnott (1995) points out, this reflects the initial and predominant focus in these explanations on the role of élites. However, by the 1970s Haas (1971) had altered his approach to take more fully into consideration the role of 'mass perceptions' (see Sinnott, 1995, 19).

Still, much of the literature on the European Union offers an incomplete account of the role of opinion. Some of the literature on European political institutions also reflects an uncertainty as to how to analyse public opinion. This is evident in a standard text entitled *Understanding the New European Community* (Nicoll and Salmon, 1994). This work provides a useful account of the historical development, institutions and key policies of the European Community, and appears also to address the question of public opinion. Chapter 11, entitled 'Attitudes of the Member States to European Integration and the Treaty on European Union' seems to promise an account not only of the way of thinking attributed to governments but an analysis of the perceptions of citizens in different nations. Table 11.1 entitled 'Maastricht and the EC's future' provides the marginals from a Eurobarometer survey of opinions on two issues: the Maastricht Treaty and the scrapping of the European Community. The results are reported for all twelve member states, and opinion is apparently divided on the question of European unity.

The first impression is of an account that focuses not only on how governments view the process of European integration, in other words, how governments might be trying to shift public opinion but also on how opinion might matter. However, the entire chapter does not actually discuss Table 11.1. One can only conclude that the authors were less concerned about public opinion than with why particular governments, at particular times, were either warm or lukewarm or uninterested in different aspects of European unification. Although the authors discuss referendums on membership of the European Community, one is left with the impression that what counts is the manner in which governments (and other political organisations, like opposition parties) were apparently shaping public opinion. This explains the ghost-like appearance of Table 11.1 in the book.

Although there may be valid empirical and normative grounds for treating public opinion as something that can easily be manipulated or influenced by government, it is a core concept for political leaders seeking to reshape or defend political institutions. There are, as I shall elaborate later, some valid grounds for being cautious about how one interprets the findings of opinion polls, particularly about the dangers of accepting the assumptions that lie behind some of the questions that are used to measure opinions. An important consideration is that the focus on mass opinion about European integration also appears to assume that we are dealing with a single social and political space whereas there are still huge differences in the kinds of issues being addressed by different countries (see Dahrendorf, 1996, 7).

The increase in awareness about the character and importance of public opinion, even if it does take these factors into account, also draws attention to a number of crucial difficulties for contemporary élites. Dahrendorf (1996) reminds us of the credibility gap that has emerged between citizens and élites and of some of the constituents of change that may have impinged on the relationship between political élites and ordinary citizens. These changes, some of which are not so recent, include the decline in the salience of traditional political cleavages like social class, the emergence of corporatist forms of intermediation and governance which have made, in some countries, for a 'cosy' (and at times corrupt) relationship between business, unions and governments, the hostility of civil society, including social movements, towards those who govern, and the rise of localism or regionalism as a political force.

Another important set of considerations is the role of national populism and how it has been mobilised against European integration. Hugo Young notes that in Britain the views of 'euro-sceptics', even though they may have been a minority, have been the most widely reported by the media:

'The tabloids appear to become physically incapable of alluding to Brussels without epithets of ridicule and hatred. If a pro EU group dares to raise its head with modest and balanced, albeit favourable, opinions on the single currency, as Lord Howe did last week, depend upon this Tory press to depict him as a treacherous lunatic whose actual words do not deserve the smallest effort in accurate reporting. Yet this performance rests on a false account of public attitudes, which are closer to indifference than hostility' (*The Guardian*, 15 June 1995, cited by Taylor, 1996, 162).

As Taylor points out, the image conveyed by the media was even more strongly at odds with how people feel about issues of sovereignty and transnational cooperation than suggested by Hugo Young (see below). Still, in Britain, as in other countries, national political élites are inclined at strategic moments to mobilise popular support against the European Union or, as in the case of Jacques Chirac during the 1995 French presidential elections, against the 'technostructure' of experts (Hayward, 1996, 28). Yet efforts by the 'technostructure' to introduce reforms, for instance to render them more legitimate, often meet resistance, for instance from countries like Britain and Norway (Hayward, 1996, 29).

The European Union therefore faces several dilemmas. Any efforts to render the institutions more accountable can be regarded as a further threat to national sovereignty. Any attempt to manage the institutions more efficiently and effectively can be viewed as an attempt by the experts to tighten their grip on power and undermine the sovereign nation states.

While the European Union may have always been vulnerable on grounds of accountability, it has a far stronger track record in administration. Rule by experts or by expert committees has been highly effective over several decades and they have made colossal progress in achieving consensus on a wide range of issues, despite being national civil servants who would be highly sensitive to concerns about national sovereignty (Wallace, 1996, 244). However, this success has been at the expense of parliaments and political parties and has apparently led to a loss of public confidence in the process of government by expert committees (Wallace, 1996, 246). The complexity of the decisions taken at the transnational level and the attempts, for instance in the Maastricht Treaty, to achieve compromises between 'incompatible' objectives like efficient decision-making, accountability and national autonomy, have left commentators puzzled as to how the gap will be bridged between 'the disillusioned public and their collective governors' (Wallace, 1996, 248).

Other writers have pointed to the difficulties of creating a 'European consciousness' that will support common European institutions. Bogdanor, in an effort to provide some constructive solutions to the problems of accountability, has advocated direct elections to the Commission (1986). However, he has also been aware of many of the constraints, and has cast doubt on the effectiveness of proposals for direct elections to European institutions on the grounds that they will be unlikely to achieve functions which are usually performed by national elections. These functions include the potential for elections to enable voters choose a government, how elections offer at least a guide to public policies that may achieve majority support and how they facilitate the emergence of someone people can recognise as a leader of the government ('a recognisable human face for government in the form of a political leader') (1996, 107). Although Bogdanor acknowledges that the national arena remains pivotal and that the cleavages that characterise national electoral politics remain distinctive and render cooperation across countries difficult, he does mention, without elaborating or speculating on the possibilities, the one factor that could change all this: the attainment of monetary union (1996, 114). One can only speculate on the political implications of monetary union, and on how it might stimulate a chain of events that leads to a stronger identification with 'Europe' among citizens of the member states.

Even if a sound basis could be achieved for creating a 'European consciousness' that will support common European institutions through direct elections, there remain a number of fundamental challenges to bridging the gap between political élites and the mass public.

Drawing on a well-established body of research on this topic, Lane (1996, 47-50) notes that mass publics are less likely than political élites:

- to be interested in and to discuss politics
- to support open discussion of conflicting opinion
- to tolerate and to defend disliked groups
- to support legal due process for those charged with crimes
- to be morally rigid and moralistic
- to adopt nationalistic rather than international perspectives
- to balance the cost of one policy against another
- to have unstable and inconsistent views in the face of counter-arguments.

All these arguments amount to a fairly strong case against the likelihood of a consensus on European Union, particularly if it is led by political élites. The following section pursues this theme by considering evidence on citizen attitudes, on beliefs about national sovereignty and about the kinds of responsibilities that should or should not be taken on by the European Union.

Recent Trends in Public Opinion

The current state of opinion on an issue (like political integration) does not necessarily provide a reliable indicator of the future state of opinion (Sinnott, 1995, 29 draws on Key 1961; see also Bourdieu, 1979). This observation is all the more important when one considers that analyses of opinion have found that the calculations by individuals of the economic costs and benefits to them of membership of the European Union are not consistently associated with support for or opposition to it (Bosch and Newton, 1995).

Much of the literature therefore still focuses on the crucial role played by established political élites and organisations in shaping opinion.

However, by contrast to some of the arguments outlined above, empirical studies have shown that there is a fairly strong connection between the opinions of élites and of the mass public towards political unification even if one cannot determine who is leading the way (Wessels, 1995, 141, Table 7.1). Again, it is worth emphasising that there are important variations between countries. In Britain, support among the mass public and among élites for joining a political federation has long been lower than in countries like Germany and France.

(a) Social and demographic factors

It is also important to identify any variation between different sections of the population in support for the European Union. In particular, there may be some correspondence in attitudes between political élites and certain sections of the population. Among those who are closest to the élites are people with higher than average levels of education, income and economic security as well as levels of political involvement. Data from the period 1973-1991 indicate that the social groups that are close to political élites are more likely than other groups to be in favour of membership of the European Union and of European unification (Wessels, 1995, 143, Table 7.2). There is greater correspondence of opinion between élites and non-élites over the issue of membership than over the question of unification. Over a long period of time (1973 to 1991) the differences between the levels of support for European unity among 'opinion leaders' and 'non-leaders' have remained fairly stable (Wessels, 1995, 144, Table 7.3).

The two strongest predictors of a European identity are levels of education and income (Duchesne and Frognier, 1995, 209), while the sense of belonging to a European community has been strongest among people who have attained high levels of formal education, express a strong (psychological) involvement in politics and endorse postmaterialist values (Niedermayer, 1995, 244).

By comparing attitudes to European unification among the supporters of different political parties with the manifestos and electoral platforms of the various political parties in different European countries, Wessels demonstrates fairly persuasively that in all nations there is a strong correspondence between the orientation of political organisations and the opinions of party followers (Wessels, 1995, 154-155). However, it is more difficult to evaluate the causal linkages between the two.

On this question of the relationship between mass opinion and leadership opinion he concludes that: 'Although the orientations of party supporters have, as expected, only a minor influence on party platforms, they do have an influence. But the content of party platforms is substantially reflected in the attitudes of party supporters in both the election and post-election periods, when party policy intentions have a high degree of visibility' (1995, 161). His analysis leads him to posit that parties, if they are in favour of European unity, need to make significant efforts to mobilise opinion: 'If there was no mobilization effort, one major precondition of European integration - a more or less stable basic level of support for the EC - might be weakened or even vanish' (Wessels, 1995, 161-162).

(b) A European national identity?

Much of this analysis presupposes that there may be an inherent conflict between an identity derived from a sense of belonging to a nation state and an orientation towards Europe. Similarly, media accounts and the rhetoric of political élites sometimes give the same impression of a deep-seated tension between national objectives and transnational ones. This need not be the case, as demonstrated by the analysis of conceptions of identity. As Duchesne and Frognier point out, although the notion of a European identity does not evoke 'a real community of belonging of the kind experienced in nation states' and represents a 'vanguard phenomenon' (1995, 223), views on national identity are independent of views on European unification. Respondents (in Eurobarometer surveys conducted in 1987 and 1988) were asked to give their views on two statements:

> If one day the countries of Europe were really united, this would mark the end of our national, historic, cultural identities and our national economic interests would be sacrificed.

> The only way of protecting our national, historic, cultural identities and our national economic interests against a challenge put up by the Great World Powers is for the countries of Europe to become truly united.

In both instances the responses proved to be 'totally independent of national pride' (Duchesne and Frognier, 1995, 206). Interestingly, the responses from Britain did show an association (that was statistically significant) between these two sets of considerations, though the connection was weak and 'unlikely to be stable over time' (Duchesne and Frognier, 1995, 225, footnote 12).

All this seems to confirm that we are a long way from achieving a strong European identity. National agendas, national cultures and symbols and national sovereignty apparently continue to hold sway. The shift towards majority voting by the Council of Ministers in the Single European Act (and in the Maastricht Treaty) has not posed a fundamental threat to sovereign states. The latter have after all retained the right to annul much of what they perceive to conflict with their national interests or they have adapted to the situation by evoking principles like subsidiarity advocated by the European Union: 'Neither accession to the European Communities, nor the terms for the Single European Act or the Maastricht Agreement, had altered the underlying legal and constitutional circumstances of national sovereignty. Indeed, the fear that this had happened was strikingly absent in most member states' (Taylor, 1996, 154).

Taylor then goes on to examine how citizens perceive all this, drawing largely on the Eurobarometer surveys carried out at regular intervals by the European Commission. The Commission uses the term 'permissive consensus' to describe how 'approval and support' for the European Union has been high 'but not deeply felt by many'. 'Europe' has apparently been identified, by survey respondents, with 'peace, friendship and mostly beneficial economic cooperation' (cited in Taylor, 1996, 154-155). As Taylor notes: 'The point relevant to sovereignty was that such a consensus, being permissive, could not be interpreted as a transfer of expectations to the new centre: 'permissive' required that there be some other primary player, like the national governments' (1996, 155).

Between 1992 and 1994 the proportion of respondents who answered in the affirmative to a question on whether or not they were in favour of 'the formation of a European Union with a European Government responsible to the European Parliament' was around 50 per cent (51 per cent in 1992, 47 per cent in December 1993 and 50 per cent in 1994) (cited in Taylor, 1996, 156). In 1992, 56 per cent of respondents were in favour of 'the European Community having a European Government responsible to the European Parliament and the European Council of Heads of National Government', and even in the United Kingdom there was a majority (55 per cent).

Does this imply that citizens in European states are willing to give up national sovereignty? Does it also represent a powerful rebuttal of arguments that have been promoted by the media and by political élites, especially in countries like Britain?

Before presenting further evidence on these questions, it is important to emphasise the point made earlier about the presupposition in the minds of many that there is an intrinsic conflict between an identity derived from a sense of belonging to a nation state and an orientation towards Europe. The research carried out by Duchesne and Frognier (1995) shows that for citizens in most European countries this is not the case. It is not surprising, given the immense pressure by the media and by some sections of the political élites, that in Britain there was a modest association between the responses to the two issues.

Yet the reality is that even in Britain there is a lack of correspondence between the way many people feel about transnational cooperation and/or sovereignty and the representation of these issues by large sections of the media or by members political élites.

This presents a number of dilemmas for the European Union which has argued that the vision of Europe rejected by the mass public 'is neither foreseen in the Maastricht Treaty nor is it represented by the current EC in spite of many a shortcoming'. Even more significantly, the idea of Europe which is acceptable to the public appears to be 'the very Europe designed by 'Maastricht' and in many respects already existing and functioning within the European Community', the problem being that 'the public, and the Euro-sceptical part of the public in particular, *does not know*' (Commission of the European Communities,. ix-x. cited in Taylor, 1996. 158).

The paradox of popular opposition to a Europe that threatens national identity and of an orientation towards Europe is partly explained by research carried out by the Commission:

They [the public] are against a Europe:

- which threatens national identity and cultural diversity;
- which gives citizens insufficient democratic influence;
- which gives their country and its governments no say in European decision-making;
- which centralises 'everything' in Brussels; and
- which is run by an enormous Brussels bureaucracy that is out of touch with the real world of citizens.

They are, however, in favour of a United Europe

- where national and regional identities and cultural diversity are respected, protected and defended;
- where democratic channels of citizen influence exist and visibly function, including their democratically established

national government having an important role in common decision-making;
- where sovereignty is pooled and exercised through common institutions only in such policy areas where national or regional governments can no longer solve problems effectively;
- where such policies are prepared and executed by an administration of adequate, limited size which is directed by a body (the Commission or later European government) responsible to a powerful democratically elected European Parliament, and to the European Council consisting of democratically established national Heads of State and Government'

(Commission of the European Communities, Eurobarometer, cited in Taylor, 1996, 158).

Further survey data from the Eurobarometer also showed, in 1994, majority opinion in favour of a joint European role for science research, protection of the environment, immigration policy, fighting unemployment and the management of currencies. While these might be regarded as technical issues, Taylor (1996, 160) also cites evidence of an overwhelming majority of people being in favour of managing foreign policy at the European level (despite setbacks in ex-Yugoslavia) and a marginal minority of respondents in favour of policies on joint defence.

Although there are variations between countries, even the case of the United Kingdom demonstrates that opinion may be at variance with efforts by sections of the media and by members of political élites to criticise transnational cooperation. On some issues there was a correspondence with policies promoted by national élites. For instance, in 1994, a majority in the United Kingdom preferred national control over permission for political asylum and over immigration. Yet even in Britain, there was majority support for 'European-level action on the environment, cooperation with the Third World, research policy, and most interestingly, on foreign policy towards non-EU countries' (Taylor 1996, 161). The majority in Britain were also in favour of the establishment of a European Central Bank.

Although there is evidence that those who are closest to political élites in terms of education and income are the most likely to support moves towards European integration, the evidence cited in this section also shows that political élites, for reasons of their own, give a very partial account of public sentiment towards Europe. As Taylor points out, the problem is not peculiar to the states, like Britain, that are wary of or cautious about

European unification: 'politicians in the cautious states, but also in the mid-1990s in the original six members, often pretended that public resistance was greater than it was for reasons of their own, presumably because losing competence would lose them power' (Taylor, 1996, 161).

Conclusions

Still, there remains the overall question of the 'democratic deficit', of the legitimacy of institutions like the European Parliament. The modest support for such institutions among the mass public in member states is not only a characteristic of Britain and is reflected both in responses to surveys of opinion and in very low turnouts in elections to the European Parliament (Niedermayer and Sinnott, 1995, 294-307).

The empirical evidence points both to the possibilities for consolidation or expansion of support among some groups for European unification and to the potential for strong resistance. Political and other élites may be tempted, according to what they perceive as their interests, to manipulate opinion in any of these directions. Their success is far from guaranteed since public opinion may move independently of their intentions.

As Beer (1974) has pointed out, there are at least two ways of viewing public opinion, the modernist approach, adopted by many political élites, that regards opinion as the result of ignorance, confusion and manipulation, and the classical model which regards opinion as creative, consecutive and democratic. The modernist account is derived from Francis Bacon and his technocratic vision of rule by a scientific élite who govern not by command but by communicating new knowledge to the citizens at large. The classical approach is, by contrast, interested in what the citizens at large think. For Beer this is best expressed by Socrates in *The Symposium*, particularly in the account of Diotima and her 'tale of love'. The focus here is on 'expressive symbolism', on the unity of emotions and thought. There is no such thing as 'dispassionate opinion'.

There are a number of other considerations, particularly as regards the meaning of public opinion, which have been presented by social and political theorists. These include questions around the issue of whether or not public opinion matters. What is the impact of government on public opinion? What impact does opinion polling have on opinion? What impact does public opinion have on government? Another set of questions centres on the significance of public opinion to democratic politics. One approach is to highlight the dangers of treating opinion in an uncritical manner (Bourdieu, 1979). However, one can also elaborate on what some of the benefits of public opinion are to the democratic process (Yankelovich, 1991). The two perspectives are not necessarily in conflict. A critical view of how élites set about manipulating opinion may serve a longer term objective, namely, to contribute to the clarification and resolution of issues rather than to promote adversarialism for its own sake.

In that regard, the concept of public judgement may be worth considering further. The focus by Habermas on public opinion as 'considered judgement' (Habermas, 1989), as reason and as the basis for 'intersubjective understanding' and dialogue (see for instance Habermas, 1981), rather than mass opinion and its manipulation, has influenced and been adapted by survey researchers who differentiate between 'top-of-the-head' or superficial responses to opinion polls and opinions that represent thoughtful, considered judgements of policy options (see Yankelovich, 1991). This approach has the potential to provide us with an understanding of the possibilities for popular sovereignty based on dialogue and consensus rather than on manipulation and control.

The problem with focusing on manipulation and control is not confined to political élites. Yankelovich argues that contemporary political science emphasises the notion of an 'attentive public' or, more frequently, an inattentive one (see the influential work by writers like Converse, 1964 and Campbell et. al., 1960). Again, this corresponds with what Beer has to say about the approach by Bacon and its influence on public opinion research. The guiding assumption of this cognitive approach to public opinion is that the public is poorly informed about and not particularly interested in politics. Yankelovich labels this approach as élitist: 'Élites define quality by their own standards of ideological coherence and being well-informed. The concept of the attentive public presupposes the élite definition and seeks to find among the public that minority of people whose thought processes mirror this model most closely' (Yankelovich, 1991, 19).

Yankelovich identifies a tendency towards valuing information at the expense of thoughtful judgement. The gap between how élites conceptualise public opinion and how ordinary citizens view policies is part of this propensity, which he labels a 'Culture of Technical Control' because it privileges the role of experts and assumes public apathy (see Yankelovich, 1991, 8-9). It could be argued that more often than not political élites in Europe have privileged this culture of technical control.

However, Yankelovich does not assume that this tendency is inescapable. Influenced by writers like Habermas, he posits a three-stage process to overcome ambivalence in and the manipulation of public opinion. The first stage entails public awareness of an issue, usually generated by media attention. In the second phase, the public might 'work through' the issue, in other words, become actively involved or engaged in the issue and experience changes in attitudes. The third stage involves 'resolution' of the issue in three ways: cognitive resolution (resolving inconsistencies), emotional resolution (confronting ambivalent attitudes and reconciling the differences) and moral resolution (placing ethical considerations above narrowly-defined self-interest) (Yankelovich, 1991, 63-5).

Most of what is reported as public opinion remains in reality, and for a long time, in the first stage. In other words, what is reported as public opinion is popular awareness of an issue - but not much else. Furthermore, contemporary institutions often hinder rather than facilitate the processes of working through or resolving issues. This has been evident both in media accounts and in the publicity created by political élites about the effects of membership of the European Union on national sovereignty, particularly in the United Kingdom. In these circumstances it is hardly surprising that public opinion may be characterised as ambivalent or ignorant or manipulated.

The crucial contribution by writers like Habermas and Yankelovich is that they go beyond the negativity that characterises some of the literature on public opinion. There are of course immense problems with the interpretation and use of public opinion polls. Habermas (1989), like other intellectuals (see Bourdieu, 1979), has been scathing about this. Still, there are possibilities for experiencing the beneficial effects of public opinion, and of judgements that represent both an awareness of policy issues and the resolution of conflicting perspectives. Public opinion can and does breathe life into a democracy.

The model proposed by Yankelovich can be used to ascertain the state of public opinion on all policy issues and, as Page and Shapiro (1992, 391) have argued, in one of the most exhaustive studies of the relationship between public opinion and government policy, there is considerable evidence to support the view that public opinion 'has often been "refined and enlarged" through public debate'.

If we apply the criteria posited by Yankelovich to issues that affect Europeans, we can plausibly argue that some governments, under pressure from social movements, have been successful in raising public awareness on some issues (for instance, concern about the environment) and in animating the process of working through the tensions between different points of view (for instance, in debates about environment and development), though they often fall short of resolving ambivalence in attitudes. Similarly, the model proposed by Yankelovich could be applied to the whole range of other issues being addressed by the European Union, to policies on a single currency, on democratic structures and national sovereignty, on economic reforms, on a free market, on social policy and on security. This model enables us to identify the different stages in the development of public opinion.

It is tempting, following the comments by Bourdieu (1979), to regard all efforts to measure public opinion, all attempts by government to influence the political agenda and all efforts to improve on the quality of survey research as manipulation and as an attempt to dupe an ignorant and uninterested public. This would be a mistake since it would deny us one of the most significant ways in which we can make express our preferences. At any rate, even if public opinion is open to manipulation, it is worth considering the following points. A significant and growing number of citizens is inclined to question established political authorities, and governments 'ignore voters' expectations at their peril' (Charlot, 1996, 99). Though it is dangerous to rely simply on the current state of opinion or on past trends as a basis for predicting the future, as often occurs in the interpretation of opinion polls, public opinion remains a crucial mechanism in the process of making democracy work and of addressing questions about national sovereignty and the democratic deficit.

References

Beer, S. 1974. 'Two Models of Public Opinion: Bacon's 'New Logic' and Diotima's 'Tale of Love'", *Political Theory*, 2, 163-80.

Bogdanor, V. 1986. 'The Future of the European Community: Two Models of Democracy', *Government and Opposition*, 21, 2, 161-176.

Bogdanor, V. 1996. 'The European Union, the Political Class, and the People' in J. Hayward (ed). *Elitism, populism, and European politics*, Oxford: Clarendon Press.

Bosch, A. and K. Newton. 1995. 'Economic Calculus or Familiarity Breeds Content?' in O. Niedermayer and R. Sinnott (eds.), *Public Opinion and Internationalized Governance*, Oxford: Oxford University Press.

Bourdieu, P. 1979. 'Public Opinion does not Exist' in A. Mattelart and S. Siegelaub (eds) *Communication and Class Struggle*, New York: International General, pp. 124-30.

Campbell, A., Converse, P., Miller, W. and D. Stokes, D. 1960. *The American Voter*, New York: Wiley and Sons.

Converse, P. 1964. 'The Nature of Belief Systems in Mass Publics' in D.E. Apter (ed.), *Ideology and Discontent*, New York: Free Press.

Charlot, J. 1996. 'From Representative to Responsive Government?' in J. Hayward (ed.), *Elitism, populism, and European politics*, Oxford: Clarendon Press.

Commission of the European Communities. *Eurobarometer*, 38. December 1992.
Dahrendorf, R. 1996. 'Mediocre Élites Elected by Mediocre Peoples' in J. Hayward (ed). *Elitism, populism, and European politics*, Oxford: Clarendon Press.
Duchesne, S. and A-P. Frognier. 1995. 'Is There a European Identity?' in O. Niedermayer and R. Sinnott (eds.), *Public Opinion and Internationalized Governance*, Oxford: Oxford University Press.
Haas, E. B. 1958. *The Uniting of Europe*, Stanford, Calif.: Stanford University Press.
Haas, E. B. 1971. 'The Study of Regional Integration: Reflections on the Joy and Anguish of Pre-theorizing', in L. Lindberg and S. Scheingold (eds) *Regional Integration: Theory and Research*, Cambridge, Mass.: Harvard University Press.
Habermas, J. 1981. *Theorie des kommunikativen Handelns*. Vols 1 and 2. Frankfurt: Suhrkamp.
Habermas, J. 1989. *The Structural Transformation of the Public Sphere*. Cambridge: Polity Press.
Hayward, J. 1996. 'The Populist Challenge to Élitist Democracy in Europe' in J. Hayward (ed). *Elitism, populism, and European politics*, Oxford: Clarendon Press.
Key, V. O. 1961. *Public Opinion and American Democracy*, New York: Knopf.
King, P. 1991. 'Sovereignty' in D. Miller et al. (eds), *The Blackwell Encyclopaedia of Political Thought*, Oxford: Blackwell.
Lane, R.E. 1996. '"Losing Touch" in a Democracy: Demands versus Needs" in J. Hayward (ed). *Elitism, populism, and European politics*, Oxford: Clarendon Press.
Newman, M. 1996. *Democracy, sovereignty and the European Union*, New York : St. Martin's Press.
Nicoll, W. and Salmon, T. 1994 *Understanding the New European Community*. London: Harvester Wheatsheaf.
Niedermayer, O. 1995. 'Trust and Sense of Community' in O. Niedermayer and R. Sinnott (eds.), *Public Opinion and Internationalized Governance*, Oxford: Oxford University Press.
Niedermayer, O. and R. Sinnott. 1995. 'Democratic Legitimacy and the European Parliament' in O. Niedermayer and R. Sinnott (eds.), *Public Opinion and Internationalized Governance*, Oxford: Oxford University Press.
Page, B.I. and Shapiro, R.Y. 1992. *The Rational Public: Fifty Years of Trends in Americans' Policy Preferences*. Chicago: University of Chicago Press.
Pierson, C. 1996. *The Modern State*, London: Routledge.
Sinnott, R. 1995. 'Bringing Public Opinion Back In' in O. Niedermayer and R. Sinnott (eds.), *Public Opinion and Internationalized Governance*, Oxford: Oxford University Press.
Taylor, P. 1996. *The European Union in the 1990s*. Oxford University Press.

Wallace, W. 1996. 'Has Government by Committee Lost the Public's Confidence?' in J. Hayward (ed.), *Élitism, populism, and European politics*, Oxford: Clarendon Press.

Wessels, B. 1995. 'Evaluations of the EC: Élite or Mass-Driven?' in O. Niedermayer and R. Sinnott (eds.), *Public Opinion and Internationalized Governance*, Oxford: Oxford University Press.

Yankelovich, D. 1991. *Coming to Public Judgement*, Syracuse: Syracuse University Press.

IV

NATION AND REGION

12 Scotland and the New Regionalism

JAMES MITCHELL

Introduction

All states are artificial. They are constructs of very recent vintage, though the rhetoric surrounding the United Kingdom and other European states often suggests otherwise. The notion that Britain is a great, ancient and revered entity is one commonly found across the political divide. In truth, the UK's current boundaries date only from the 1920s. Its core may be ancient, but that could be said of almost anywhere in Europe. The core need not be territorial, and in the case of the UK, the core has arguably been institutional. The Crown in Parliament lies at the heart of the UK. In some quarters, challenges to it are deemed to be challenges to the state itself.

Two trends challenging the 'Crown in Parliament' have been evident in western Europe since 1945. One trend has been towards 'ever closer union', to use the phrase from the preamble of the Treaty of Rome establishing the European Economic Community. The other has been the trend towards greater decentralisation within existing states. These trends have had considerable impact on our understanding of European states and the relationship between territory, identity and politics in Europe. The traditional notion of the state as omnipotent and unified has been undermined. The view that its external borders are closed and, internally, that it is coherent, even homogeneous, is difficult to sustain today.

This has affected all states including the United Kingdom of Great Britain and Northern Ireland, to give the state more commonly called 'Britain' its correct title. The name itself should raise questions about its coherence. Like all states, it was founded as an amalgam of territories but, unlike some others, its establishment over many centuries did not involve the eradication of all traces of its constituent parts. This has been most obvious in the case of Scotland. The Union which brought Scotland and England together was one which acknowledged and accepted elements of Scottish distinctiveness. It was not an incorporating or assimilationist union. At the core of the new state, as now, was Parliament at Westminster. Its central importance, in every sense of the phrase, is difficult to understate. Theoretically, Parliament is sovereign. It can make and unmake any law. Beyond Parliament, however, Scottish distinctiveness was catered for.

The legal and theoretical limits of Parliament differ markedly from its actual position. Its role in policy-making, for example, has been described by two leading scholars as so limited that Parliament probably fulfils a more significant role as a tourist attraction (Jordan and Richardson 1987: 57), but this does not detract from either its symbolic or its actual significance in political debates. In debates on European integration and devolution of power within the state, parliamentary sovereignty has been crucial. From one perspective, these two phenomena are viewed as threats to the UK as a state. From another perspective, Parliamentary sovereignty and the myths that surround it are viewed as debilitating, warping our understanding of contemporary politics and how we should be governed.

State Nationalism in the UK

British nationalism is a complex phenomenon. Its malleability and dynamic qualities must be taken into account. A distinction needs to be drawn between its outward and internal projections. The key institutions and symbols require to be identified. One significant feature is that it is a nationalism without a name. Richard Rose asked what name could be given to the nation associated with the United Kingdom and concluded, 'One thing is certain: No one speaks of the "Ukes" as a nation.' (Rose 1982: 11) Britain and British are used as short-hand, but these are inaccurate terms which cause offence in Northern Ireland. That does not mean, of course, an absence of nationalism. Indeed, it might be argued that it signifies the strength of British nationalism. British nationalism typifies what Michael Billig has called 'banal nationalism' (Billig 1995); it is the mundane, everyday reproduction of habits, beliefs and assumptions which are taken for granted.

British nationalism has been more evident in the outward projection of the state. In external cultural relations, British Governments have been willing to project an image of the country as a multi-national state, celebrating the diversity within it. However, in political and economic relations with others, it has been determined to project a more coherent message and image of itself. The fear that it might be perceived to speak with more than one voice has been a powerful constraint on diversity. In Britain's dealings with the European Union, this nationalism has been in everyday evidence. The infamous Sun newspaper headline, 'Up Yours Delors!' in response to some proposal from the then President of the European Commission typifies a strain of xenophobic British nationalism.

There were remarkable similarities in arguments deployed against membership of the European Community by people with very different political positions. A British nationalist argument was heard from Enoch Powell on the right-wing of British politics to Tony Benn and Michael Foot on the left which focused particularly on the position of Parliament following EC membership. Parliamentary sovereignty remains a matter of concern to 'Euro-sceptics'. In 1962, Hugh Gaitskell, Labour's leader, warned that joining the Common Market would mean the 'end of Britain as an independent European state. I make no apology for repeating it. It means the end of a thousand years of history' (Labour Party 1962: 12). Tony Benn warned his Bristol constituents in December 1974 that Britain's continued membership of the European Community would mean the 'end of our democratically elected Parliament as the supreme law-making body in the United Kingdom' (Benn 1996: 38). On the right, Enoch Powell told a French audience in 1971 that the creation of assemblies elsewhere in Europe was the result of recent and deliberate political acts and that the notion that a new sovereign body can be created is as 'familiar to you as it is repugnant, not to say unimaginable, to us' (Powell 1996: 85). In her memoirs, Margaret Thatcher asked rhetorically, 'Were British democracy, parliamentary sovereignty, the common law, our traditional sense of fairness, our ability to run our own affairs in our own way to be subordinated to the demands of a remote European bureaucracy, resting on very different traditions?' (Thatcher 1993: 743)

On the other hand, internally, Britain has been a territorially pluralist state. The process of creating and redefining the state was not accompanied by the eradication of the local communities and nations which preceded it. To use the terms adopted by Rokkan and Urwin in their comparative study of territory, identity and economy in Europe, the United Kingdom was formed not as a unitary state 'built up around one unambiguous political centre [which] enjoys economic dominance and pursues a more or less undeviating policy of administrative standardisation. All areas of the state are treated alike, and all institutions are directly under the control of the centre' (Rokkan and Urwin 1982: 11). It conformed more with the union state model of state formation which was 'not the result of straightforward dynastic conquest. Incorporation of at least parts of its territory has been achieved through personal dynastic union, for example, by treaty, marriage or inheritance. Integration is less than perfect. While administrative standardisation prevails over most of the territory, the consequences of personal union entail the survival in some areas of pre-union rights and institutional infrastructures which preserve some degree of regional autonomy and serve as agencies of indigenous elite recruitment' (Ibid.).

The formation of England may have conformed to the unitary state model, but the new state of Britain/UK formed when England joined with Wales, Scotland and Ireland did not. This was most obvious in the case of Scotland, for which the definition of a union state might have been specifically written. The Treaty of Union of 1707 pronounced that Scotland and England would henceforth no longer exist and that Britain would come into being but protected the continued existence of Scots Law and the Church of Scotland. The structure of local government, local administration and the poor law were different from that in England and developed differently from this base. Scotland did not disappear as a political entity.

The key British central institutions from the outset were Parliament and the monarchy, which came together in notions of the 'Crown in Parliament' or Parliamentary sovereignty. Parliament had a very limited role in the lives of most people in Britain. This changed as the state's role changed, and it had implications for its territorial organisation. Grants to help pay for education, for example, were paid by the state at the centre during the early part of the nineteenth century. Public health regulations were passed by Parliament. Pressure from industrialisation and urbanisation was to alter the relationship between subject and Parliament fundamentally. The centre, in the shape of Parliament, increasingly became significant in the lives of people across Britain.

From a Scottish perspective, this development could have taken either of two directions. The more active role for the state could have led to a more unified polity, a unitary state in which 'all areas of the state are treated alike, and all institutions are directly under the control of the centre' or the union state foundations of Britain could have been maintained through new measures to take account of Scottish distinctiveness.

What happened was a mixture of these two developments. Territorially, the state grew more complex as its reach and remit widened. Special provision for the established Church of Scotland is still maintained, but in contemporary Scotland it is almost meaningless, as the role of religion has declined, especially in the secular twentieth century (Brown 1987: 209-248). New bodies of law were established which were applied uniformly, or almost so, across Britain. Labour law, aspects of welfare law and company law were generally British, thus undermining the union state nature of Britain. In other respects, the union state was maintained, indeed revivified. A sense that Scottish interests were not being well served developed in the middle of the nineteenth century and complaints were made that insufficient Parliamentary time was allocated to specifically Scottish affairs. These grievances coalesced around campaigns for a government minister with responsibility for Scottish affairs. This was conceded in 1885 when the office of Secretary for Scotland was set up. It proved the single most important development ensuring the survival into the twentieth century of Scotland as a distinct political entity. Its responsibilities grew: education and local government were its main responsibilities on establishment, but responsibility for law and order in Scotland were taken from the Home Office and added to those of the Scottish Office within two years. This was just the beginning of an incremental accretion.

As the state cut out an increased role for itself in agriculture in the first decade of the twentieth century, there were calls for a Ministry for Agriculture which was conceded, but a separate Scottish Board of Agriculture was established under the Scottish Secretary. Similarly, a Scottish Board of Health under the Scottish Secretary was set up in 1919. Over time, the Scottish Office became the 'centre' for Scots over a wide range of matters. Crucially, however, it was an administrative centre. The political centre remained Parliament at Westminster. Scottish Secretaries were appointed by British Prime Ministers and were accountable to Parliament as a whole, not just to Scottish members. A distinct Scottish dimension was maintained through the Scottish Office, but ultimate control lay at Westminster. Parliament remained the key integrating institution of the state.

State nationalism has been a complex phenomenon in the UK. Outwardly, especially in times of crisis such as during wars but also in the everyday handling of European Union affairs, it could be bombastic. Internally, it has tended to be pluralistic. There appeared to be no contradiction between Scottish and British. This pluralism did not apply to every community within the state. There remains, for example, ample evidence that this pluralism does not apply to being British and Asian. Compared with France, however, with its constitutional reference to the 'one and indivisible' nation, there was little sense of such indivisible unity in Britain. There was no conscious nation-building programme. However, the union state foundations changed. Changes in the nature of state intervention had territorial implications but a constantly changing balance between the Scottish and British elements of the constitution was maintained.

Parliamentary Sovereignty

As has already been argued, Parliament lies at the heart of Britain. It has been the key unifying body in British politics. Challenges to its authority might be seen as challenging the authority of the state itself, at least as viewed from the perspective of a unitary state. The notion of Parliamentary sovereignty can be traced back to the work of early legal theorists, but particularly to the verve and tenacity with which Albert Venn Dicey, a legal theorist and political campaigner in late nineteenth and early twentieth century, articulated its central tenets. Dicey's contribution was probably greater as a populariser of the idea than as one who contributed to the intellectual development of the doctrine of Parliamentary sovereignty. Even more significant was his role in applying it to contemporary concerns of late Victorian politics. In his book *England's Case against Home Rule*, first published in 1886, Dicey argued that the establishment of an Irish Parliament was incompatible with Parliamentary sovereignty. Independence for Ireland, he maintained, made legal sense as this would simply involve removing Ireland from the state in a clean and clear manner, though he questioned the financial sense for the Irish people of going down this road. He opposed devolution because it was, he asserted, incompatible with Parliamentary sovereignty.

Dicey's intellectual honesty might be questioned, given the demands he made in the early twentieth century for a referendum on the status of Ulster and his support for armed resistance to Irish home rule. His main goal appears to have been to oppose Irish home rule, and articulating the case for Parliamentary sovereignty merely a phase in pursuit of this. Dicey's contribution to constitutional politics highlights the manner in which rules can be invented given the lack of any written, entrenched constitution. As Geoffrey Marshall remarked on British constitutional conventions, they are 'somewhat vague and slippery - resembling the procreation of eels' (Marshall 1984: 54-55). Nonetheless, the doctrine of Parliamentary sovereignty took hold and influenced later debates on constitutional and political change.

This reverence for the 'mother of Parliaments' has been important in twentieth century debates on constitutional reform. In the 1970s, many supporters of Parliamentary sovereignty opposed membership of the European Community on the grounds that it would undermine Parliament's authority and opposed the use of the referendum on EC membership as this too by-passed Parliament. Devolution was also opposed as this would have the same effect. They were unsuccessful in the first two cases but successful in blocking devolution by then insisting, ironically, that referendums should be held in Scotland and Wales.

Though some anti-devolutionists have been strong supporters of European Union membership, fewer Euro-sceptics have been devolutionists. The most fervent anti-devolutionist in the Labour Party in Scotland in the 1970s was Tam Dalyell - a baronet, old Etonian and former chairman of Cambridge Conservative Club - and Labour MP for West Lothian, the constituency outside Edinburgh in which his family estate, dating back centuries, is situated, and which has long been a solid Labour supporting area. Dalyell was the late twentieth century equivalent of Dicey. As he insisted in the conclusion of his book *Devolution: The End of Britain?*, published at the height of the debate twenty years ago,

> The people of Scotland must be made to realise that there is not, and never can be, a tenable half-way house between remaining an integral part of the United Kingdom and opting for a Scottish state. As we have seen, one of the rocks on which the Scotland and Wales Bill [an early legislative proposal for devolution] foundered in the House of Commons was the realisation that one cannot have a subordinate Parliament in part - though only part - of a unitary state (Dalyell 1977: 306).

The experience of having a Parliament at Stormont in Northern Ireland for fifty years until 1972 was an unhappy precedent for Scottish devolutionists. This experience of devolution was remarkable in a number of ways. It came to the one part of the UK which had been most vehemently opposed to devolution, at least devolution for Ireland as a whole. It was rarely cited as a precedent which might undermine notions that devolution was not possible in the UK. Policies pursued by successive governments in Northern Ireland which discriminated against Catholics and the subsequent 'Troubles' had given devolution a bad name. In the 1970s, Scottish supporters of devolution were understandably reluctant to refer to Stormont as an example. Northern Ireland was treated as a detached entity which neither proponents nor opponents of devolution wanted to refer to.

Dalyell was correct. Devolution is incompatible with a unitary state, at least as understood in Rokkan and Urwin's definition quoted earlier. With devolution, the political centre would not be unambiguous, policy would deviate across the state and different areas of the state would be treated differently. The question for Dalyell, however, is whether his premise - that Britain is a unitary state - is correct. Even without devolution, while the centre is unambiguous, policy deviates across the state and different areas are treated differently. For Britain to become a unitary state, the Scottish Office, the separate system of Scots law and education and the vast paraphernalia of Scottish distinctiveness would have to be dismantled. This notion of Britain as a unitary state rests firmly on the central position accorded to Parliament at the exclusion of other political and other institutions.

The Dicey-Dalyell argument that there could be no half-way house between being an integral part of the UK and a separate Irish or Scottish state found many adherents in the late nineteenth century and the late 1970s. The idea appealed across the political divide to traditionalist supporters of

Parliament's position in Labour and Conservative Parties. Labour opinions were of particular interest. Apart from the doctrine of Parliamentary sovereignty, Labour thinking on the constitution was fairly centralist. The view that a strong central state was necessary in order to deliver welfare and equality had influenced the Attlee Government. Home rule, which had been part of Labour's programme for government since its foundation, was cast aside. Parliamentary sovereignty assumed an importance in Labour thinking because of the belief that this was a strong centre and the most effective way of achieving socialist goals. As Gordon Brown, future Chancellor of the Exchequer, wrote in his doctoral thesis on the Labour Party in Scotland in the 1920s, no Labour theorist had been able to reconcile the 'conflicting aspirations for home rule and a British socialist advance. In particular, no one was able to show how capturing power in Britain - and legislating for minimum levels of welfare, for example, could be combined with a policy of devolution for Scotland' (Brown 1981).

Europeanisation of British Politics

Challenging the orthodox view that Parliament was sovereign and that more than one political 'centre' was possible were amongst the influences which membership of the European Community had on domestic politics in Britain. A growing awareness of experiences elsewhere in Europe was inevitable amongst political elites who had to take account of the growing significance of the European dimension. British parochialism was challenged as never before. Europeanisation, however, was not a straightforward phenomenon. There was evidence of a reaction against the experience of Europe amongst sections of the political elite as much as there was evidence of Europe rubbing off on others.

As students of nationalism and identity formation had long understood, close contact between peoples could lead to a diffusion of attitudes, values and shared outlooks, but it could also provoke a reaction and backlash. This had, after all, happened in the case of Scotland within the UK. There had been a growing sense of common British identity but when the sense of Scottish identity and Scottish interests were perceived to be under threat, there could be a reaction and demands that Scotland should be treated differently, even calls for political separation. A similar situation pertained in Britain's relations with Europe.

In time, a type of British nationalism emerged inside the Conservative Party which was domestically assimilationist, rejecting notions of a multi-national state and and assuming uniformity, and which was almost belligerently anti-European. Simultaneously, and as much in reaction to this development in Conservative thinking, an alternative vision of Britain emerged inside the Labour Party which was more pluralist domestically and more consciously pro-European, at least rhetorically. This had long been the view of British Liberals who had supported home rule within the UK since Gladstone's time (though they failed to do anything about it under Asquith) and over the post-war period had consistently supported European integration. But at another level, Europe was having an impact on British politics. Local authorities were increasingly conscious of the European dimension. European funds for regional development, regulations affecting a wide range of local authority services and the impact of economic integration all had local government implications (Audit Commission 1991: 7). Local authorities started to acknowledge the importance of Europe, with Strathclyde Region, then the largest local authority unit in western Europe and covering over half Scotland's population, establishing one of the first British local authority lobbying offices in Brussels. A growing appreciation of the diversity of structures of regional and local government elsewhere in Europe developed. Scottish local authorities, which in the 1970s had been amongst the most vociferous opponents of devolution, began to see merit in a level of government somewhere between themselves and central government in London.

Even the one and indivisible France established regional government in the 1980s and the German state, widely deemed to have been uniquely successful, was a federal republic. By the late 1980s, Britain looked rather odd as one of the few EC member states without a tier of regional government. The presidency of Jacques Delors brought a new style of leadership to Europe. In speech after speech, Delors stressed the importance of subsidiarity, an idea new to British politics though familiar elsewhere in Europe. By the late 1980s, it had almost become a shibboleth in British politics, though its precise meaning was unclear. Decisions should be made at the most appropriate level, according to the subsidiarity principle, but who decided what the most appropriate level was? For Delors it meant the European and regional levels to a greater extent than then was the case, at the expense of the member state. He stressed the role of regions within member states, much to the annoyance of the Conservatives. In an article written when she was challenged for the leadership of the Conservative Party in 1990, Margaret Thatcher argued for the 'liberty in devolution of power away from the centre' but the centre in question was not London:

> That is why what is called subsidiarity is so important. The [European] Community should be involved in taking action only where it is demonstrably clear that member states acting on their own cannot achieve a particular objective. (Thatcher 1990)

But this did not extend to domestic politics, as the Scottish National Party (SNP) and other supporters of a Scottish Parliament frequently remarked.

It is difficult to assess the precise impact which Europeanisation had on domestic constitutional debate. Europe and the British regions were emerging as allies if only because they had a common enemy - London. The language of politics had altered. Federalism and subsidiarity were commonly talked about, even if they were ambiguous and, in the case of federalism, vehemently opposed by sections of public opinion and the elites. If nothing else, federalism was on the political agenda as never before, and there was a growing appreciation that Britain was unusual in not having a system of regional government; proposals for a Scottish Parliament seemed more attractive. Devolution and European integration were alternatives in a highly centralised system of government. They became part of the language of 'modernisation', however imprecisely.

Domestic Pressures

It would be wrong to suggest that Europe had the most significant impact on the debate on Scotland's constitutional status in the 1980s and 1990s, or that support for a Scottish Parliament came into existence only then. Polls since the late 1940s showed consistently high levels of support amongst Scots for some measure of home rule (Mitchell 1996). In the 1980s, there was a deepening in this widespread support for change as the issue of Scotland's constitutional status became more politically salient. Parties in opposition had long 'played the Scottish card' to embarrass the government of the day. Accusing the government of ignoring Scottish distinctiveness was a hallmark of opposition in Scotland, but it had an added piquancy under Margaret Thatcher.

The Conservatives may have had a majority in the Commons but they were a minority and declining force in Scotland. The opposition parties - Labour and Liberal Democrats as well as the SNP - questioned the legitimacy of Conservative rule in Scotland through the Scottish Office. In the early 1980s it was argued that the Tories had 'no Scottish mandate' and Labour's Scottish conference passed a resolution proclaiming this in 1984. Comparisons were drawn between the role of Conservative Scottish Secretaries and colonial Governor-Generals with Malcolm Rifkind, who served as Scottish Secretary from 1986 to 1990, himself making this comparison on one occasion. There may have been a distinct office responsible for Scottish affairs, but it was controlled by a party with little support. Scottish distinctiveness was catered for, but not Scottish democracy.

The introduction of legislation for a poll tax, a regressive tax replacing the local property tax, shortly before the 1987 general election caused a furore in Scotland. It was introduced in Scotland a year ahead of England, leading to accusations that the Scots were being used as a guinea-pigs. Its regressive nature was attacked and a massive civil disobedience campaign was launched. The anti-poll tax campaign had all the potency of a movement combining Scottish nationalism and left-wing politics. The obvious argument was made that no Scottish Parliament would ever have imposed a poll tax on Scotland. No issue had ever before been so tied up with debate on Scotland's constitutional status as the poll tax. Scottish nationalism was no longer seen as a romantic movement concerned with cultural matters, but a left of centre political movement.

The SNP had been struggling to make a breakthrough during most of the 1980s, but the combination of Europe and the poll tax gave the party a boost. By the late 1980s, the Labour Party was beginning its transformation into New Labour, shedding its radicalism. Officially, Labour would not support a non-payment campaign though many individual members, including some senior party figures, decided to participate in the campaign. The SNP had no such scruples and became the main supporter of the mass non-payment campaign. It managed to out-manoeuvre Labour on the left. In addition, the SNP abandoned its previous hostility to European integration and finalised a gradual process in support of the European Union which began in the early 1980s when in 1988 it launched its 'independence in Europe' campaign. Having fairly unanimously opposed EC membership in the 1975 referendum, just over a decade later the SNP had become Euro-enthusiasts. This signified a change in the SNP but had a wider symbolic significance. Support for European integration and support for a Scottish parliament (whether devolved or independent) were no longer seen as incompatible. Indeed, these aspirations had come to have more in common than had previously been acknowledged.

Changes were afoot inside the Labour Party too. Labour's hostility to Scottish home rule on the grounds described by Gordon Brown above had led the party to come out against it officially in the late 1950s. The rise of the SNP in the 1960s had forced Labour to think again. After the SNP breakthrough in the first election in 1974, when the Nationalists won seven seats with 22 per cent of the vote, Labour did a U-turn and the party, once more in power, found itself committed to a policy which had been arrived at largely due to electoral pressure. Labour thinking remained centralist and it had difficulty reconciling its traditional centralist predisposition with the electorally expedient policy of devolution. It was hardly surprising, then, that the party was unable to maintain a united front in the referendum in 1979, and that Labour supporters, without a clear cue from the party as to how to vote, failed to turn out in large numbers for the party's official policy. Though a narrow majority voted for devolution in that referendum, it was smaller than devolutionists had expected and was insufficient to overcome the hurdle set by Parliament. Forty per cent of the eligible electorate were required to vote for devolution before the measure was implemented. In the event 32.9 per cent of the eligible electorate (constituting 51.7 per cent of those who voted) were in favour with 30.8 per cent voting against and the remaining 36.3 per cent not voting. The 40 per cent rule had defeated devolution and was seen by supporters of a Scottish parliament as unfair, especially as no such provision had been required in the 1975 referendum on continued membership of the European Community.

Labour's lukewarm attitude to devolution changed in the 1980s. The party in Scotland gradually became committed to the policy. SNP electoral pressure continued to play its part, but Margaret Thatcher proved a more important influence. Thatcherism became associated, particularly in the minds of Scottish local authorities overwhelmingly dominated by Labour, with centralisation. As Labour in Scotland did well in successive elections while the party south of the border did poorly, the Scottish party began to appreciate the opportunities which devolution offered as a means of at least blocking the excesses, as Labour members saw them, of the Tories and perhaps allowing for alternative, progressive policies to be pursued. During the eighteen years Labour was in opposition in Parliament, the party inevitably looked for alternative sources of power and legitimacy. Europe, local government and devolution came to have attractions in sections of the party which they had never had before.

The emergence of New Labour, however, did not involve a complete rejection of centralisation. Party rhetoric placed a heavy emphasis on devolution and a positive role in Europe, but the practice of the leadership under Tony Blair suggested something quite different. If Blair was to lead his government when in power as he led his party while in opposition, then centralisation would not be a thing of the past. Blair was known to have doubts about devolution and was determined that his ambition would not be thwarted by any suggestion that Labour was the party of the Celtic peripheries, unsympathetic to 'middle England'. He was determined to play down devolution in the election but the commitment to Scottish devolution was not one he could afford to ditch. Clause four was abandoned because the main political pressure came from the right in middle England. Devolution, however, could not be abandoned as the main pressure in Scotland came from the Nationalists. Indeed, Scottish Labour would have exploded. Clause four, Labour's commitment to socialism could be jettisoned, but devolution could not. Such was the state of opinion in Scottish Labour by the time of the 1997 election.

Ironically, those most in favour of devolution in the Labour Party in Scotland were on the left. These were people whose commitment to equality and welfare might have led them to oppose devolution in the past. But many such Labour supporters and members came to believe that the best means of defending the social and economic policies they supported was a Scottish Parliament. They felt that gaining a majority for their views in Westminster would prove difficult. New Labour, under Tony Blair and Gordon Brown, had abandoned socialist policies. There was no need to attempt to 'reconcile the aspirations for home rule and a British socialist advance', as Gordon Brown had written as a student, when Gordon Brown, as Chancellor of the Exchequer, abandoned a British socialist advance in pursuit of Conservative voters in middle England. With a mixture of pragmatism and principle, Labour supporters in Scotland remained entirely consistent in their support for the same state over the period since 1945 - not the British state, nor the Scottish state, but the welfare state, which in pragmatic terms meant looking towards a Scottish Parliament and away from Westminster.

Conclusion

The outcome of the 1997 election and the planned election of a Scottish Parliament in 1999 mark a dramatic change in British politics. The second referendum on Scottish devolution held five months after Blair's victory was remarkable not only in the convincing majorities recorded for devolution with tax raising powers, but in the fact that those who questioned the need for a referendum were those who supported devolution. The argument which had been used at the time of previous referendums that such a device undermined Parliamentary sovereignty was not raised. Indeed, referendums have been proposed for other matters. Devolution for Scotland, Wales and possibly Northern Ireland will have an impact with implications going beyond these constituent parts of the UK. In the conclusion to his *History of Europe*, Norman Davies noted that the independence movement in Scotland was gathering pace as he was finishing the work. The Scots have the 'power to destroy the United Kingdom, and thereby to deflate the English, as no one in Brussels could ever do. They may make Europeans of us yet' (Davies 1996: 1134). It is not that the Scots are destroying the UK or that the English are ever likely to be deflated, but that Scotland and Europe have been part of a process of change. At the heart of this is Parliament. A more genuinely pluralistic form of politics may yet emerge, with Parliament at Westminster having its proper place.

References

Audit Commission (1991), *A Rough Guide To Europe: Local Authorities and the EC*, London, HMSO.
Benn, Tony (1996), 'The Common Market: Loss of Self-Government' in M. Holmes (ed.), *The Eurosceptical Reader*, Houndmills, Macmillan.
Billig, Michael (1995), *Banal Nationalism*, London, Sage.
Brown, Gordon (1981), *The Labour party and Political Change in Scotland, 1918-1929: The Politics of Five Elections*, Edinburgh University PhD unpublished.
Dalyell, Tam (1977), *Devolution: The End of Britain?*, London, Jonathan Cape.
Davies, Norman (1996), *Europe: a History*, Oxford, Oxford University Press.
Labour Party (1962), *Britain and the Common Market: Texts of speeches made at 1962 Labour Party Conference by the Rt. Hon. Hugh Gaitskell MP and the Rt. Hon. George Brown MP together with the policy statement accepted by the conference*, London, Labour Party.
Jordan, A.G. and J.J. Richardson (1987), *British Politics and the Policy Process*, London, Allen & Unwin.
Mitchell, J. (1996), *Strategies for Self-Government*, Edinburgh, Polygon.
Mitchell, J. (1997), 'The battle for Britain? Constitutional reform and the election', in A. Geddes and J. Tonge (eds.), *Labour's Landslide*, Manchester, Manchester University Press, pp.134-145.
E. Powell (1996), 'Britain and Europe', in M. Holmes (ed.), *The Eurosceptical Reader*, Houndmills, Macmillan.
Rose, Richard (1982), *Understanding the United Kingdom*, London, Longman.
Thatcher, Margaret (1990), 'My vision of Europe: open and free', *Financial Times*, November 19.
Thatcher, M. (1993), *The Downing Street Years*, London, HarperCollins.

13 An England of the Regions in a Europe of the Regions?

JOHN MURPHY

Introduction

Present-day discussion of future types of government is often formulated in terms of the forces of globalisation, tribalisation and supra-national trading blocs competing for supremacy over the corpses of nation states. There is a widespread belief that nation states are doomed because they are too small to resist the transnational influences which ignore formal frontiers and make decisions which no individual nation can deny. This undermines the nation states' sovereign and central powers, releasing forces which might lead to the disintegration of some of the less well-structured.

One road to safety lies in joining some larger supra-national grouping to help hold the forces of tribalisation in check, diverting them into acceptable forms such as regional identities within the borders of what remains of the nation states. A trading bloc like the European Union (EU) encourages regional identities, or controlled tribalisation, in order to break down the national barriers that might inhibit the emergence of the seamless super-state which it has the potential to create.

The advance of globalisation in the form of trade liberalisation, privatisation and reliance on market forces has aided the growth of transnational corporations which now control some 70% of all world trade. In its transnational form, globalisation takes little or no account, as its name implies, of the nation state when carrying out its activities. Although this disregard is not uniform either in its openness or its degree, it may be taken as read that it will override most nationally-based opposition. If Britain is ready to send a spade-carrying prime minister to cut the first sod for a new Siemens factory in Newcastle or a Hyundai works in South Wales, then what chance does an underdeveloped Third World country stand of insisting on respect for its sovereignty from an incoming transnational? The very concept, national sovereignty, is becoming quaint.

However, as far as transnationals are concerned, it is the individual nation state, despite its declining powers, rather than the bloc which is still the more likely of the two to inhibit their operations. Trading blocs like the EU are easier for transnationals whose home base is not in one of the countries belonging to a bloc to deal with. Penetrating just one member state can turn it into a Trojan horse from which to infiltrate the rest. The fact that they form a bloc then makes the process of operating simpler than if the frontiers of each separate nation had to be crossed.

The United Kingdom

The situation of the United Kingdom (UK), as things stand today, is especially interesting because all the main issues arising from globalisation, tribalisation and membership of a trading bloc are present there. The UK is both a home base for some major transnational corporations and among the largest overseas capital investors, while at the same time being a favoured target for inward foreign direct investment and a place where many of the world's largest foreign-owned transnationals have daughter companies. In terms of tribalisation it possesses both the benign and malign varieties in that Scotland and Wales are to be given their own devolved assemblies according to a peaceful process, while the violent aspect is found in Northern Ireland where civil war and incipient ethnic cleansing lurk. For the last quarter of a century the UK has also belonged to what today is the EU.

In its relations with the EU, Britain is in disagreement over many policies which affect her national sovereignty. Although the new Labour government is trying to work more closely with the EU than its Conservative predecessors, the present line is that EU cooperation should extend little further than the operation of the single market. Accordingly, while Britain may accept the Euro once public opinion has been prepared, and with that the inevitable surrender of some national control over the economy, other areas seem more problematic. Further losses of parliamentary sovereignty would be resisted as would interference in foreign and defence policies including the UK's right to retain border controls. And, if the evidence of the past serves as a pointer, there would be an English refusal to yield any significant extent of central government authority to the English regions either in line with EU regionalisation strategies or in continuation of Labour's commitment to Scottish and Welsh devolution.

In what follows it will be argued that on the evidence of her history over the past two thousand years, England is unlikely to conform to the EU's desire for the extension of regionalisation. Although a country the size of England naturally has regions, if only for the purposes of weather forecasting, as well as strong regional identities, English history points towards a centralising imperative which denies regional autonomy. In what appears to be a natural manifestation of utilitarianism, the English have accepted the rejection of particularism in the interests of some greater national good. Despite the existence of numerous regional organisations and the many claims concerning the living reality of regional identities, the possibility seems very remote of English regional governments emerging whose powers might grow at the expense of those at the centre, no matter how hard the EU may wish to promote this.

The English historical evidence

From an historical viewpoint, extending from the Roman occupation until today, the English historical/geographical identity, and the Welsh too within limits to be suggested, presents a remarkably uniform picture where unifying tendencies in the end have always predominated over centrifugal forces. Of course it could be that the outcome so far only reflects the triumph of centralisation over regionalisation in circumstances which were all essentially different to those in operation today but that time alone can reveal and, in the meantime, the evidence from the past has at least to be considered when attempting to foresee the future.[1]

Roman Britain

The Roman colony of Britain defined not only what has become present-day England and Wales, but also the division of the British Isles. Wales was included because its tribes were Britons and so were overrun along with the rest. Ireland was a nuisance, but as offering no threat could be ignored and Caledonia, which was a danger, could be sealed off with a wall built at a strategic point. Although the division of the major portion of Great Britain lying south of that wall varied over the 400 hundred years of Roman administration, sometimes with the province divided into two approximately equal parts, at others into quarters, the probability is, in the absence of real evidence, that these dividings and re-dividings were mostly attributable to the usual tendency for administrations to shake things up now and again. More recent colonial history in Africa and the Americas suggests the arbitrary imposition of boundaries by the ruling powers and there is no reason to imagine that the Romans were over-sensitive to native regional preferences, though that is not the same as saying that they were not responsive to perceived regional threats.

Angleland

The effect of Roman withdrawal at the start of the fifth century was tribalisation, as the Anglo-Saxon tribes poured in and the Romanised Britons fell apart. Many were driven into Wales, Cornwall and Cumberland, while the Germanic invaders set up a variety of petty kingdoms within the approximate borders of modern England. Over the course of the next four to five centuries a process of consolidation and unification occurred in Anglo-Saxon territory which in the end proved sufficiently strong to shake off the violent impact of the ninth century Viking invasions. The Saxon kingdoms consolidated around Wessex to defeat the Danes, though the more disparate Angles, despite having given their name to the country, collapsed under the waves of Viking invaders. That collapse, however, only served to make the later stages of Saxon hegemony all the easier once the Viking threat had been contained. By the beginning of the eleventh century, the heptarchy of the Anglo-Saxon kingdoms and the territories of the Danish earls had been subsumed into one unit of English rule. Although this single authority was still shadowy in places, only the Celtic parts retained a truly separate identity as well as the indeterminate region where Northern England merged with the south of Scotland.

The Norman conquest

The Norman conquest greatly strengthened the process of homogenisation. Uniform laws gradually replaced local systems and by the 13th century these were administered throughout the length and breadth of England by centralised legal authorities. The spread of the common law through the agency of the Norman law courts also played an important part in the re-emergence of the submerged English identity. An early sign was the statement of 1236 which declared "Nolumus leges angliæ mutare"[2] followed over a century later by a statute of 1362 which ordered that common law pleas should be heard in English, though recorded in Latin. Despite Norman French remaining in practice the chosen language of most lawyers for a least a century longer, the records of the Chancery court established in 1357 were kept in English from its inception.[3]

The English identity

As the Normans strove to unify their conquered English possessions, the English were showing other signs of freeing themselves from their conquered status. As the most numerous population, they were gradually asserting themselves by displacing Norman French in a process of absorption and making governance dependent on consultation. This produced a system recognisable as a modern parliament by the end of the 13th century whose records from the start, like the Chancery court, were kept in English. The English parliament was a single entity representing the towns and counties of the entire country and, from the start, mediated between the king and tax-paying subjects. This was quite unlike the way the many French *parlements* developed, which only resembled the English version in name. Those in France grew into focal points of regional identity and the inflexible guardians of separate legal systems.[4]

At about the same period, the French territories of the kings of England gradually ceased to be regarded as Norman and became English. By the time the Hundred Years' War broke out in 1360, the underpinnings of an English national identity were there in terms of language, a sense of geographic space and a shared culture. English court music, as opposed to French or Burgundian, was an important part of national recognition and among the earliest examples of cultural propaganda. Being part of an island with defined borders certainly helped, as did the recognition that those against whom the English fought were not like them but foreigners. Conversely, the wars against the English were the reason for the early emergence of a French, and for a time a Burgundian, sense of national identity. At the conclusion of the Hundred Years' War, when the English lost Bordeaux in 1453, they withdrew to England and, by then, there could have been nowhere else for them to have gone.

The English palatinates

In the thirteenth century, the only parts of England which were truly separate from the rest were the regions bordering on Wales and Scotland, the two lay palatinates of Chester and Lancaster and the ecclesiastical one of Durham. At the Conquest, the Norman kings had been careful to divide up the territories granted to reward their followers into parcels scattered up and down England. The only places where there was a real coherence of possession was in the marches of Wales and Scotland because of the need to grant virtual autonomy to lords like the Mortimers along the Severn and the Percys in Northumberland in return for their guarding the English frontiers.

Durham

The Durham palatinate, whose head was its bishop, was a second line of defence behind the Percys in case of a Scottish invasion. In fact the whole area as far south as York was at risk and a potential no man's land until as late as the mid-fifteenth century. When the present Durham cathedral was begun in 1093, its foundation stone was laid by the king of Scotland, Malcolm III, together with the Norman bishop. Nevertheless, over time the area became steadily more settled and it was the Borders, the region of southern Scotland beyond the English frontier where the no man's land finally lay. By then the Durham palatinate had ceased to exercise its autonomous functions, although Celia Fiennes, who revelled in a taste for antiquity, made much of its separate status when she visited the city in the early eighteenth century.[5]

Chester

The Chester County Palatine, under the control of an earl, was established as part of the defence of the Anglo-Welsh border. In this case, the cure turned out to be worse than the disease because the earl's powers were so considerable as to cause disruption in England itself. In 1241, Henry III brought the area back under the direct authority of the English crown, and the title, earl of Chester, eventually became one of those of the prince of Wales. Thus, at an early point, the danger of such regional autonomy to the unity of England was recognised, and in this case dealt with.

Lancaster

It is consequently surprising to find that the most powerful of all such medieval regional entities, the County Palatine of Lancaster, was set up by the same king, Henry III, shortly after the extinction of Chester. Henry's second-born son, Edmund, a hunchback, was made earl of Lancaster and ruler of this county palatine.[6] Although much of its extensive territories lay on either side of the Pennines in Northern England, its existence could scarcely be justified as a barrier or a buffer like Chester or Durham. With its own government apparatus, laws, revenue raising and taxation powers it was to all intents and purposes a state within a state.

In 1399, a little over a century after its foundation, it served as the springboard from which its then possessor, Henry Bolingbroke, overthrew and murdered his cousin Richard II and made himself king as Henry IV. 1399 was, however, the last time that such a possibility was allowed to exist. Ever after, the English monarch has always been Duke of Lancaster as well, and the county palatine, though retaining its separate identity in an insubstantial form (the Chancellor of the Duchy of Lancaster still sits in the cabinet), has been subsumed into the larger entity of England. The elimination of the palatinates in fact, if not in name, is an important demonstration of the movement away from regionalism towards centralisation.

The ending of English border military autonomies

By the mid-sixteenth century the last of the English autonomous areas had its independence curtailed. The Welsh marches had been dealt with earlier, partly with the decline of the Mortimers following the defeat of their forces, the last of the independent Welsh and the Northumberland Percys at Shrewsbury in 1405. The marcher lords of the Scottish borders were needed for another century, which preserved a good deal of their autonomy. However, the scale of English victories over the Scots at Flodden in 1513 and Solway Moss in 1542, combined with the religiously-based civil wars which tore Scotland apart at this period, meant that the role of the northern English border barons rapidly approached its end under Elizabeth I (1558-1603), and definitively with the accession of James VI of Scotland as James I of England, the first monarch to unite the two crowns.

English regional councils

Nevertheless, these former military structures did not disappear entirely as they were changed into civilian-based regional authorities with vice-regal powers. This happened in part because of the threat of religious strife which exploited regional economic distress to challenge national authority. Three regional administrative bodies came into being in the wake of serious unrest at the Reformation, in particular the 1536 northern Pilgrimage of Grace. Two, the Council of the North and the Council in the Marches corresponded approximately to the former Scottish and Welsh marcher territories and were based on rudimentary bodies some fifty years older. A third new one was in Devon and Cornwall, presumably because of the West Country's remoteness and lingering Celtic separatism combined with its contemporary economic importance.

The Council of the North was established in York, and had a continuous existence lasting from 1537 until 1641 when it became one of the earliest casualties of the as yet undeclared English Civil War.[7] It was abolished by the Long Parliament because it represented royal powers outside parliamentary control. Its main fault, in their eyes, lay in its having furnished the earl of Strafford, executed in 1640, with a power-base from which to implement arbitrary royal policies during the 1630s including levying taxes without parliamentary approval.

The Council in the Marches (also known as the council for Wales), situated at Ludlow from 1536 until its abolition in 1689, was responsible for law and order in Wales and four of the English counties along the Welsh border. It was important because it was part of the process through which a union between England and Wales was established by an act of annexation passed by the Reformation parliament in 1536. From then on, Wales was treated identically to England for administrative purposes. The old marcher lordships were dissolved, new Welsh counties added to the existing ones and Welsh MPs brought into the Westminster parliament. In 1689, following the Glorious Revolution and in the new atmosphere of the bill of Rights, this council had outlived its purpose.[8] The third council, that of the West, was very short-lived. Formed in 1539, it ended in 1547, the year of Henry VIII's death. The demise of these councils, for various reasons and at different times, points once again towards the long-term strength of the forces of centralisation.

The British regions

With the creation of the United Kingdom of Great Britain in 1707 the existing royal union of England and Scotland changed into a political one. The Scottish parliament closed and 45 Scottish MPs and 16 lords joined the English and Welsh at Westminster. This union ended any contemporary prospect of reviving English regionalism. Scotland and Wales became "the regions". No matter what was claimed about the creation of a new British identity encompassing all the people of Great Britain, the eighteenth century's equivalent of today's encouragement of EU citizens to see themselves first as Europeans, the English national identity strengthened in reaction to the Scots and at the expense of English regional identities.

When Wales was incorporated there was no sign of English anti-Welsh feeling. Henry VIII was of Welsh descent, which may have kept some dissent unvoiced, and "Taffy was a Welshman, Taffy was a thief" was a sentiment only current in the border areas where cattle were stolen. There was no influx of Welsh fortune seekers such as characterised relations with the Scots who were an entirely different proposition. The first Scottish carpet-baggers arrived with James I and soon made themselves very unpopular. The worst example was Robert Carr, created earl of Somerset in 1613, who not only seriously offended the English ruling class, but became involved in an unsavoury murder.[9] Scots were seen as unscrupulous intruders, cashing in at English expense. This sense of injury lessened in the course of the 17th century as ties with Scotland weakened. England became a significant European, and even world, power while Scotland languished after mid-century in poverty and obscurity. England to the south was a magnet to the ambitious and impoverished Lowland Scots, but their penetration prior to 1707 was held in check.

After that date the efforts to create a new British persona were warmly welcomed by the Scots,[10] and the Welsh too. If anything, this only reinforced English national consciousness. The Scots remained outsiders, easily identifiable by their speech and occasionally their dress. They were poor relations saved from national bankruptcy by the Union and, even worse, politically suspect for the first 40 years because their country provided the main hope for the overthrow of the Hanoverian settlement whereby both nations would have the same Protestant king, a crucial objective behind the Union's creation. Jacobitism only ceased to be a threat after the failure of the 1745 rebellion.

A notable low point came when the Scottish earl of Bute was prime minister between 1762-3. His main qualifications appeared to be that he had been George III's tutor, and probably his mother's lover. Incompetence soon put him out of office, but not before confirming the English view that the entire Scottish political elite was a venal collection of place-hunters. It was this reputation which led to remarks like Dr Johnson's that "the noblest prospect that a Scotchman ever sees, is the high road that leads him to England!"[11] Others expressed their dislike for Scots on the make by complaining about those who acquired estates in England for planting Scotch firs, instead of hardwoods. This suggested either that they were shallow opportunists wanting to see their trees full grown in their lifetimes, unlike the English who planted for posterity, or barbarians who lacked gentlemanly taste.[12] Scots could well call the Georges kings of Great Britain, but to the majority of the island's inhabitants they remained kings of England.

London dominance

The onset of the Industrial Revolution in the 1760s was accompanied by vast changes which further weakened the English regional identities of the past. Regional metropolises like Norwich, York, Exeter or Worcester were turned into backwaters by the growth of huge new industrial cities such as Manchester, Leeds and Birmingham, or by their own hastening pace of decline into provincial obscurity. Mrs Gaskell's "North and South" pointed to a new form of an old division in England, but any possibility of a rift emerging to separate the two was prevented by the enormous influence of London. Apart from being the seat of government, and with a population some ten times larger than any other city, the capital never ceased to be a major manufacturing centre in its own right, though not mass, machine-powered production as in the English North and Midlands.

Another major reason for London's hold over the rest of England was that no significant portion of its financial and political dominance was yielded to those regions where the new wealth was being created. Leading companies and banks often had their head offices in London far from the scene of their actual operations and, even when they kept their headquarters closer to their activities, their representative London offices frequently outdid their provincial seats. Politically, the newly represented English cities of the Industrial Revolution were incorporated into the national fabric after parliamentary reform began in 1832, and their new MPs went like lambs to London where the national centre of decision-making remained unchallenged at Westminster.

The railway age and English regionalism

A glance at any map showing communications will confirm the fact of London's all-pervading influence. Whereas one for canals would show that industrial areas predominated in being served for the transport of coal, raw materials and manufactured goods, a map relating to the carriage of people would reveal the extent to which all the roads and railway lines from the regions of England, and from Wales and Scotland too, led to London. While road maps indicate more provision for east-west travellers, the rail maps, those absolute markers of nineteenth century progress, leave no doubt - the railway lines radiated like wheel spokes from the capital. These railways also promoted the growth of a London-based national press whose nationwide influence acted to reduce the likelihood of the emergence of self-consciously regional alternatives to London's dominance which the wealth of Manchester, Leeds and Birmingham might otherwise have fostered. This is unlike what happened in Germany, Italy and the USA where large provincial centres like Munich, Milan or Chicago retained their regional autonomy.

Scotland and Wales until the 1970s

Although parts of Scotland and Wales became heavily industrialised, fewer people there were actively involved than in England. However, for those who were, and for those who wanted to be because they were tempted by the material rewards, there were more serious internal regional barriers to be overcome than in England. To move from the Scottish Highlands to Glasgow or to South Wales from the centre or the north involved far greater dislocation than comparable English internal migration. In South Wales, for instance, there was an inflow of both English capital and management so that the work force, whether local or drawn from other parts of the Principality, had to surrender something of its identity, in particular, the native Welsh language. As the self-made 19th century millionaire, David Davies, said ".. if you are content with brown bread, you can, of course, remain where you are. If you want to enjoy the luxuries of life, with white bread to boot, the only way to do so is by learning English well."[13]

Scotland remained for long content with its bargain, in particular the Empire, and many Scots preserved an identity by emigrating to places like Canada and New Zealand which were theirs as much as they were England's. There they could retain traditions while bettering their condition. Those who stayed at home could take pride in these pioneers, the heroism of individuals like Dr Livingstone, or rejoice in the stereotype of the indomitable Scots engineers who kept the British merchant fleet steaming thanks to will-power and bits of bent wire.[14] Sharing the Empire more than compensated the Scots for remaining within, unlike most Irish who wanted their independence, perversely failing to appreciate being allowed to share in the greater British glory. As late as 1954, an English professor of history, long resident in Scotland, could write in an article on the quarter millennium of the UK "..that so long as common interests are thought to outweigh separate interests, the Union of 1707 will survive in something like its present form."[15]

Thatcherism and regional identities

By 1979, that picture had altered considerably. There were still some common interests, but more and more separate ones. The Commonwealth had less appeal than the Empire and, when the UK became a member of the European Economic Community in 1973 and turned its back on the Commonwealth, this accession also gave rise to the argument that Scotland would be better served at Brussels as an independent entity than under Whitehall's management where English interests would predominate. At the same time, the discovery of North Sea oil suggested a viable economic basis, at least as good as Norway's, for Scottish independence. The Labour Party, well aware that the parliamentary seats won in Scotland and Wales were vital for its chances of forming the UK government, offered both regions devolved assemblies in 1979 to head off the nationalist challenge. The Labour government, with a wafer-thin Commons majority, was forced to accept amendments to its devolution bills which required the approval of 40% of the total Scots and Welsh electorates, rather than simple majorities. In the referendums, Labour fell just short of this in Scotland and well short in Wales, though there was a majority for devolution in Scotland of those who bothered to vote.[16] A month later, Labour was out of office and Mrs Thatcher had taken over.

The next 18 years saw the steady growth of resentment among Scots and Welsh voters because, although both countries elected a majority of Labour MPs, they were ruled by Conservative governments. Mrs Thatcher's centralising policies, especially in local government, meant less and less autonomy despite her pledge "to roll back the frontiers of the state". In the 1997 election, a consequence of this stored-up resentment was the total elimination of all Conservative parliamentary representation in Scotland and Wales. It also meant that the new Labour government had to fulfil its pledges to give Scotland a parliament and Wales an assembly which is why it was the first bill presented to the new parliament. Labour knows that any failure to make the Scottish parliament into a real legislative body, and not just an Edinburgh talking shop, would provide the Scottish Nationalist Party with the biggest boost for its campaign for complete independence since North Sea oil. Failure in Wales would be less serious; Labour would suffer at the next election, but Plaid Cymru would not necessarily be the main beneficiary.

The English effect

No good ship, it is claimed, was ever launched whose design was changed on the stocks after its keel was laid. The 1974 local government reform's origins lay in the Macmillan era, its major investigation and research period in Wilson's first spell as prime minister and its implementation in Heath's turbulent times. The reforms failed to provide a system able to match either contemporary or future needs. A weak point was its inability to meet demands made by the new notion of subsidiarity. Local government became less local. There was generally an increase in the physical distance between most electors and their local authorities because the elimination of smaller units, in the hope of making savings, inevitably made administrations more distant.

On the credit side, some subsidiarity aims were fulfilled by the creation of metropolitan councils in six of the main English urban concentrations. These were not regional councils *per se*, but they were the closest England had come to such bodies since the abolition of those founded in the Tudor era. The county councils set up in 1888, though possessing real powers, had given no sign of forming the basis for some separate regional identity. Only Yorkshire and Lancashire possessed industrial, geographical and population bases large enough, while Norfolk and Lincolnshire, though big in area and remoteness, were too thinly populated and agricultural. The post-1974 metropolitan counties, though large in population, were too small geographically, however, to be really regional, being hearts or heads without bodies.

The metropolitan councils were meant to carry out, along the lines of the Greater London Council (GLC) of 1963, a mass of functions ranging from town and country planning, transport, waste disposal, etc., best done by larger, rather than more local, authorities. A major drawback, as it turned out, was that all these metropolitan second tiers were held by Labour, then very weak at Westminster. By virtue of the relative national vacuum they came to represent some of the most coherent Labour opposition in the country at large, which made them the object of Conservative wrath and also involved them in the feud between Mrs Thatcher and the leader of the GLC, Ken Livingstone. This ended with the abolition of all seven metropolitan authorities in 1985, in the case of the GLC against the wishes of 7 out of 10 Londoners.

It is arguable that the metropolitan councils might have formed the nuclei of wider regional authorities. This is because the North/South divide which emerged in the Thatcher era gave rise in some parts of England to the same feelings of frustration as in Scotland and Wales - that although they had not voted Conservative, they were ruled by an alien and unsympathetic Westminster regime.[17] Perhaps the most serious legacy of their abolition, however, is the lasting impression left in the public mind that such tiers of local administration were a waste of public money. The "unnecessary" tag was always more to do with that than anything else and remains a difficult first obstacle. Tony Blair remains vague about the introduction of regional councils, stressing their optionality. He must be aware of the danger, first pointed out by the previous Conservative Lord Chancellor, the Scot, Lord Mackay, that to give the English regions real powers would have the effect of reducing a Scottish national parliament to the status of a mere English regional assembly, which would offend the very people he wants to please in Scotland.

Transnational regions

The validity of these historically-based arguments in the case of England's predilection for a centralised as opposed to a regionalist solution is partly affirmed from what may at first sight may seem an unlikely quarter, that of the transnational regions which are emerging as part of the EU process of regionalisation. Taking Denmark as an example, there is the possibility of three such transnational regions emerging there in the near future. One in the south links Southern Jutland and North Schleswig,[18] a second covers islands off the west coast of Denmark forming the northern end of a Friesian fringe stretching as far as Germany and the Netherlands,[19] while the third may result from the building of a road and rail bridge across the Sound to Sweden.[20]

Their common link is their re-creation of the patterns of the past, and EU policy is promoting the re-emergence of submerged identities. In all three, there are strong arguments in favour of the restoration in modern form of earlier historical realities. National affiliations may have changed, but the other reasons and imperatives for their existence - geographical, economic, social and cultural - still speak across time. England's history merely expresses the same forces more explicitly by confirming the existing *status quo*.

Conclusion

If England is unlikely, therefore, to adopt any regional form of government, then are there signs suggesting other forms of change? Obstacles stand in the way of even modest alterations. First is the general democratic deficit implicit in the British first-past-the-post electoral system. Second is the central government stranglehold over local authorities in limiting them only to those functions permitted under national law, with any other action being illegal as *ultra vires*, ie, beyond the power or authority of local government. Third is the lack of genuine local tax-raising powers, still affected by the reductions caused by Mrs Thatcher's Poll Tax, which is an almost insuperable obstacle to the freedom of action of local government. Here, though, the creation of more unitary local authorities since 1995 gives a little more sense of their being masters in their own houses.[21]

A possible line of approach involves a return to the village moot whose modern grassroots equivalent is the parish council. Dr Alex MacGillivray, who is on the council of the National Association of Local Councils, which represent England's 10,000 parishes, has started a debate which might lead to their receiving the power of "general competence". This ought to be theirs under the 1985 European Charter of Local Self-

Government and, though less explicitly, according to the subsidiarity principle of the Maastricht Treaty. The Charter has been ratified by most European governments, but not so far in the UK.[22] At the end of 1996, John Gummer, then Secretary of State for the Environment, proposed a bill to promote the well-being of rural life. Although the 1996 White Paper on central/local government relationships had specifically opposed the Charter, the bill's proposals carried an implicit message that local democracy needed strengthening.[23] It is a long way from the parish to the region, but the journey might start there.

The harsh realities

In 1996, a report on regional government in Britain concluded that while Scotland and Wales had most of the necessary structures in place, based on what had been built up through the Scottish and Welsh Offices, there was hardly any sign of the same in England. While it would be welcome in democratic terms, the chances of it happening were very remote.[24] Regional Government Offices, set up in England in 1994, had their own regional boundaries and offered no more than a fig-leaf at a time when Maastricht was urging EU governments into regional activity. The EU's Committee of the Regions, with yet another set of regional boundaries, has so far made little impact and, though time is on its side, there is little else in its favour at present.

One way forward might be to revive, at least in name, one of the Tudor councils or set up transnational regions covering Northumberland and the Scottish borders or Sussex and Normandy linked by the channel tunnel. Much depends on Scottish devolution. If it works, it might provide the missing spark - though nothing will happen until the idea of regional autonomy takes root in many more English heads and hearts than today.

Notes

1   What is, in essence, information from standard sources such as the Cambridge or Oxford standard histories of England will not be referred to by footnote.

2   A proclamation issued by Henry III in response to attempts by the Church to introduce the principle "legitimio per matrimonium subsequens". In D. Tamm, *Roman Law and European Legal History*, Copenhagen 1997, p. 228.
3   J.A.F. Thomson, *The Transformation of Medieval England*, London 1983, p. 293 and R.J. Walker, *The English Legal System*, 5th edn., London, 1976, p. 8.
4   A. Cobban, *The Parlements of France in the Eighteenth Century*, in History, the Journal of the Historical Association, Vol XXXV, London 1950, pp. 64-81. This article outlines how the 12 provincial parlements and that of Paris thwarted French central government attempts to reform the country's taxation and legal systems as well as acting as bastions of regional identity.
5   *The Journeys of Celia Fiennes*, ed. John Hillaby, London 1983, pp. 383-5. As an ardent Whig, she was very struck by the bishop of Durham's open championship of the Jacobite cause, which she attributed to his being the head of a county palatine.
6   It is not beyond the bounds of possibility that Edmund was the elder of Henry III's sons, but was replaced by his brother, later Edward I, because he was a hunchback. Henry III made great efforts to secure a crown for Edmund in the Near East before making him earl of Lancaster and head of the palatinate.
7   There were many disputes over custom and precedence between York and the vice-regal Council of the North recounted in the *History and Antiquities of York*, 1785, based on F. Drake's 1736 edition of his history. For instance, in 1608, a case was decided in York's favour at the High Court in London over the lord mayor's right to have the city's sword of state carried point upward in the presence of the president of the council. Vol 2, pp. 7-11.
8   It is possibly best remembered today for its connection with John Milton, whose *Comus* was performed as a masque at Ludlow castle in 1634 to mark the inauguration of the earl of Bridgewater as president of the council.
9   This was the poisoning of Sir Thomas Overbury in 1613 whose poem, "The Wife", was seen as criticism levelled at Carr's future wife who actually arranged the murder.
10 North Britain became an acceptable way of addressing letters to Scotland.
11 J. Boswell, *The Life of Johnson*, 1791, Penguin books edition, 1973, p. 106.
12 For instance John Byng, fifth viscount Torrington who wrote in his account of a tour in Sussex in 1788: "We soon came to the seat of Genr. Murray; thro whose domain I rode: this Scottish *haro* is ill-placed amidst the woods and enclosures of Sussex; as with the rest of his countrymen he wou'd feel more at home on a bleak-heath; but the General is trying what pleasing alterations he can make, by grubbing up hedges, and oaks, and introducing the fir; "The

Scotch fir that's never out of place". The Hon. Jon Byng, *The Torrington Diaries*, London 1934, Vol I, p. 360.

13 Quoted in Rhys Davies, *The Story of Wales*, London 1943, p. 36.

14 Even here, though, the Scots were not spared sarcastic comment; in this case a nice comment on the Opium Wars and the seizure of Hong Kong in 1840 to further the interests of Scots merchants like Jardine and Matheson.

> "You had a formidable opponent, Lord Marney told me," said Sir Vavasour. "Who was he?"
>
> "Oh, a dreadful Scotsman, richer than Croesus, one McDruggy, fresh from Canton, with a million of opium in each pocket, denouncing corruption, and bellowing free trade."
>
> Benjamin Disraeli, *Sybil*, London, 1845
> Penguin books edition, 1980, p. 74

In this anti-Scottish connection it may be noted that Christopher Booker writing in the *Sunday Telegraph* on 4/5/1997 claimed that with the Labour victory, the UK was now to be ruled by "a Scots mafia" most of whom were from the Lowlands. The other side of the coin was illustrated in the case of Gerry Malone, a Scot, who formerly held Winchester for the Conservatives. At the general election on 1/5/1997 he lost his seat by 2 votes. After discovering that he might have won if a small number of spoiled ballot papers had been allowed (they were excluded on a technicality), Mr Malone won a High Court ruling which called for a new election to be held in the constituency. This resulted on 20/11/1997 in a landslide victory for the new sitting member, Mark Oaten, a Liberal Democrat whose majority increased to 21,556. Mr Malone then blamed "anti-Scottish racism" for his rejection. Reported in the *Guardian*, 22/11/1997.

15 R. Pares, "A Quarter of a Millenium of Anglo-Scottish Union", in *History, the Journal of the Historical Association*, Vol XXXIX, London 1954, p. 248.

16 See J.D. Murphy, "The Survival of the United Kingdom", in *Memory, History and Critique, European Identity at the Millenium*, proceedings of the 6th International ISSEI Conference, Utrecht 1996, MIT, CD-ROM, 1997, p. 3.

17 See D. Smith, *North and South*, London 1989.

18 The duchies of Schlesvig and Holstein were part of the Danish sphere of influence stretching to the Elbe until 1864 when the territories were lost to Prussia. A new border established in 1920 restored some lost territory to Denmark and is the present frontier.

19 These islands stretching from Jutland in Denmark to the southern coast of the Netherlands were probably the home of the Jutes who invaded England along with the Anglo-Saxons. Friesians share a common life-style based on their shared geographical and climatic conditions.
20 Southern Sweden was Danish territory until 1659 and has more in common with Denmark from a geographical and climatic point of view than it has with the rest of Sweden. There is also a lingering pro-Danish sentiment among some of its population.
21 One outcome of the Local Government Commission established in 1992 to put to rest the Poll Tax disaster.
22 Articles in the *Local Council Review*, Vol 48, No 6, 1997, p. 7 and Vol 49, No 1, 1997, pp. 7-8.
23 *Rural England*, the Rural White Paper, Third report of the Environment Select Committee, London 1996
24 A. Harding, R. Evans and M. Parkinson, *Regional Government in Britain: an economic solution*, Bristol 1996.

14 Regional Inequality: the New Germany and the European Union

HANS JOACHIM MEYER*

Discussing terms and concepts like that of a region should be the business of legal studies or political science. Since I am only a practitioner in politics, possibly not wholly uneducated, but certainly unlearned, I decided to fall back on my academic past as a linguist and to start by considering the meaning of the word "region". Normally, words are used to refer to a fact or to denote a concept or to express an idea. At least, it should be so according to linguistic theory. In reality, however, words are quite often used to cover up the truth that there is neither a fact nor a concept nor an idea but rather some necessity to fill a hole or a vacuum. The suspicion that a word is used for such a purpose is irresistible whenever a precise definition or at least a clear description of the semantic content of a word is difficult to find. What is a region in the European Union? This is indeed not easy to define. So what is a region in general? According to the *Oxford Advanced Learner's Dictionary of Current English*, a region is an area or a division with or without definite boundaries or characteristics. Obviously, there are three elements in this definition: First of all, that the region is an entity in itself, i.e. an area, or that it is part of a larger or higher entity, i.e. a division; secondly, that a region can be defined externally, i.e. by boundaries, or internally, i.e. by characteristics; and thirdly, that these boundaries or characteristics may be definite or not, or probably, that they may be quite definite or not so definite but rather vague.

Looking now at the regions within the European Union, we will easily find that they differ in all three respects. In constitutional terms, the basic difference is whether they must be considered an area or a division, because this is directly related to their legal status as well as to their political importance. The *Länder* of the Federal Republic of Germany are states in their own right and in this sense they do not depend on federal assent. In the framework of the definition of a region, they are areas, although to German legal experts this is probably still too weak and hence unacceptable. In contrast, the regions in France are divisions of the French Republic which has introduced them and could just as well abolish them.

The political importance of a region is of course closely bound up with its distinct appearance in public thinking and, particularly, with the existence and the expression of regional identity. Identity results from a common cultural heritage and has its roots in history. Practically, all important regions within the European Union which may come to our mind have an impressive history of their own, and quite often it is their history which provides the arguments for strengthening their rights and broadening their possibilities. However, a long history is not automatically the basis for a strong legal or political position of the region. Scotland in Britain is certainly as old as Bavaria in Germany, if not older, and Scottish boundaries and characteristics could not be more distinct, but it is only Bavaria which has a parliament and a government of her own. And even if Scotland, as a consequence of the recent political changes in Britain, should get her own institutions, she would still have a long way to go before she had achieved a position which would equal that of Bavaria.

I could go on illustrating regional inequality like this for some time, if we take the term to denote the legal and political inequality of the regions within the European Union. And if we considered at some length the economic and cultural characteristics of these regions and their differences, the impression of inequality would consolidate. The question is why, on such uneven and unsafe ground, a new pillar of the European Union should be erected in addition to the pillar formed by the nations, or rather, by the nation-states which are the constituent members of the Union. What sense does it make to add further complex problems to the difficulties and troubles that are inevitable if one attempts to unite or, at least, to bring together, highly different nations and national states which quite often were divided by a long and bitter history of tensions, conflicts and wars into a new economic and political entity called European Union? Why should the European Union try to promote the cooperation of widely differing entities which are collectively given the vague name of a region?

In my view, the answer to this question must be sought in at least three directions. First of all, there is a growing mental or psychological necessity to strengthen the roots of the European Union in the public life of the member states. Immediately after the Second World War, there was a quite active European movement in the free part of the continent, particularly in those countries which later formed the nucleus for the process of European integration. What this movement was striving for was a European democracy rather than a European bureaucracy. However, the path towards European unity - in spite of the immense success of integration - has met with many obstacles. More democracy would mean strengthening the rights of European Parliament, which would inevitably reduce the position of national parliaments and governments. So far, the governments of the member states have preferred to keep the power of final decision in their hands. This leads to the absurdity that the national governments which in their own countries are in the position of the executive decide on European legislation which is constantly reducing the scope of legislation by the national parliaments, while the European Parliament is not much more than a consultative body. As a consequence, there is no European political debate, practically no European press, and, above all, there are no real European political parties. Too often the European Union, in the lives of ordinary citizens, appears in the form of new regulations which rather provoke their anger than engage their support. In other words, it is not enough to construct the European Union from the top down. What we need is to build up Europe from the bottom up, or rather, from the roots.

For quite a long time, a network of contacts and cooperation between the various local communities has been spreading across the European countries. You will hardly find a city or town in Europe without European partners, and quite often they proudly refer to them in their street signs and on official occasions. Quite undoubtedly, this network of local communities which involves a large number of people provides a popular basis for the European idea. However, the distance between the local level and the European level is too wide to allow the development of a continuous interest in the daily routine of European politics and European administration in Brussels. Moreover, the last decades have brought a remarkable revival of regional identity even in those Western European countries which for a long period had more or less exclusively pursued the concept of the central state, at least in their official national policy. In Britain, the constitutional status of Scotland and Wales has been a topic of political debate for more than two decades. And now it no longer seems totally impossible that the term "United Kingdom" may get a new meaning. For Spain, the recognition of regional autonomy was one of the conditions for the stability of the state and for the success of Spanish democracy. Italy is still grappling with the problem, but the concept of regions has been more or less accepted at least as a principle. Belgium has been transformed into a federation and its regions and cultural communities have most of the attributes and privileges of states. Even France, the one and indivisible French Republic, has rediscovered her historical landscape, which had been so radically and systematically neglected by the departments installed by the revolution, and has introduced regions reminiscent of her old provinces and former semi-independent feudal territories.

There was also a growth of regional thinking in both parts of Germany in the late seventies and in the eighties. And this regional thinking concentrated on history and culture. In view of the different and even contradictory conditions in the two Germanies, the question of what the reasons might have been is of some interest. One common motivation, though nourished from different sources, was the difficulty in referring to oneself as a German. In the GDR, the communist leadership had decided in the early seventies that there was no longer one German nation, but that there were now two nations - a socialist one in the GDR and a capitalist one in the Federal Republic. By the way, this change of the communist mind was a reaction to the attempt by Willy Brandt's government to come to some agreement with the GDR on the basis of the principle "two states but one nation". Hence there was an official pressure to speak of "GDR citizens" when referring to the Germans in the GDR - an expression which was of course not very popular. Instead, people increasingly preferred to use the old names like Saxon or Thuringian. In the Federal Republic, in clear contrast to this, there was a growing tendency, particularly but not only among intellectuals and people of left-wing persuasion, to think and speak of themselves as Europeans and as people from Hamburg or from the Rhineland or from Bavaria, but not as Germans. Walter Jens, an outstanding West German intellectual, said at that time that one could speak of Germany only in the past tense. For people like him, speaking of Germany meant not to recognise the division of Germany and coexistence with the GDR, which could only lead to war.

A remarkable example of the revival of regional thinking, although Walter Jens would most probably not have liked it, was the rediscovery of Prussia as an historical and a cultural phenomenon. The catastrophe of Nazi dictatorship had thoroughly destroyed any glorious image of German history and spoilt practically everything which might have been an element of it. In the late seventies and early eighties, however, people began to examine the individual bits and pieces of their history. One of them was Prussia, which immediately after the war had been regarded only as the very embodiment of authoritarian rule and aggressive militarism. West Germany took the lead and staged a huge and very ambitious exhibition which, according to the catalogue I was able to see, was in fact a critical, though well-balanced analysis of Prussian history. I still remember the vicious criticism published in the GDR media about this malicious attempt of West German imperialism to whitewash a bulwark of German reaction. Soon after, however, the GDR published a book by Ingrid Mittenzwei, an eminent Marxist historian, who gave a critical yet quite positive account of the life and work of the Prussian King Frederick the Great. To be honest, she called him *Frederick III*! A spate of films, plays and TV productions followed, which underlined the positive aspects of Prussian history. And the impressive monument dedicated to Frederick the Great and his time which, since 1949, had been hidden in a remote corner of the Park of Sanssouci, was set up again quite centrally in Berlin, at its old place on the famous street "Unter den Linden". Yet certainly no one can hope, or needs to fear, that Prussia will be reestablished. I mention this example because it shows that regionalism is not always primarily economically motivated, but is quite often bound up with historical memory and cultural heritage.

There were also clear indications of regional protests in the GDR against the neglect of towns and cities in favour of East Berlin, the capital of the highly centralised GDR. When in 1980 the 750th anniversary of the foundation of Berlin was celebrated, there were stickers on cars in Dresden saying that in the same year their city was 774 years old. And in Erfurt, a representative of the local administration surprised a group of foreign visitors with the question whether they knew what this city had celebrated in 1492. It was in fact Erfurt's 750th anniversary.

I am fully aware of the fact that one could discuss these tensions in terms of conflict between centre and periphery. But I do not believe that this could also be applied to the Federal Republic, new or old. The provisional capital at Bonn has never been a centre in the European sense of the word, and cannot compare with Munich, Hamburg, Stuttgart and Düsseldorf, to name only a few. This will be different with Berlin, although I doubt that it will regain the position it had at the time of Bismarck's Reich and the first German Republic, that is, from 1871 to 1933.

Although the regions in the various European countries differ considerably in legal status and political power, it is nevertheless true that all of them exercise rights and duties which could be or so far had been the prerogative of the national governments. As a result, there is a practical necessity, or it is at least practically convenient, for those who are responsible at the regional level to come to immediate contacts or to establish more or less regular relations with other European regions. In fact, a sub-national networking is slowly but continuously developing which may become an important element of the political structure of Europe. The European Union has responded to this development by setting up the so-called Committee of the Regions as a kind of consultative body in addition to, though not equal with, the European Parliament. So far, however, the Committee of the Regions is a very weak institution, hopelessly heterogeneous and ineffective, the very embodiment of regional inequality in Europe. What is urgently needed for it to become an elective institution is the right to institute proceedings against the decisions of other institutions as far as the principle of subsidiarity and regional matters are concerned, the right to be heard in all decisions relating to environment, vocational education and the information society, the right to put questions to the commission with regard to regional affairs and, last but not least, to have an organisational basis of its own.

Generally speaking, the regional structure of the European Union is still in flux, and, in my view, it is still unclear what the final outcome will be. What will European regions be like when inequality is no longer the most fitting word for their general characterisation? In such an open situation, particular specimens of the category of European regions might prove influential and set a reference point for those who are hoping to increase their importance because the legal status and the political influence of certain regions could be considered as the apex of regional development. You may already guess that I'm referring to the position of the States or *Länder* in the Federal Republic of Germany. And I do hope that you are not going to regard this as an expression of German nationalism if I now say a few words about their rights and responsibilities, because this might have an impact on future developments in other parts of Europe. Let me first remind you that in the German language federalism does not mean centralism. Quite the contrary, federalism in Germany means to keep the power of the central or national government at the lowest possible level. Federalism in this sense has very deep roots in German history. The German emperors and kings of the Middle Ages had not been able to centralise power in their hands for a long time, in contrast to the kings in France and England. After the end of the Thirty Years' War in 1648 the German princes and the few free cities were in fact the real powers in the Holy Roman Empire of the German Nation till it collapsed in 1806. The German Confederation which was set up after Napoleon had been finally defeated had the explicit aim of protecting and preserving the sovereignty of the individual German states against liberals and democrats who were striving for national unity. In the end, national unity did not come about as a liberal democracy, but as an alliance of princes under Prussian leadership. But this German Empire too, which had been forged by Bismarck, was a federation. The first German republic, well known as the Weimar Republic, was also a federation. In fact there were only two periods in history when a centralised state was set up in Germany and any trace of federalism was eradicated. These were the dictatorship of Adolf Hitler and his so-called National Socialist Party from 1933 to 1945, and from 1952 till 1990 in the GDR, when the traditional *Länder* were abolished under communist rule. I do not want to imply that Fascism and Communism are identical twins. In fact, during the German revolution of 1848 Karl Marx had already proposed to follow the French example of the one and indivisible republic, because he thought that only in this way would democracy have a chance against the reactionary princes, who in fact retained their power. But in spite of this necessary historical differentiation, it is obvious that these two historical episodes created a solid barrier of suspicion in Germany against any kind of centralised government. Today there is practically nobody in German politics who demands or even considers the abolition of the federal structure. It would be of no avail, anyway, as the federal principle, together with human rights, has been enshrined in the German constitution as immutable.

The German states thus come before the German Federal Government, the *Bund*, both historically and constitutionally. Nevertheless, as probably in most federations, the central government is quite strong, not only because a number of important fields such as foreign affairs and defence are its prerogatives and because of its strong position in the all-German taxation system, but because it is usually much more effective in dealing with the needs of the society than 16 state governments can ever hope to be. Nevertheless, their constitutional competence is quite large. Police, education and culture are their exclusive domains. Other fields such as social welfare and research are the joint responsibility of the federation and the states. The representatives of the states or, to put it more precisely, of the governments of the states, form the federal council or *Bundesrat*, the upper house of the Federal Republic of Germany which has quite a strong position in the federal legislature. One major reason for the difficulties of the present German government under Chancellor Helmut Kohl is the fact that - in contrast to the situation in the lower house, the *Bundestag* - he has no majority in the *Bundesrat*.

Although foreign affairs and international relations are federal domains, the governments of the German states are also active in this field. All of them have representation in Brussels, though without diplomatic status, and most of them cultivate relations with certain foreign states and with some European regions. The question is whether the privileged position of the German states will motivate and encourage other European regions, at least those regions which have already some state or state-like functions, to aspire to the same position as the German states? The German pattern may well have had some influence on developments in Spain and Belgium, but I am also convinced that the internal forces in these countries calling for a regionalisation of the national state were much more important for the development towards a federal structure. When some weeks ago I was in the French region of Brittany, which is Saxony's partner, I got the impression that, despite the very distinct character of this old cultural landscape and the outspoken pride taken in their own history, including some anti-centralist resentment, the representatives of the region seemed much more interested in being involved in decision-finding at every stage of the political system, that is, at the local, the regional *and* the national level, than in the clear separation of different fields of competence. Sharing power, so characteristic of France, seems to be more attractive to them than having only their own portion.

At this point I should like to turn briefly to Saxony as an example of regional inequality in the European Union. Let me start with a few words of introduction: Saxony must be a confusing name to people outside Germany. You may be familiar with Lower Saxony (*Niedersachsen*), as it was already one of the *Länder* of the Federal Republic of Germany before 1990. Since Niedersachsen is situated in the North of Germany, it is quite close to Britain - not only geographically, but also economically and even mentally. In fact, Lower Saxony was created in 1946 by the British Military Government, which united four smaller *Länder* or provinces in the then British Zone of Germany to form one larger *Land*. Until then there had never been a state called Lower Saxony in German history. Possibly some British officers had a faint recollection that the Angles and Saxons, Germanic tribes who in the fifth century invaded and conquered England or rather the then Roman Province of Britannia - had come from Northern Germany. So much for Lower Saxony.

The Saxony I come from is situated in the South East of Germany and until 1990 it was part of the GDR. In 1952, Saxony was abolished together with the other East German *Länder*, as I've already mentioned, because the Communists wanted the GDR to be a centralised state. A strong feeling of regional identity, however, survived the decades of communist rule, so that in 1989 it soon became one of the demands of the peaceful revolution to reconstitute the former East German *Länder* as member states of the Federal Republic. Accordingly, the last People's Chamber of the GDR, the only parliament of this state which had arisen from free and democratic elections, decided to reestablish the original five *Länder* in East Germany. Elections were held for the five regional parliaments, the *Landtage*, on 14th October 1990.

But history is not a matter of a few years or decades, and if we neglect the comparatively short period from 1952 to 1990, Saxony can be regarded as one of the oldest states in Germany. The preamble to the present Saxon Constitution, which was adopted in 1992, locates the origin of the State of Saxony in the Meissen Marches set up by the German King Henry I and his son, the Emperor Otto the Great, in the years 929 to 936. You may ask why a region which originally was called Meissen is now referred to as Saxony. Like almost everything which seems strange and puzzling, this can be explained historically. Originally, the seat of the Dukes of Saxony had been near or in the city of Braunschweig, which some of you may know from English history as Brunswick (the city and the region of Brunswick are now part of Lower Saxony). In 1423, as the result of a long and complicated story whose detail I shall spare you, the German Emperor Sigismund gave the title, the position and the land of the Dukes of Saxony to the Margraves of Meissen. And since in the order of aristocratic ranks, a duke is higher than a margrave, all the territories ruled by this prince and his successors became to be regarded as Saxony. In the course of the following centuries, Saxony was reduced to its present size and lost all territories in Northern Germany, so that, ironically, only those parts were left which five hundred years ago were not called Saxony. It was this Saxony which in the beginning of the 19th century, when the Holy Roman Empire of German Nation fell apart, was made a kingdom by Napoleon. The Kingdom of Saxony was at first independent but later became one of the states of the united Germany set up as the result of Bismarck's policy. The revolution of 1918, that is, at the end of the First World War, turned Saxony into a republic or "free state", as one of the states, of course, of the Weimar Republic. This is now once again its official name: *The Free State of Saxony*.

Why do I try to condense a very long and highly complicated story into a few sentences? What is the relevance for our topic? It shows, I think, that Saxony has played an historical role of her own for more than one thousand years and that for a few centuries Saxony was a factor in European politics. People in Saxony are still aware of old historical and cultural ties with other European countries and regard their country less as a border region of Germany than as a bridge to Central and South East Europe. Today, this "bridge" function particularly pertains to our neighbourhood with the Czech Republic and with Poland. The contacts with the Czech republic are especially close and also have their origins in history.

Historically, Saxony consists of two parts - the Meissen Marches and Lusatia. Lusatia was once a crown land of the Kingdom of Bohemia, which is today the Czech Republic. In 1635 Lusatia was given to the Duke of Saxony as a security. In effect it became a hereditary property of the Duke of Saxony, but it was not until 1831, when the first Saxon Constitution was adopted, that the legal difference between the two parts of the country was abolished. Of course this history is no longer of any immediate importance, but over the centuries many cultural and economic relations developed. Hitler's annexation of Czechoslovakia in 1938/39 and the expulsion of the Germans from Czechoslovakia in 1945/46 meant a radical break in history, but slowly new ties have grown. In fact, already in the seventies and eighties, during the time of the GDR, people in Dresden felt closer to Prague than to East Berlin, their capital.

There were also close historical ties between Saxony and Poland, particularly between 1697 and 1763, when the Dukes of Saxony were elected Kings of Poland, often in rivalry with other European princes. The best known and most popular of the Saxon Kings of Poland was Augustus the Strong, a highly talented, well-educated and recklessly ambitious personality, a man of incredible physical strength and famous not least for his numerous mistresses. In Dresden you can still admire a golden monument showing him on a horse and with all his titles "Duke of Saxony, Elector and Archmarshal of the Holy Roman Empire, King of Poland". And in Warsaw you can still see the ruins of the Saxon Palace destroyed during the Second World War which is now houses the memorial to the unknown soldier. At the time of the Polish-Saxon Union, a Polish nobleman established an academy dedicated to the study of Polish literature in Leipzig, which together with Dresden, the capital, is the most famous city in Saxony. The academy still exists and is older than the Saxon Academy of Arts and Sciences. And in the 19th century Dresden was a place for Polish refugees whose names you can still find in the Old Catholic Cemetery. As a result of the terrible crimes committed in Poland after Hitler's attack, the expulsion of the Germans from the former East German territories and the expulsion of Polish people from the former East Polish territories following the displacement of Poland on the European map after the Second World War, a relationship which had been growing for centuries seemed destroyed for ever. Yet more than fifty years after the most terrible catastrophe in European history, new ties have been knit. This year, the 300th anniversary of the beginning of the Polish-Saxon Union was celebrated officially by a brilliant exhibition in Warsaw and by an outstanding historical conference in Dresden.

Since 1990 the Free State of Saxony, as a member state of the Federal Republic of Germany, has continued to develop a close cooperation with Poland and the Czech Republic. This has been done both at the governmental and the local level. The Premier of Saxony has repeatedly visited Prague and Warsaw for talks with the Presidents of the Republic and the Prime Ministers there, and contacts between the ministries have meanwhile become a matter of course. If this cooperation is placed in a European context, both in its historical and in its contemporary dimensions, then Saxony's present role is certainly part of the emerging regional structure of the European Union, but it cannot simply be reduced to that level. I should add that Saxony's activities are by no means unique among the German states. At the same time it must be emphasised that the international activities of the German states are restricted to those domains in which they exercise responsibilities of their own, i.e. in the fields of economy and culture in the broadest sense of the word. For specific activities in these fields, particularly for those on both sides of a border, a cover term has been coined which must be mentioned in any discussion of regional inequality in present-day Europe. It is the term "Euroregion", which will certainly add to the confusion about what a region in Europe really is. Euroregions are certainly not areas or divisions with definite boundaries or characteristics. I would define a *euroregion* as a working formula for promoting and organising local cooperation by means of joint efforts and projects. The term is vague, but highly useful. Meanwhile we and our partners have established four so-called euroregions to promote economic and cultural cooperation between towns and districts in the border areas of Saxony, in the Northern Bohemian areas of the Czech republic and in the Silesian areas of Poland. There are no regional institutions, but there is a local network constituting a region of practical cooperation and, more or less regularly, there are definite regional activities. The advantage is that many common tasks in immediately adjacent towns and districts can best be done by the people who are responsible at the local level without involving the ministries in the capitals, provided, of course, the local representatives have been given the necessary legal competence to act. Both the Polish and the Czech Republics remain centralised states, following both their socialist heritage and their long standing admiration for the French model of state administration. I assume that there is still a remnant of suspicion in Warsaw and Prague that the German partner, even if represented only by local mayors, could still be too powerful and too dangerous for the Polish and Czech border areas. We do not complain, accepting that more time is needed to overcome the bitter experience of a catastrophic past.

From an East German point of view, both German federalism and European regionalism provide an opportunity to secure political domains which are decided by the East Germans themselves, to gain some influence on all-German and European affairs and to reduce the danger of being treated as an appendix to West Germany forever. One might describe the East German states as a kind of shelter for a poor minority, and there is some temptation to interpret East German regionalism as the attitude of economic underdogs. But I do not believe that this provides a really convincing explanation. The most characteristic expression of regional identity in Germany, both in East and in West, is pride in one's own cultural heritage, the cultivation of its particular traditions and, quite generally, a feeling of belonging to the region. It is unlikely that this will decrease if Saxony succeeds, as we hope, in again becoming a leading industrial region, just as Bavarian identity certainly did not dissipate when their land, which was once poor, became rich.

I have tried to show that in the European Union an intermediate, "regional" level is emerging between the national level which, notwithstanding the great advances made towards European unity, is still the basis of political responsibility and political decision-making, and the local level, at which, more or less spontaneously, a loose network of contacts has been knit. Regions are highly heterogeneous in status, character and stability. They range from member states of federations which are constituents of the European Union to administrative divisions of centralised states and even to working formulas and cover terms for local cooperation across political borders in vaguely defined areas. The question remains: what will be the importance of the regional concept in future? Considering the fact that regional and national tasks and domains overlap in Europe, one could ask more precisely: which will be more important in the European Union of tomorrow - the national states or the regions?

To the member states of the Federal Republic of Germany this is a vital question. Almost every week, the Saxon Government has to decide whether our representatives in the German *Bundesrat* should approve or reject a new regulation proposed by the European Commission in Brussels. Such regulations clearly restrict the range of possible national decisions in the future. Who will decide on the rest - the federal government or the governments of the states? It is difficult to imagine that Germany will not be represented on the European level by her national government. But it is certainly in the interest of peace and political balance in Europe that Germany continues to have a federal structure. So both layers of power will survive, but which of the two sides will be the winner or the loser of the consequences of European unity in Germany - the federation or the states? The weakness of the latter lies in the inequality of their partners - their partners in Germany and their partners in Europe. The sixteen German states differ widely in their economic strength and financial stability, ranging from those with the size and population of a medium European country like Bavaria or North Rhine-Westfalia to cities such as Hamburg and Bremen. The worst mistake we made in East Germany after 1989 was to restore the five *Länder* of 1952, instead of establishing only two which would have had the potential to become stable and successful in a foreseeable future. Unfortunately it has proved enormously difficult, if not impossible, to unite German *Länder* into larger units. Two of the larger new states owe their existence to the political wisdom of Britain as one of the occupation powers in postwar Germany - Lower Saxony and North Rhine-Westfalia. One came into existence as the result of a plebiscite, namely Baden-Württemberg. A recent attempt to unite Berlin and Brandenburg by a plebiscite was not successful, although Brandenburg surrounds Berlin and both were parts of the former Prussia.

Regional inequality is much greater in the New Germany than it was in the old Federal Republic. The five East German states have increased the number of those *Länder* which are dependent on financial contributions from the richer ones. In the early seventies, when there was a steady growth in prosperity, it was decided to set up a unified taxation system which provides compensation for those states whose tax revenue is below the national average. As a result of German unification, the burden on the richer states has risen considerably. In fact, two of them, Bavaria and Baden-Württemberg, have decided to go to court because, as they see it, they are punished for their successful economic management, while others are not obliged to reduce their public expenditure. There is some truth in this argument, although one should not forget that, when it was one of the poorer states with a predominantly agricultural structure, Bavaria itself profited greatly from the principle that there should be equal living conditions all over Germany.

So the German states which seem the backbone of European regionalism are not as strong as they look. At the same time there is little reason to hope that in the near future all or most of the member states of the European Union will develop a coherent regional or federal structure with an essential share in political decision-making. Inequality will remain a conspicuous feature of European regions. It is thus my view that in the relationship between nation and region, the nation will continue to be the decisive factor in the political life of the European Union. This seems to be true for the challenges of globalisation and individualisation as well. We can see at the moment how in times of economic instability and social unrest people in the countries of the European Union direct their attention and their expectations to their national governments rather than to any other political authority. Yet the regions, despite and even because of their inequality, present our most important challenge, because it is at the regional level that the conditions for the economic and cultural cohesion of the European Union must be created. And without economic and cultural cohesion there will be no stable European Union.

Note

[*]   Hans Joachim Meyer, Professor of English at the Humboldt University in Berlin and a member of the GDR delegation which negotiated the German Unification Treaty, is now State Minister for Higher Education, Research and Culture in the Saxon State Government.

V

REFRACTIONS

15 Europhobia in the New Tory Historiography*

ANDREW BONNELL

The contemporary debate on European integration is still prey to distortions through the deployment of outdated national stereotypes and, in the case of some British Conservatives, an insularity arising from nostalgia for lost greatness, which is manifest in some recent controversies over British history. There is insufficient space in this chapter to provide a comprehensive survey of works which might be included under the rubric of the "new Tory historiography". Nor do I wish to argue that such works constitute a wholly consistent body of thought on Britain's past (any more than there is a united Conservative view on European integration). It is also outside the scope of this chapter to canvass in detail the merits of the political and economic arguments advanced by British Conservative Eurosceptics, many of which may have a rational basis. Instead, this chapter will focus on the latent "Europhobia" which manifested itself in the controversy around John Charmley's 1992 revisionist biography of Churchill (*Churchill: The End of Glory*). Following an examination of this controversy, Charmley's Churchill biography will be considered in the context of his not inconsiderable *œuvre*, and in relation to the broader context of "new Tory historiography".

The bold syntheses of Marxian and radical British historians of the 1960s have been followed by a period of scholarly revisionism in fields such as the English Civil War, the Industrial Revolution and the emergence of working-class radicalism.[1] To take just one example, Jonathan Clark's work on English society from 1688 to 1832 might be viewed as (at least in part) an "Anti-E.P. Thompson", stressing the socially cohesive properties of Anglicanism and deference where Thompson saw plebeian radicalism and nascent class consciousness.[2] Some of the revisionist historiography has been the product of the normal academic business, in a time of specialisation and professionalisation in historical research, of modifying big pictures by insisting on more carefully detailed studies (and, perhaps, of the PhD industry's propensity to slice salami ever thinner). This trend has shown itself in what Perry Anderson characterises as "the reassertion of the particular and the piecemeal, the contingent and the episodic".[3] Or, as David Cannadine put it in 1987, "British historians today are mainly concerned to show that less happened, less dramatically, than was once thought".[4]

What Anderson describes as a "historiographic backlash" against both Marxian and Whig traditions of historical explanation,[5] has clearly had an ideological and political aspect in addition to the usual processes of scholarly revision and contestation. Despite the shrill Philistinism of Thatcherism, and Margaret Thatcher's apparent suspicion of intellectuals, the history of England and of Britain was clearly an ideological battleground to which the Conservative government (and Margaret Thatcher personally) attached great importance, as shown by the drive for a revised national history curriculum.[6] The right sort of history curriculum was supposed to foster patriotism and national cohesion, and, at the same time, an "enterprise culture".

British history constituted an ideological resource which could be mobilised at times of actual or putative national emergency. During the Falklands War, Margaret Thatcher drew encouragement from the fact that Chequers, Churchill's wartime residence, "played a large part in the Falklands story", as the location for important talks and planning meetings: "Churchill had used it quite a lot during the Second World War and its atmosphere helped to get us all together".[7] In February 1985, Margaret Thatcher took a bronze statue of Churchill with her to Washington to stiffen the resolve of the Western Alliance, when she went to express her support for Ronald Reagan's Strategic Defence Initiative in an address to the US Congress.[8]

Considering Winston Churchill's career as a political maverick, his posthumous status as a Conservative icon might seem odd. However, the way in which he powerfully epitomised a patriotic nation united in resistance to the threat of Nazi tyranny was of considerable utility to post-war Conservatives not least for the way in which this image eclipsed the memory of the less than inspiring response of mainstream conservatives to the rise of Hitler in the 1930s. By the 1990s, however, Churchill's legacy as the standard-bearer of the wartime consensus and the broad welfarist consensus of the post-war period in Britain was increasingly coming under question on both the foreign-policy and the domestic front, even if right-leaning historians preferred the label "Butskell consensus" to "Churchill consensus".[9] Correlli Barnett, for example, concentrated his fire on the "'enlightened' Establishment" of middle-class do-gooders and intellectual mandarins, whom he did not scruple to rank with Adolf Hitler in the class of "romantic fantasist[s]",[10] while identifying Churchill himself and his "bulldog personality" with the struggle for national survival and subsequent attempts at re-asserting British national interests.[11] Ultimately, though, if Churchill is not personally singled out for criticism in Barnett's book, his wartime coalition government is harshly censured. Following on the controversy over Martin J. Wiener's *English Culture and the Decline of the Industrial Spirit 1850-1980*,[12] Barnett's polemic was something of a tract for Thatcherite times, with its call for a more positive orientation towards "enterprise culture" on the part of British cultural élites echoing similar exhortations from Sir Keith Joseph in the mid-1980s.[13] In turn, Barnett's *Audit of War* was invoked by the then Chancellor of the Exchequer Nigel Lawson "as a major source of authority for his fiscal and social policies".[14]

As 1993 dawned, with Prime Minister John Major promising a "new era of Thatcherite prosperity", after "what he admitted had been a miserable year for many",[15] and with the Treaty of Maastricht causing continuing division among the governing Conservatives, a review by former Minister of State for the Ministry of Defence, Alan Clark, of a new biography of Winston Churchill sparked off a spirited controversy over the Churchill legacy, with the focus on the latter's foreign rather than domestic policy, and his achievements as Britain's war leader. Alan Clark had been a military historian of some note, with well-regarded books on the failure of British generalship in the 1915 Western Front campaigns (*The Donkeys*) and on the campaigns on the Eastern Front in the Second World War (*Barbarossa*), before his political career took him to a position in the Thatcher government and a more recent publishing success as a famously indiscreet diarist. A loyal Thatcher lieutenant to the last, Alan Clark had visited his Prime Minister on the eve of her involuntary retirement in November 1990 to urge her to go down in a "Wagnerian ending" fighting the "nonentities" besieging her.[16] Not long after her fall, Alan Clark had speculated in his diary that John Charmley, who then had books on Duff Cooper, Lord Lloyd and Neville Chamberlain to his credit, might be a suitable ghost writer for the Thatcher memoirs.[17]

Clark hailed Charmley's *Churchill: The End of Glory* as "probably the most important revisionist text published since the war".[18] Clark's review began by describing the situation of Britain in May 1940, just after Churchill became Prime Minister, when Churchill rejected Lord Halifax's suggestion that Mussolini be "bought off" with concessions.[19] Clark suggested that Churchill's "single-minded determination to keep the war going" was a reflection of the extent to which his political career had become dependent on opposition to Hitler, rather than being dictated by the national interests of Britain. According to Clark: "There were several occasions when a rational leader could have got first reasonable, then excellent, terms from Germany", such as July 1940, before the Battle of Britain, on terms which were "still available, now weighted more in Britain's favour" after the air battle, and again in spring, 1941, when Hess flew to Britain before Operation Barbarossa commenced. Churchill's persistence in ignoring German peace offers led him to ignore the defence of Singapore, costing Britain her Far Eastern empire, and also necessitated "the abasement of Britain before the United States". The fruits of Churchill's ultimate victory were that at the end of the war, "the country was bust... The old social order had gone forever. The empire was terminally damaged...". For Clark, it was a sign of the docility of the Conservative Party that "to assert these facts has been heresy".[20]

The Clark review was followed by media reports of reactions by historians. Martin Gilbert, author of the multi-volume "official" biography of Churchill, found "nothing new" in Charmley's book, and argued: "You can't argue that the Nazis were not as bad as was thought at the time. If anything they were worse. Given what was known then, which was pretty comprehensive, there was no way a British government could have made peace with Nazi Germany without being overthrown."[21] Ben Pimlott concurred, pointing out that "Churchill was made prime minister by the House of Commons because it felt that the war was not being prosecuted with sufficient vigour".[22] The biographer of Lord Halifax, Andrew Roberts, found Charmley's work "a very important revisionist book", but was unconvinced by its thesis.[23]

While the initial scholarly response was hardly dramatic, *The Times* kept the story going with a full-page spread on page 5, three days after the Clark review, under the title "Could Churchill have stopped the war?". *The Times* proclaimed that "John Charmley's revisionist biography of Winston Churchill has shattered the scholarly consensus and broken taboos... Never has a work of historical revisionism upset so many in so short a time."[24] Interviewed for the article, Charmley distanced himself somewhat from Clark's claim that Churchill should have made peace with Hitler, although he maintained that "Churchill's obsession with Hitler" was "a grave error", and claimed that after the invasion of the Soviet Union in June 1941, British diplomacy could have induced Hitler to withdraw from Western Europe. Among the benefits of a peace settlement in the West, in Charmley's view, would have been the reinforcement of "the position of the traditional ruling class", and such a peace "would not have allowed the egalitarian emphasis to develop".[25] In the days that followed, *The Times* published excerpts from Charmley's book, an editorial, more responses by other historians, and another interview with Charmley, along with a stream of letters to the editor. While professing neutrality as far as Charmley's claims were concerned, the *Times* editorial praised the nature of the revisionist enterprise as "cathartic", noting that "all history has an agenda" and is inextricable from "present politics".[26] Not surprisingly, Winston Churchill's defenders in the dispute included a number of Conservative politicians, including his eponymous descendant (and Sir Nicholas Fairbairn, MP, who described Alan Clark as a "goon".)[27]

The controversy did not confine itself to the pages of *The Times*. *The Guardian* ran a critical article by Norman Stone, which was more of a response to Alan Clark than a review of Charmley.[28] Other critical responses included those by Robert Rhodes James in the *Times Literary Supplement* (expanding on criticisms he had already expressed in the columns of *The Times*), who argued that however many mistakes Churchill made before 1939, his instinct to resist Hitler in 1940 without compromise was fundamentally correct;[29] Richard Lamb in *The Spectator*;[30] Edward Luttwak in the *London Review of Books*, who seemed highly bemused by British idolatry of Churchill, but still thought Charmley wrong about Churchill's decision to fight on after Dunkirk;[31] and Noel Annan in *The New York Review of Books*, who regarded Charmley's book and the "twaddle" by Alan Clark which it had excited as falling outside the category of "serious revisionist history".[32] In due course, and with due delay, the reverberations of the debate reached the academic journals. The most energetically hostile assessment of the views on Churchill of Alan Clark and John Charmley that I have so far encountered has been in a recent review article by Robin Prior and Trevor Wilson, who had been supplied with fresh ammunition by Clark's and Charmley's reiteration of their views in a 1995 television panel discussion marking the fiftieth anniversary of the end of the Second World War.[33]

As has often been the case with recent historical controversies fought out in the public arena, the net gain in historical knowledge seems to have been small. One is therefore led to enquire how much substance there is in Charmley's work, as well as why it enjoyed such considerable attention (apart from Alan Clark's evident talent for attracting notoriety).

Charmley was not the first "revisionist" biographer of Winston Churchill, and he will certainly not be the last. (Indeed, 1994 saw the publication of Clive Ponting's revisionist Churchill biography, which

Andrew Roberts branded as libellous.)[34] Robert Rhodes James' study of Churchill's career up to 1939, to name perhaps the first major example of the genre, dates from 1970.[35] In his treatment of Churchill's career before the outbreak of the Second World War, Charmley acknowledges Rhodes James' influence. His book also followed Martin Gilbert's multi-million word monument to Churchill, and Charmley admits being indebted to the "quarry" which Gilbert's volumes constitute for the Churchill scholar, a debt which is readily apparent on a perusal of Charmley's end-notes (although Gilbert has complained that these notes employ "a rarely used bibliographical device that causes him to omit my name!").[36] While Charmley also displays evidence of great industry in his researches in the published and unpublished papers of Churchill and his contemporaries, readers would be entitled to be sceptical as to whether yet another large tome on Churchill could have all that much to say that could be new.[37] As far as interpretation is concerned, Charmley's reading of appeasement largely follows Maurice Cowling's 1975 work *The Impact of Hitler*, Cowling having since become the doyen of the "Peterhouse school" of conservative revisionism. (Cowling's influence has not been confined to the cloisters of the University: his former students and political contacts include prominent Eurosceptic Tory Michael Portillo.)[38]

As Rhodes James indicated in one of his responses to Charmley's book, its coverage of issues is sometimes haphazard.[39] The reader seeking, for example, systematic treatment of Churchill's social policies would be better served by Paul Addison's work on the subject, which appeared just before Charmley's book.[40] A major collection of essays edited by Robert Blake and Wm. Roger Louis, based on the proceedings of a conference in Texas in 1991, appeared not long afterwards, illustrating the range of opinions and intellectual concerns in the field of Churchill studies.[41] For Richard Lamb, author of a critical study of Churchill as war leader, neither Charmley's biography nor the Blake and Louis collection contained much new material, but he found the latter "the more important and the better buy".[42]

At the height of the controversy started by Alan Clark, Charmley observed that he had not gone as far in his book as Clark had.[43] One can certainly find Clark's arguments in Charmley's book, but they are not always developed systematically. For example, Charmley devotes considerable space to discussions in the War Cabinet from 26 to 28 May 1940 over Halifax's proposal to explore the possibility of peace talks, and Churchill's address to the wider cabinet on 28 May ("perhaps the most crucial meeting of 1940") in which he managed to "polarise the issue in a way which made Halifax's suggestions for exploring the possibilities of a negotiated peace look defeatist".[44] Charmley raises the question of a negotiated peace with Hitler again in discussing (what appear to have been) indirect Foreign Office peace feelers in mid-June 1940 and calling Churchill's judgement in resolving to fight on into question, on the grounds that it was based on an "over-optimistic" assessment of underlying German weakness.[45] At the end of July 1940, Lloyd George outlined what Charmley calls "a compelling case" for discussing terms with Hitler once the brunt of the Battle of Britain had been withstood. The principal reason for this view, one which Charmley strongly endorses, was that the price of eventual American assistance in the war would prove to be the bankruptcy of Britain and the loss of the Empire.[46] Charmley does not go into the question of what peace terms would have been available to Britain at this time, however. Instead, he harps on the irony of the old imperialist Churchill presiding over the "liquidation of the British Empire" in his attempt to buy American aid, remarking: "Ironically, the posture of stern, heroic defiance of Germany could be purchased only by the most servile grovelling to the Americans".[47] Charmley does concede elsewhere that it "was certainly better be an American rather than a German protectorate", but he declines to expand on this insight.[48]

In Charmley's view, Churchill "let slip" another "opportunity" to rethink Britain's position with Hitler's invasion of the Soviet Union,[49] preceded as it was by Rudolf Hess' flight to Britain. Oddly, Charmley mentions the Hess flight only briefly, with no attempt at analysing what the flight meant as far as the Nazi regime was concerned. He does, however, express the view that "Churchill would have been well-advised to have profited from the Russian uncertainty" to which it gave rise.[50] Precisely what Churchill might have gained from feeding the paranoia of Stalin, who was suspicious of the West at the best of times, is not spelt out. In the light of the Alan Clark controversy, the lack of detail Charmley provides about the terms which might have been available to Britain, and the lack of consideration given to the deliberations on the German side, is disappointing.

After the Nazi occupation of the remnant of the Czech lands in March 1939, even Chamberlain, in Charmley's account, believed that Hitler was not to be trusted. This objection to the suggestion that deals could still have been struck with the Nazi regime in 1940 or 1941 is not dealt with in Charmley's *Churchill*. In the course of the post-Clark debate, Charmley suggested that it might have made sense to have cultivated Göring and other "non-ideological Nazis", and to follow a "line of diplomacy which would have detached Hitler from his chieftains".[51] Again, this suggestion is not substantiated in the work itself, with only one oblique reference to Göring appearing in the text.[52] Nowhere does Charmley have anything substantial to say about the nature and inner workings of the régime which Churchill rightly saw as threatening to inaugurate a "new dark ages" in Europe. Charmley's critics are on firmer ground in pointing to the consequences of German occupation for Nazi-occupied Europe. Such an argument does not rest solely on hindsight: there was plenty of detailed and accurate information about the nature of the Nazi occupation in Poland and elsewhere available at the time.[53] Charmley refuses to let contemplation of the plight of the peoples suffering under the Nazi New Order (including, of course, many Germans) to spoil his central thesis: that the "liquidation of the British Empire" was too high a price to pay for Churchill's "finest hour".

At this point, it is worth giving some consideration to Charmley's other works. His works prior to *Churchill* show the extent to which he was on the way to becoming a prominent Conservative biographer and historian (and a potential candidate to become the Thatcher administration's historian laureate), while his subsequent books have continued to reflect his preoccupation with the loss of Empire and Britain's loss of primacy to America.

Having written his Oxford D.Phil. on British policy towards de Gaulle, John Charmley was well qualified to write the authorised biography of Duff Cooper, Churchill's ambassador to de Gaulle, who is perhaps best remembered as having been one of the first British politicians in the 1930s "to sound the tocsin about the dangers of Nazism".[54] It is a breezily narrated book, which evinces warm sympathy for the Francophile diplomat, author and politician Duff Cooper. In 1986, Charmley warmly praised Duff Cooper for having had the "distinction" and "the honour of having been one of the first to point out the menace of Hitler".[55] In contrast, the pro-appeasement *Times* had "a disgraceful record of pandering to Hitler's Germany". Duff Cooper "had been right when it had been wrong".[56]

Towards the end of the Second World War, Cooper was an advocate of a strong Anglo-French alliance as a step towards a Western European Union, but found himself struggling against Churchill's and de Gaulle's outbreaks of mutual animosity, and against the Foreign Office's caution lest suspicion be aroused on the part of either the United States or the Soviet Union. Although an Anglo-French treaty did eventuate in early 1947, Cooper remained disappointed at what he saw as the historic failure of the Foreign Office to grasp the opportunity of having Britain take a leading role in the movement towards Western European Union.[57] Almost as ardent a Germanophobe as he was a Francophile, Cooper saw an Anglo-French alliance as a safeguard against any resurgence of German power, and also as a basis for a new role for Britain. Charmley quotes Cooper as writing to Ernest Bevin, in October 1947:

> Britain has now become part of the Continent of Europe, and she has to decide whether she will place herself at the head of a confederation of Western democracies or whether she will become a satellite of the United States.[58]

By 1949, Cooper was writing that Britain had lost the opportunity to exercise hegemony in Europe, where Britain's future lay.[59]

Charmley's Duff Cooper biography was quickly followed by another authorised biography of one of Churchill's contemporaries, George, Lord Lloyd, imperial proconsul in India (as Governor of Bombay) and Egypt, and Colonial Secretary in Churchill's first wartime cabinet. This work was written, originally at Lloyd's son's request, out of Charmley's "long-standing interest in the imperialist wing of the Conservative party", and set out to challenge the stereotypes propagated by "left-wing polemicists".[60] Charmley argued that "Lloyd's imperial vision" was more prescient than the views of his Whiggish adversaries, and of most historians, in seeing that "without her Empire Britain must become a small overpopulated island off the coast of Europe which would soon be impoverished and of little account in world affairs".[61] Charmley defended Lloyd against the charge of being a "die-hard" imperialist, while presenting events from Lloyd's point of view, which included the belief that Indians "are children and must be treated as such..."[62] and a belief in "the fundamental unsuitability of modern western democratic methods of government to any Oriental people".[63] While the book is based on impressive research in British official papers and the private papers of Lloyd and others, there is scant use of sources depicting either Indian or Egyptian nationalism from any perspective other than Lloyd's, a perspective apparently shared by Charmley, who characterises Gandhi, for example, as a "pestilential" nuisance.[64]

In his opposition to any form of Indian self-government, Lord Lloyd had an ally in Churchill. Interestingly, in his later assault on Churchill's reputation, Charmley tends to take a more sympathetic view of Churchill's stubborn defence of British rule in India than of Churchill's position on other issues (to the point of suggesting parallels between "appeasement" of Hitler and "appeasement" of Gandhi).[65] Lloyd also concurred with Churchill in advocating British rearmament in the 1930s. He regarded the Munich agreement as a national dishonour,[66] but avoided breaking with Neville Chamberlain personally. Charmley suggests that the way in which Chamberlain made use of Lloyd as an unofficial envoy in the Balkans and elsewhere, while serving as chairman of the British Council, should be seen as showing that there was an "element of steel" in Chamberlain's foreign policy, and not solely "conciliation or appeasement".[67]

It was Neville Chamberlain who furnished the subject for Charmley's next work, and the basis for further reflection on the fate of the British Empire. Compared with the evaluation of appeasement and the Munich agreement evident especially in *Duff Cooper*, the book on Chamberlain reflected, in Charmley's own words, "a change of mind".[68] The official biographer of Duff Cooper had endorsed Cooper's insistence, when he resigned after the Munich conference, that Britain had fought in 1914, as in previous wars against Napoleon Bonaparte, Louis XIV, and Philip II, "in order that one great Power should not be allowed, in disregard of treaty obligation, of the laws of nations and the decrees of morality, to dominate by brutal force the Continent of Europe", as a definitive "statement of the classic principle of traditional British foreign policy".[69] The revisionist chronicler of Neville Chamberlain and the "lost peace", a few years later, distinguished between "two schools of thought on British foreign policy: the cosmopolitan and the insular", the former school being represented by well-travelled, and often Francophile, figures such as Cooper, Churchill, Lloyd, and others.[70] Chamberlain, Lord Halifax, and most Conservatives, had "a more insular cast of mind".[71] It is with this latter, more "insular" approach that Charmley clearly sympathises, arguing that Chamberlain's policy leading up to the Munich conference was the only realistic course to pursue in the light of what Chamberlain knew about the political and economic realities, especially the limits of the British Empire's resources in the 1930s.

Unfortunately, the insularity extends to Charmley's research methods. He draws almost exclusively on sources and literature in English. As with his previous works, he displays considerable knowledge of both government and private papers pertaining to British diplomatic and "high" political history, combined with an apparent absence of curiosity as to how events looked from non-British perspectives.[72] At its best, this method conveys an understanding of how things appeared from Neville Chamberlain's perspective. It does not, however, permit a rounded interpretation of the Munich crisis. If a much earlier re-appraisal of the Munich crisis, A.J.P. Taylor's *Origins of the Second World War*, could be faulted for treating German foreign policy in isolation from Nazi domestic politics or Hitler's racial ideology, such charges can be levelled *a fortiori* at Charmley's work. Charmley does not, for example, give any serious consideration to the potential of the German military resistance to Hitler in 1938. (While it may be a trivial detail, it is symptomatic that the name of almost the only figure connected with this whom Charmley mentions, Ewald von Kleist-Schmenzin, is repeatedly mis-spelt.)[73] Rather, he refers dismissively to "disgruntled Germans" who fed information to the anti-appeasement foreign policy adviser Sir Robert Vansittart.[74] The prospects of the Czechoslovak army offering serious resistance to a German invasion are also brushed aside, without any analysis of either German or Czech sources.[75] In his discussion of Lord Runciman's mission to Czechoslovakia, a diplomatic manoeuvre that from the Czechoslovak point of view was both transparently clumsy in conception and inept in execution, Charmley empathises with Runciman's plight of having to listen "to interminable ramblings by dim nationalist politicians with unpronounceable names and unrealisable objectives".[76] Charmley omits to mention that Runciman was briefed by anti-Nazi Sudeten Germans on the "terroristic methods" used by the Sudeten Nazis to gain control of the German minority and by Jews who feared "annihilation" in the event of incorporation into the Third Reich.[77]

In his work on Chamberlain, Charmley defends the reputation of Nevile Henderson as British ambassador to Berlin, although he does not quote Henderson's fulsome praise for the "great social experiment" of the Third Reich, nor Henderson's view that the German was "certainly more civilised than the Slav, and in the end, if properly handled, also less potentially dangerous to British interests".[78] Charmley repeatedly endorses Henderson's conception of pointing Hitler eastwards, that is, of allowing Hitler to undertake revision of the Versailles Treaty at the expense of Germany's eastern neighbours.[79] As for Chamberlain's reluctant guarantee to Poland, Charmley invokes "[Oswald] Mosley's sensible ideas on foreign policy... why die for Danzig?"[80] Charmley's conclusion is that Chamberlain's policy of appeasement had been "the only policy which offered any hope of avoiding war- and of saving both lives and the British Empire".[81] In other words, the existence of the British Empire could, and should, have been prolonged, even at the cost of Nazi domination of Central and Eastern Europe.

It is instructive to compare Charmley's completely Anglocentric account of the Munich crisis with the recent study by Igor Lukes, based on research in Czech archives, as well as published British, French, German and Soviet documents. Lukes shows Czechoslovakia as an actor in, and not merely an object of, international diplomacy, and even if he is not uncritical of aspects of Edvard Benes's diplomacy, he makes it clear that Benes had fewer illusions about Hitler and the Nazi regime than did Chamberlain.[82] His account of the Czechoslovak mobilisations of May and September 1938 also indicate a formidable defensive capacity and will to resist on the part of the

Czechs.[83] As R. W. Seton-Watson pointed out at the time, Munich deprived the Western powers "of an ally possessed of a highly efficient army of 1,500,000 men and 2,000 planes", and left the munitions factories of Skoda and Vitkovice within easy reach of the Wehrmacht.[84] Seton-Watson's *Munich and the Dictators* appeared before Hitler's occupation of the remaining part of the Czech lands, that is, without the benefit of hindsight. Charmley does not mention Seton-Watson anywhere in either his *Chamberlain* or *Churchill*, apart from a passing reference in the latter,[85] despite the fact that Seton-Watson was, at that time, arguably Britain's leading expert on that part of Europe, whose works offered a compelling contemporary critique of appeasement. In contrast, Charmley can always find space for the views of the ultra-right, pro-fascist MP and socialite Sir Henry "Chips" Channon, "to whom", in Noel Annan's words, "hardly anyone attached much weight".[86]

Charmley has described his works on Chamberlain and Churchill as forming two parts of a "triptych", which was completed by his 1995 *Churchill's Grand Alliance. The Anglo-American Special Relationship 1940-1957*.[87] In his book on Churchill, Charmley had been highly critical of the illusions Churchill had harboured about the unity of the "English-speaking peoples" and about the benefits of his own "special relationship" with Franklin D. Roosevelt. In reality, Americans were "foreigners who disliked the British Empire even more than did Hitler".[88] Charmley repeats the themes of the earlier work, arguing: "In retrospect, the 1930s were to be promoted (not least by Churchill) as a decade of lost opportunities..., in fact, it was a decade in which the last opportunity to save the civilisation of Western Europe was lost",[89] as well as the British Empire, which to Charmley perhaps amounts to the same thing. Again, and at length, Charmley is more critical of Churchill's "appeasement" of the wily and anti-imperialist Roosevelt than of Chamberlain's "appeasement" of Hitler. Again, there is the suggestion that Churchill's fixation with defeating Hitler blinded him to Britain's long term interests and accelerated the loss of Empire. From the perspective of the 1990s: "It was all very odd. The British had fought two world wars to prevent Germany from dominating Europe, and they had still ended up in a German-dominated Europe. They had fought to preserve their independence, but they had lost it all the same."[90] Charmley does not pause to reflect on the difference between the Germany of 1942 and that of 1992. For him, European Union was a product of the "fanciful notions" of men like Paul-Henri Spaak, a failure of national will on the part of the Western European political classes in the 1940s, and self-interested American policy.[91] He praises Anthony Eden for not being (in the words of

Sir Edward Bridges) "misled by the kind of mysticism which appeals to European catholic federalists", unlike Macmillan.[92] Charmley sums up his "central theme" as follows: "that America wanted a compliant, non-imperial Britain as part of a European federation".[93]

Nothing if not prolific, Charmley followed *Churchill's Grand Alliance* with a short history of the Conservative Party in the twentieth century.[94] This somewhat impressionistic narrative is unlikely to replace Robert Blake's account as the standard one-volume history of the party, but it displays some significant differences from Blake's "liberal Conservative" account.[95] In this short but opinionated book, Charmley wears the label "Thatcherite historian" with some pride.[96] The extent of his anti-Europe sentiment is indicated by a hint that as a young Conservative supporter in 1974 he was among those who followed Enoch Powell's advice to vote for Labour as the more "Euro-sceptic" party.[97] His normally flippant style becomes unusually fervent when discussing how Margaret Thatcher embodied "the voice of British nationalism" in her foreign policy (leaving aside the inconvenient question of the extent to which British and English identities increasingly diverged under the impact of her domestic policies).[98] Towards the end of his history, surveying the scene after Thatcher's involuntary departure, he evidently identifies with the faction around John Redwood: the "Tory Likud", as Matthew Parris recently called them. Charmley praises Redwood, the most "Eurosceptic" of Tory leadership contenders, for his "tough-minded realism".[99]

Charmley's works since his book on Chamberlain have been characterised by a revisionist blend of nostalgia for the British Empire, a right-wing Conservative political outlook disdainful of egalitarianism, and a championing of an "insular" interpretation of British foreign policy interests. This last tendency manifests itself in a neglect of continental European historical sources and views which sometimes amounts to a highly developed form of solipsism. Charmley's iconoclasm as far as Winston Churchill is concerned may seem to put him in a somewhat isolated position among Conservatives (other than Alan Clark), but it is possible to see his work as part of a wider right-wing Anglocentric historical revisionist enterprise. Andrew Roberts' *Eminent Churchillians* may have grabbed public attention for its claim that Churchill was racist, as most late-Victorian imperialists were, but it was more concerned with attacking, from a Thatcherite perspective, the "liberal Tory" tradition which followed in Churchill's wake in the 1950s and 1960s for its share in contributing to British decline, not least through "appeasement" - that word again - of the trade unions.[100] Roberts has been perhaps the most notable of the youngest generation of new Tory historians who work as much through political and media connections as through academia, congregating loosely around the *Spectator* and the *Times* and *Sunday Times*, the Murdoch newspapers being important sponsors of Eurosceptic Tory opinion.

Another prominent Conservative revisionist, Jonathan Clark, has been quoted as arguing that revisionism is giving rise to a "more honest patriotism" which will guide Britain in its new relations with Europe and changing relationship with the United States.[101] Jeremy Black's 1994 survey of the history of British-European links, *Convergence or Divergence?* has also been mentioned in this context. This work takes a "Eurosceptic" view of the continued relevance of national identities, although it avoids an essentialising view of the latter, and is rather more carefully reasoned in its reading of the British-European connection than Charmley's works tend to be.

Scepticism is generally a good thing, but it is questionable whether it is the right term for the retailing of outdated national stereotypes which is sometimes practised under that label in discussions of Britain and Europe. The Charmley view that Britain had fought a war to avert German domination of Europe only to succumb to it fifty years later is reminiscent of the utterances of Nicholas Ridley, Secretary for Trade and Industry and a Thatcher confidant, in 1990, describing European Union as "a German racket designed to take over the whole of Europe", and arguing that to give up sovereignty to the European Commission would be equivalent to giving it up to "Adolf Hitler". The media reports on the discussions on "The German Character" held for Margaret Thatcher's benefit in Chequers in March of that year of German unification seem to have reflected the conviction that there was such a thing as a trans-historical national character, which operated regardless of political régime (even if the substance of the actual expert presentations at Chequers did not support this assumption).[102] For the debate on Britain and Europe to advance, a genuinely sceptical and realistic view will have to look beyond out-dated national stereotypes. A solipsistic "insular" historiography, characterised by nostalgia for the days of the Raj, is unlikely to be of much help in this.

Notes

*   My thanks to the participants in the "Britain in Europe" conference, especially Dick Geary, Doug Newton and William Wallace, for their comments and advice, and to Tony Cahill for his reading of the manuscript.

1 See Perry Anderson, "A Culture in Contraflow", in *English Questions*, London/ New York, 1992, pp. 281f..
2 J.C.D. Clark, *English Society 1688-1832*, Cambridge, 1985.
3 Anderson, *op. cit.*, p. 282.
4 David Cannadine, "British History: Past, Present - and Future?", *Past and Present* 116, August 1987, p. 183; also quoted by Anderson, *ibid.*
5 Anderson, *op.cit.*, p. 285. This is not to suggest, of course, that all "revisionists" in British historiography are politically Conservative. For example, Conrad Russell, a major revisionist in the field of seventeenth-century British history, is a Liberal Democrat.
6 See Bernard Porter, "'Though Not an Historian Myself...'. Margaret Thatcher and the Historians". *Twentieth Century British History*, 5, 1994, pp. 246-256.
7 Margaret Thatcher, *The Downing Street Years*, New York, 1993, p. 193.
8 *ibid.*, p. 468.
9 See the review article by R.A.C. Parker, "Churchill and Consensus", *The Historical Journal*, 39, 2 (1996), pp. 563-572; for a useful critique of the term "Butskellism", see Neil Rollings, "'Poor Mr Butskell: A Short Life, Wrecked by Schizophrenia'?", *Twentieth Century British History*, 5, 1994, pp. 183-205.
10 Correlli Barnett, *The Audit of War*, London, 1987 (first published 1986); quotation on p. 19.
11 *ibid.*, p. 3, 11. Barnett views Churchill as personally relatively reluctant to engage in "New Jerusalemist" projects of social reconstruction. *ibid.*, pp. 31-33.
12 Cambridge, 1981; on the controversy, see Bruce Collins and Keith Robbins, eds., *British Culture and Economic Decline*, London, 1990.
13 Keith Robbins, "British Culture versus British Industry", in Collins and Robbins, *op. cit.*, p. 3.
14 José Harris, "Enterprise and Welfare States: A Comparative Perspective", *Transactions of the Royal Historical Society* (Fifth Series), 40, 1990, p. 177. Harris' paper is an important critical discussion of Barnett's thesis as far as social policy is concerned. Cf. also David Edgerton, "The Prophet Militant and Industrial. The Peculiarities of Corelli Barnett", *Twentieth Century British History*, 2, 1991, pp. 360-379.
15 Philip Webster, "Major sees new era of Thatcherite prosperity", *The Times*, 2 January 1993.
16 Cf. the account in Thatcher, *Downing Street Years*, p. 853, beginning: "... even *Macbeth* has the porter's scene", and Clark's account in his *Diaries* (paperback ed.), London, 1995, p. 366, beginning: "She looked calm, almost beautiful. 'Ah, Alan...'".
17 Clark, *Diaries*, p. 385.
18 Alan Clark, "A reputation ripe for revision", *The Times*, 2 January 1993.

19 Cf. John Charmley, *Churchill: The End of Glory*, London, 1993, pp. 402-408.
20 Clark, "A reputation...".
21 Ian Murray, "Historians rally to defend Churchill", *The Times*, 4 January 1993.
22 *ibid.*
23 *ibid.*
24 Matthew d'Ancona, "Could Churchill have stopped the war?", *The Times*, 5 January 1993.
25 *ibid.*
26 "The Other Churchill" [Editorial], *The Times*, 6 January 1993.
27 D'Ancona, "Could Churchill...".
28 Norman Stone, "Gunning for Hitler", *Guardian Weekly*, 17 January 1993.
29 Robert Rhodes James, "Chipping at the Churchill memorial", *Times Literary Supplement*, 8 January 1993; idem, "Leader who galvanised the British into a nation of do-or-die warriors", *The Times*, 5 January 1993.
30 Richard Lamb, "All great men make mistakes", *The Spectator*, 20 February 1993.
31 Edward Luttwak, "World's Greatest Statesman", *London Review of Books*, 11 March 1993.
32 Noel Annan, "How Wrong was Churchill?", *New York Review of Books*, 8 April 1993. This article discusses the Charmley controversy as an introduction to a review of other books. Cf. Annan's more detailed treatment of Charmley in *Daedalus*, Vol.122, 3, Summer 1993, pp. 263-272.
33 Robin Prior and Trevor Wilson, "Review Article: Reassessments of Winston Churchill", *International History Review*, xviii, 1, February 1996, pp. 113-126. Cf. Charmley's reply in the same journal, xviii, 2, May 1996, pp. 371-375.
34 Andrew Roberts, "Baiting Britain's Bulldog", *The Times*, 2 May 1994.
35 R. Rhodes James, *Churchill: A Study in Failure 1900-1939*, Harmondsworth, 1973 (first published 1970).
36 Charmley, *Churchill*, p. x; Martin Gilbert, "Churchill and the welfare state", *Guardian Weekly*, 17 January 1993.
37 For all his industry, Charmley's productivity levies its toll of errors, albeit mostly minor ones. See John Grigg, "Reputation bruised but still intact", *The Times*, 7 January, 1993, and R. Rhodes James, "Chipping at the Churchill memorial", for examples.
38 For Cowling's involvement with the Conservative Philosophy Group and the Salisbury Group in the 1970s, see Richard Cockett, *Thinking the Unthinkable. Think-Tanks and the Economic Counter-Revolution*, London, 1995, pp. 218-219. See also Cowling's own account of the "Peterhouse Right" in the Preface to the 2nd ed. of his *Mill and Liberalism*, Cambridge,

1990, which includes Jonathan Clark and John Vincent among the historians associated with this group.
39 Rhodes James, "Chipping...".
40 Paul Addison, *Churchill on the Home Front, 1900-1955*, London, 1992.
41 Robert Blake and Wm. Roger Louis, eds., *Churchill*, Oxford, 1994 (first published 1993).
42 Lamb, *op. cit.*, p. 32.
43 D'Ancona, "Could Churchill have stopped the war?".
44 Charmley, *Churchill*, pp. 403-408, quotations pp. 405, 406.
45 *ibid.*, pp. 422-424.
46 *ibid.*, pp. 431-432, 448f.
47 *ibid.*, p. 430.
48 *ibid.*, p. 440.
49 *ibid.*, p. 452.
50 *ibid.*, p. 455.
51 D'Ancona, "Could Churchill have stopped the war?"; Valerie Grove, "The man who rewrote history", *The Times*, 8 January 1993.
52 Charmley, *Churchill*, p. 526.
53 See, for example, *The German New Order in Poland* (published for the Polish Ministry of Information), London, [1941]; Paul Einzig, *Hitler's "New Order" in Europe*, London, 1941; Shiela Grant Duff, *A German Protectorate. The Czechs under Nazi Rule*, London, 1942. These are merely samples of what was on the public record at the time.
54 J. Charmley, *Duff Cooper. The Authorised Biography*, London, 1987 (first published 1986), p. 75.
55 *ibid.*, pp. 75, 76.
56 *ibid.*, p. 2.
57 *ibid.*, Ch.21-23; also J. Charmley, "Duff Cooper and Western European Union", *Review of International Studies* (1985), 11, pp. 53-64.
58 Charmley, *Duff Cooper*, p. 218; "Duff Cooper and Western European Union", p. 62.
59 Charmley, "Duff Cooper and Western European Union", p. 63.
60 Charmley, *Lord Lloyd and the Decline of the British Empire*, London, 1987, p. 1.
61 *ibid.*, p. 172, cf. also p. 261.
62 Cited in *ibid.*, p. 94.
63 *ibid.*, p. 170.
64 *ibid.*, p. 82.
65 Charmley, *Churchill*, pp. 244-246, 255-259, 275-278, 286-290. For a contrasting assessment, see Sarvepalli Gopal, "Churchill and India", in Blake and Louis, *op. cit.*, pp. 457-471.
66 Charmley, *Lloyd*, p. 219.

67   *ibid.*, p. 22.
68   John Charmley, "'Reassessments of Winston Churchill': A Reply", *International History Review*, xviii, 2: May 1996, p. 372. Charmley states (*ibid.*, p. 372) that his edition of the diaries of Evelyn Shuckburgh, *Descent to Suez: Diaries, 1951-6*, London, 1986, contributed to his critical assessment of Churchill's judgement on appeasement, among other things.
69   Charmley, *Duff Cooper*, p. 128.
70   J. Charmley, *Chamberlain and the Lost Peace*, London, 1989, p. 111. Cf. also p. 7, where Charmley questions the significance of the 1907 "Crowe memorandum", the "*locus classicus*" of the view of British foreign policy to which Cooper appealed.
71   *ibid.*, p. 112.
72   Other than a very few references to French sources in *Churchill. The End of Glory*, and references to American sources when he discusses Anglo-American relations.
73   Charmley, *Chamberlain*, pp. 91, 246.
74   *ibid.*, p. 97.
75   *ibid.*, pp. 73, 94f, 133f.
76   *ibid.*, p. 90. For the Czechoslovak perspective on Runciman's mission, see Igor Lukes, *Czechoslovakia between Stalin and Hitler*, Oxford, 1996, pp. 181-185.
77   *ibid.*, p. 184.
78   Richard Griffiths, *Fellow Travellers of the Right. British Enthusiasts for Nazi Germany 1933-39*, Oxford, 1983, pp. 281, 282f.
79   Charmley, *Chamberlain*, pp. 6, 10, 77, 144, 201.
80   *ibid.*, p. 186.
81   *ibid.*, p. 212.
82   Lukes, *op. cit.*.
83   *ibid.*, pp. 144-147, 236-238, 248.
84   R.W. Seton-Watson, *Munich and the Dictators*, London, 1939, p. 134.
85   Charmley, *Churchill*, p. 349, which is confined to the question of whether or not Churchill and Eden joined in the standing ovation for Chamberlain in the House of Commons on 28 September 1938.
86   Annan, "Review of John Charmley...", p. 268.
87   Paperback ed., London, 1996, p. xiii.
88   Charmley, *Churchill*, p. 430.
89   Charmley, *Churchill's Grand Alliance*, p. 7.
90   *ibid.*, p. 359. In another passage (p. 252), he compares Britain's relationship with the USA to the status of Vichy France!
91   *ibid.*, pp. 30, 247.
92   *ibid.*, p. 300.
93   *ibid.*, p. 350.

94 J. Charmley, *A History of Conservative Politics, 1900-1996*, New York, 1996.
95 See *ibid.*, p. 182.
96 *ibid.*, p. 197.
97 *ibid.*, pp. 195, 267n17. Charmley clearly has great respect for Powell. Referring to the latter's praise for Thatcher after the Falklands/ Malvinas War, he writes (p. 214): "coming from the source it did, this was the highest possible compliment".
98 *ibid.*, p. 212.
99 *ibid.*, pp. 246-248.
100 Andrew Roberts wrote that the purpose of his chapter on "Churchill, Race and the 'Magpie Society'" was "not to make specious and anachronistic value judgments about Churchill's lack of political correctness, still less to criticise him for assumptions which were overall to work more for Britain's benefit - especially in 1940 - than to her detriment, but to ask objectively how and why he of all Prime Ministers allowed Britain to become a multi-racial society." Roberts presents post-war immigration as another failure of nerve on the part of "liberal Toryism" which damaged British national interests. *Eminent Churchillians*, London, 1994, Ch.4, quotation here from p. 211.
101 Cited by Matthew d'Ancona, "History men battle over Britain's future", *The Times*, 9 May 1994. My thanks to Rebecca Langlands for drawing this reference to my attention.
102 On the "Ridley" and "Chequers affairs", and other British responses to German unification, see Harold James and Marla Stone, eds., *When the Wall Came Down*, New York/ London, 1992, pp. 221-250.

16 "Grass Roots": Eric Cantona, Jürgen Klinsmann and the Europeanisation of English Football

ANDY SMITH

Introduction

Despite European integration's social content and impact, the study of this process remains dominated by research objects centred upon European Union, national and local institutions together with their organisational partners. Such analyses have usefully identified the contours of a "European space of public action" which now structures the resources and behaviour of institutional actors (Muller, 1995). However, apart from questionnaire-based analysis of often dubious scientific quality, little energy has been devoted to the impact of European integration upon social ties within or across the member states. Worse still, currently available theoretical foundations for such study remain decidedly shaky and dominated by nation-state thinking. In short, approaches which target an "interest in European-level politics" continue to overshadow more fundamental questions about the state of contemporary identities in European societies (Belot & Smith, 1998).

This chapter is a by-product of a research project which runs counter to dominant perspectives on European integration for reasons which are as much methodological as empirical. Idealistic perspectives which see Europe as a society in the making (Ferry, 1992; Habermas, 1992) are thus rejected along with quests for precursors of a "European identity". Instead I am interested in developing and testing the sociological and anthropological hypothesis that the continent of Europe is a profoundly "fragmented space" (Poche, 1996). Within this space, territorial belonging is nevertheless constantly being recomposed around the concrete objects of what we political philosopher Charles Taylor disarmingly calls "daily life". Seen from this angle, change in territorial identities is not sparked by political interaction and interdependence, rather it emerges from complex forms of "selfness" and "otherness" (*altérité*). These are embedded in history but also constantly reinvented by and around contemporary social practices.

From this point of view, the "thickness" (Geertz, 1973) of the relationship between the peoples of England[1] and the continent ought to get more serious treatment than is often the case. What images do the English have of their geographical neighbours? Indeed, what vision do they have of themselves and of their territory? In both cases, what social practices are actually seen to matter? From the point of view of political science, detailed study of the origins and effects of selfness and otherness could begin to provide answers to Helen Wallace's pertinent observation of the absence of a British epistemic community in favour of European integration (1995, 169). For sociology, reassessing the role of territorial identity is of even greater importance at a time when the study of political and media defined "social problems" threatens to overwhelm analysis of the causes of, and challenges to, social cohesion.

From this perspective, the "Europeanisation" of sport as a public spectacle offers a field of study that has thus far been largely ignored, particularly from the point of view of its supporters and followers.[2] Through questioning supporters themselves[3] and reflecting upon the meaning of sport for the self definition of social groups, my point of departure is that watching and following sport are not simply entertainment, but activities which are socially constructed and possess social meaning[4]. Self-definition of territory may in many cases be linked to political factors, but an additional working hypothesis is that other social institutions have more deep-seated influence upon the construction and maintenance of "spatial imaginaries" (Anderson, 1991).

The validation of such hypotheses could have stimulating consequences for European integration theory. Firstly, seeing Europe as a fundamentally fragmented space implies considering integration as inevitably partial and disjointed. Secondly, nation-nation and nation-European Union oppositions would lose their essentialist character and thus become a series of relationships that merit placing alongside, rather than automatically above, other territory-linked tensions (between regions, cities, provinces, etc). Thirdly, this study could counter the woolly post-modernist contention that what Europe needs is a "public sphere" similar to the national ones Habermas identified as arising in the 18th century. Finally, and more positively, our research also sets out to reconceptualise the relative contribution made by politics and public policies to the creation and maintenance of social bonds.

These academic goals are of course both highly ambitious and deeply contentious. Indeed, given that our empirical research has yet to be completed, this chapter leaves itself particularly open to violent criticism! Nevertheless, embracing the need for "refractions" on European integration, I first take the opportunity to present a socio-anthropological approach to sport and territory (I) before setting out some ideas regarding one aspect in particular of this relationship: the role of the foreign player in English football (II). Using the examples of Eric Cantona and Jürgen Klinsmann, respectively ex-heroes of Manchester United and Tottenham Hotspur, "Europeanisation" will be discussed in a very different light than is so often the case.

Sport and Territorial Belonging

The bedrock of my project's approach to social ties breaks with classical approaches to territorial belonging which emphasise legal definitions of citizenship and political rights (Tassin, 1994). On the contrary, social ties appear to involve much stronger levels of interdependence. As Charles Taylor writes of collective identity:

> the question is spontaneously phrased by people in the form who am I? But this can't necessarily be answered by giving name and genealogy. What does answer this question for us is an understanding of what is of crucial importance to us. (1989: 27)

Consequently, studying social ties cannot simply be limited to setting out the common history of social groups and assuming that the past determines the present. Identities may well possess some rather mystical properties but structuralist magic or loose definitions of culture are no help in getting closer to their understanding. Instead, research on contemporary identities needs to answer the basic question: *what dimensions of social practices possess meaning for individuals as they live their lives?* The approach of a French sociologist, Bernard Poche, provides a link between Taylor's general perspective and fieldwork. For Poche, collective identities are made up of "sociality principles" and thus constitute:

> a sociological phenomenon of self-definition (or self-reference) which can neither be reduced to a set of a priori "objective" criteria, nor to the individual under study's representation of the outside world. Rather the nature of collective identities hinges upon how these individuals see themselves and engage in specific and privileged modes of intercommunication. (Poche, 1995: 85)

When linked up with the insights of a recent study into football fandom (Bromberger, 1994), Poche's theoretical position on self-definition (or selfness) has stimulated three sets of hypotheses and questions for our study of the Europeanisation of sport:

- sport's role in the self-definition of territory;
- its contribution to the perception of frontiers;
- the role played by foreign players in self identification and in the construction of otherness.

This paper will concentrate on the third point. However, an outline of the first two will be used to illustrate the overall research perspective.

Sport, passion and territorial definition

Conceptualising the watching and following of sport as identity-forming practices (Poche, 1996: 182) means taking seriously what Bromberger identifies as "the paradoxical gap between the futility of a game and the intensity of the passions it inspires" (1995: 1)[5]. Through his ethnology of football as a popular passion, Bromberger shows that "far from being of peripheral interest, these collective passions starkly reveal and define, enlarge or even anticipate cleavages which cut across societies" (1995: 5). Indeed, in a book rich in both information and analysis, this author develops the following academic question:

> what do the impassioned seek to give shape to? What are the mechanisms, the significations, and the specific modalities behind commitments to the object of their passion? (1995: 7).

My study seeks to take this reflection a stage further by ascertaining the role played by sport in structuring forms of sociality which sustain and reveal territorial belonging. More precisely, I have sought to unpack the concept of "following" to better reveal when and how sport is the object of communication above and beyond the short span of time devoted to actual matches.[6] Contrary to journalistic approaches to spectating, methodological rigour is extremely important in order to apprehend these social practices. Initially an interviewee is asked to describe their past and present lives around the place reserved for sport spectating. The analytical *objectif* here is to be able to reconstruct the "world" of the interviewee and in particular the relative value accorded to place. Indeed, my study differs from that of Bromberger through its accent on "territoriality". In other words, my research interest is less focused upon "the fascination exerted by football"

(Bromberger, 1995: 15, 111, 196) or by other sports. Rather what I have set out to discover, and eventually explain, are the forms of intercommunication and identification which seem to develop and grow around the *following* of sport.

European competitions and frontiers between social groups

The intrinsically competitive nature of sport has no doubt influenced a generalised conception of sporting spectacles as symbols of longstanding opposition between countries or cities, opposition which the colours worn by each team illustrate and dramatise. Media depictions of titanic "clashes" between "historical enemies" such as England-Germany (football) or England-France (rugby) perpetuate the conflictual nature of such occasions.[7] The force of national representations that are mobilised around such matches cannot, and indeed must not, be underestimated. Nevertheless, as indicators of selfness and otherness they merit greater analytical deconstruction than is often given them. Firstly, one needs to bear in mind Bromberger's analysis of the links between caricaturing an "opponent" (a team but also its fans) and tactics to destabilise it (1995). As abhorrent as they may seem, violent, and sometimes downright xenophobic, chants and banners cannot simply be taken at face value. Instead, they need placing in the context of a spectacle in which supporters believe they actively participate.

More fundamentally, one needs to reconsider the contribution of frontiers and perceptions of difference to definitions of "the other". Once again, Poche offers a stimulating hypothesis: the primary *effet* of frontiers between different social groups is not that of a barrier to communication, but that of a "disjunctive" expressing contrast rather than opposition:

> A frontier's effect is not (or at least is not initially) one of separation, but of recognition - recognition of a considerable number of points, which one must not rush to call details, where the same references do not mean the same thing and thus where objects do not have the same content or meaning (Poche, 1996: 215).[8]

On this theoretical basis, my research project treats European sporting competitions as particularly privileged moments of identification involving several degrees of geographical scale. Indeed, contrary to prevailing political science analyses, it appears likely that correspondence between scale and identity is far from self-evident[9]. In this respect, my study should provide new information on the sociological nature of European nation-states. Bernard Poche for one is resolutely sceptical here, calling most nation-states "pseudo groups". More precisely, Poche points out that most nation-states are *political* orders which have over time *imposed* definitions of territory as a norm. In contrast:

> a social representation is not a norm, or something that can be imposed: it is a form (or a shape), something that is self-constructed, self-referenced, and which is never absolute, irreversible, nor even necessarily homogenous (1996: 232).

Poche thus concludes that in most nation-states it is more useful to speak of *allegiances* to a regime than of *belonging* to a territory. Poche's point of view as regards the modern nation possesses the great advantage of challenging many implicit visions of territoriality in Europe. From this perspective, territorial meaning and belonging are more likely to occur at (sociologically defined) regional levels. However, only empirical research can really test Poche's theoretical assertion.

Foreign Players, Otherness and Selfness

The examples of Eric Cantona and Jürgen Klinsmann

Over the course of sociology's history, the role played by the foreigner in the construction of social ties has been a perennial controversy that I do not pretend to deal seriously with here. Instead, Georges Simmel's approach will be recalled as a means of underlining the superficial nature of "common sense" linkages between foreigners and the destruction of territorial identities. Contrary to this contention, Simmel saw the foreigner as a positive influence upon the emergence and sustenance of group belonging through providing "a particular form of interaction" which encouraged reflection upon similarities as well as dissimilarities. (1979, 53) In presenting his anthropological approach to the study of European Union institutions, Marc Abélès develops a similar idea through the concept of "defamiliarisation". To Abélès this is not simply a matter of standing back from a people under study in order to render transparent its vision of the other. Rather, defamiliarisation ought to encourage observation of the intrinsically fragmented nature of "the games of otherness", the misunderstandings and the mismatches, that also shape selfness and identity (Abélès, 1997: 4).

Bearing these points firmly in mind, it will be argued that over and above the fleeting contact provided by international matches and tournaments, popular perceptions of "imported" players participating in national championships provide a potentially rich field for the study of territoriality, selfness and otherness. Whereas European football has featured "foreign" players for many years[10], in England their recent increase only dates from the beginning of the 1980s. So far, however, the import-export of players has provoked many journalistic accounts but little scientific analysis. Although useful, one example of the latter is inconclusive due to being founded upon the views of fans totally committed to one club. Qualifying the foreign player as a "mercenary", Bromberger is sceptical about the significance of players who, according to him, just "pass through" and thus have little effect on identification processes.[11] However, my interviews strongly suggest that for less "one-eyed" football followers, certain players do have a lasting effect upon self-identification and perceptions of otherness. What needs answering is: which factors determine that certain players attain this status and thereby play socially constructing roles? My working hypothesis is that the greater the "foreignness" of a player (ie. his territorial distinctiveness), the greater their impact upon conceptions of belonging is likely to be.

The remainder of this chapter is devoted to a preliminary discussion of these points of view centred upon two continental footballers and the English part of their respective careers: Eric Cantona and Jürgen Klinsmann.[12] Between 1993 and 1997, the former became not only a hero for supporters of his teams, Leeds and Manchester United, but a subject of identification or rejection throughout much of England. Klinsmann's experience with Spurs was much shorter, lasting only the 1994-95 season, but has also had a considerable impact. If the footballing talents of both players undoubtedly explain some of their appeal, it will be argued that the fascination with their very different personas outweighs a purely functionalist explanation of their effect upon a major part of English society. Instead, the popular impact of these men appears to have been inextricably linked with perceptions of their Frenchness, Germanness and, through a "game of mirrors", contemporary Englishness. In all three cases myths, symbols and stereotypes clearly still exist. But, as any anthropologist would claim, how could it be otherwise? My point is that through Cantona and Klinsmann interpretations of selfness and otherness have moved on, although in quite different ways. In presenting these case studies *"breathless eulogy"* (Holt & Mangan, 1996a, 5) will (hopefully) be eschewed in favour of an exploration of the social meaning of the two narratives.

Cantona's Story: The Path of Distinctiveness

For a player of his undisputed talent, Eric Cantona had many ups and downs over his thirteen year professional career. Four periods in particular will be highlighted and used to show how the personality of this man confirmed, but also challenged, many English stereotypes of the French but also conceptions of their own football and themselves. Some of these processes were of course deliberately encouraged by Cantona's self-publicisation through a series of well-known advertisements. However, it will be argued that the sociological effect of this player's distinctiveness both preceded and surpassed the impact of such marketing.

Eric Cantona: footballer and unlikely ambassador

- **May 1966**: born in Marseille
- **July 1981- November 1985**: first professional contract with AJ Auxerre
- **November 1985-June 1986**: loaned to FC Martigues
- **July 1986-June 1988**: return to Auxerre
- **July 1988-February 1989**: transferred to Olympique de Marseille
- **February-June 1989**: loaned to FC Bordeaux
- **July 1989-June 1990**: loaned to Montpellier
- **July 1990-June 1991**: return to Marseille
- **July-December 1991**: transferred to Olympique Nimes
- **February-November 1992**: transferred to Leeds United
- **November 1992-May 1997**: transferred to Manchester United
- **February-October 1995**: suspended after violent altercation with spectator
- **May 1997**: retirement

- 45 French caps (20 goals)
- 2 French championship medals (Marseille); 1 French cup winner's medal (Montpellier);
- 5 English championship medals (1 with Leeds, 4 with Manchester Utd);
- 2 cup winner's medals

---

1) *From a stormy departure to a warm arrival*

Before leaving French football for good at the end of 1991, Eric Cantona had earned himself a reputation as an artistic forward and persistent non-conformer. Repeated sendings-off, sudden transfers and outspoken comments contributed to his reputation as *un mal-aimé* (unloved) or *incorrigible*. Often dismissed as arrogance, his ideal of football as a *game*, rather than just a profession, and desire not to be just another footballer led him into repeated conflict with French managers and officials.

Arriving in England as both a virtual unknown and *"enfant terrible"*, the traits which had caused so much trouble in France ironically appeared to strike a chord with the two English clubs he subsequently joined. Beginning at Leeds United in early 1992, Cantona's first games in England coincided with his side's march to a championship victory. This on-field success was accompanied by the player's adoption by Leeds fans and their creation of a new French-referenced chant: "Ooh ah, Cantona!". If for numerous opponents and opposing fans Cantona's aloofness confirmed stereotypes of Frenchmen in general, many other English players and supporters immediately appreciated his unusual skills and frequent praise of their national championship.

Cantona's full "arrival" in England, though, can more accurately be traced to his signing for Manchester United in November 1993. Over the course of the next two seasons he became the keystone in a side that won not only its first championship in 26 years but then went on to repeat this act the following year, even achieving a rare league and cup "double" in the process. Over this period Cantona rapidly became the idol of Manchester United fans and the subject of their own chants and banners. Judging by their behaviour and paraphernalia, to these supporters Cantona was much more than a vital part of United's footballing success. Indeed, it was during this period that Cantona's suave image and regal manner earned him the unoriginal, but apparently heartfelt, nickname of "Eric the king".

For opposing fans and neutrals, however, Cantona's initial reception was more complex. The former category traditionally despise the best forwards of other teams as an obvious threat to their own club's chances of success. The feeling was no doubt intensified in this case because of the involvement of Manchester United, a team that attracts support from throughout Britain and indeed the world. Hard-core fans of teams such as Aston Villa, Coventry and Birmingham City often criticise anything to do with United for this very "denial" of territory. Neutrals, on the other hand, were often attracted to Cantona both as an individual player to admire and as "the last piece in the jig-saw of a fine, attacking team" (interview). Here it should be recalled that in the early 1980s English football was relatively short of its own footballing heroes. For example, Paul Gascoigne, the star of England's 1990 World Cup successes, was playing rather unsuccessfully in Italy. With hindsight Cantona can be seen not only as the first continental star to become a much disputed English hero, but also as a vital part in the rehabilitation of following football as a respectable and valued social practice.[13]

2) *From contested hero to sympathy for the villain*

Cantona began the 1994-95 season much as he had left off the previous one. Adored at home and revered by many neutrals, he continued to be detested by opposing fans. This situation came to a decidedly unexpected head in January 1995 over a televised and much publicised incident at Crystal Palace. Having been sent off for retaliation, Cantona was marching towards the dressing room when, taunted by the xenophobic chanting of a Palace fan, he snapped and kung-fu kicked his verbal assailant. This episode led to an eight-month suspension from the game, a conviction for assault and a lengthy sentence of community service. Newspaper accounts universally condemned the player's action and the manner in which it "brought the game into disrepute"; the *Coventry Evening Telegraph's* headline: *"Kick him out!"* (26.1.95) was representative of many initial reactions. Revealingly, the most frequent media reaction was to call for Cantona's permanent expulsion from the *English* game, an action similar to deportation, thus underlining the player's foreignness and the need to punish those who transgress English social norms.[14] A Daily Mail commentator even went so far as to conclude that: "letting loose such a volatile Gallic temperament upon this aggressive English society of ours produced some explosions of brilliance but was sure to end in disaster" (27.1.95).

If condemnation and outrage were initial reactions, subsequent media treatment of this affair is more complex. Whereas tabloid papers continued to vilify Cantona, an editorial in *The Guardian* (27.1.95) offered a partial defence of the player, arguing that he had been provoked by a racist (sic) thug with whom the English judicial system should also be dealing (thus reflecting unspoken sympathy for an act of "natural justice"). Indeed, the Crystal Palace incident was used as a reminder that anti-French behaviour is just as xenophobic and offensive as anti-black words and actions.

Today, this violent episode can be seen as having had two lasting effects. The first, paradoxically, was to introduce Cantona to a wider public, popularity and/or notoriety that the player and his entourage were quick to seize upon through lucrative advertising contracts, notably with the sportsgoods firm Nike. The second effect was to distance Cantona even further from his national team and native land.

3) *An English comeback and a French rejection*

More precisely, the Crystal Palace incident automatically led to Cantona being dropped from the French national team in its preparation for the European Nations Championship to be held in June 1996. The drama over this story of rejection was heightened by the fact that this tournament was to take place in England and, as it transpired, after a triumphant footballing comeback from suspension by Cantona himself. Returning to his club team in October 1995, Cantona not only scored in his first match but subsequently went on to captain United to a second league and cup double (even scoring the winning goal in the Wembley cup final). During this season, idolising by United fans reached new heights (singing the *Marseillaise*, mass waving of French flags). Meanwhile increasing numbers of neutral fans and non-football followers warmed not only to the player's skills but to a dramatic narrative of redemption. Biblical language was often employed by the media, as exemplified by the *Coventry Evening Telegraph's* description of the comeback game as Cantona's *"second coming"* (...) "His new halo never slipped as English football's most notorious number 7 returned to his heaven" (2.10.95).

Reclaimed as a natural part of "*English* football", Cantona's image was doubtless enhanced by the low-key way he had gone about completing his sentence of Community Service (publicised only through interviews of the children he had been directed to coach), and his impeccable behaviour on the pitch from October 1995 onwards. As one Aston Villa supporter related, "I had to do an about face on Cantona. I thought initially he should have been expelled from our game. But I really admired how he behaved after the ban" (interview). It is within this context that media coverage of the French coach's decision not to recall Cantona for "Euro 96" merits attention. Labelled "the ultimate heartbreak" by the *Daily Star* (20.5.96), much of the British media saw this rejection as an offence not only to the player himself, but to the English championship in which he had flourished. In full knowledge that French popular opinion was largely pro-Cantona,[15] during Euro 96 the English media subsequently put many of the failings of the French team down to his absence. Indeed, a paradoxical sense of pride was felt over the fact that only in England had a player of Cantona's talent and individuality been fully appreciated.

4) *A wrong-footing abdication*

One year on from international-level disappointment and after a season that once again saw Manchester United champions of England, Cantona wrong-footed football followers for (probably) the last time by abruptly announcing his retirement at the relatively young age of 31. Citing a desire to "leave at the top", Cantona then baffled reporters by "disappearing" on holiday and thus depriving them of the habitual round of sentimentality and scandal that often surround a player's retirement. Presented as an "abdication" by *The Financial Times* (21.5.97), the nobility of the man was emphasised as much as the artistry of his footballing skills. "The explosive philosopher from

Manchester will always remain in our memories for having brought poetry into English football which beforehand had been completely blocked" (*The Independent*, 19.5.97). Meanwhile in Manchester itself the retirement announcement sparked genuinely funereal behaviour (tears, black arm bands, silent disbelief). Once again, Cantona's actions overspilled the back pages to become not just the talk of Britain but of much of continental Europe as well. Although one could hardly imagine a more unlikely ambassador for his country, the "passing" of Eric Cantona was frequently discussed as bringing to an end a distinct chapter in French-English relations.

Jürgen Klinsmann: The Path of Assimilation

> **Jürgen Klinsmann: gentleman and diplomat**
>
> - July 1964: born in Stuttgart.
> - September 1982: début for Stuttgart Kickers
> - September 1984: transferred to VFB Stuttgart
> - August 1989: transferred to Inter Milan
> - July 1992: transferred to FC Monaco
> - August 1994: transferred to Tottenham Hotspur
> - May 1995: transferred to Bayern Munich
> - September-December 1997- transferred to Sampdoria Gènes (Italy)
> - December 1997-July 1998: back to Tottenham
>
> - 107 German caps (46 goals)
> - World cup winner's medal (1990)
> - European Championship winner's medal (1996)

Unlike Cantona, Jürgen Klinsmann came to England at the peak of his career, having made a name for himself as a goal scorer first in his native Germany and subsequently in Italy and in France. Although he stayed with Tottenham Hotspur for only one season, three moments during that year give some idea of the impact he had upon the English game. As we shall discuss, in contrast to his French rival, Klinsmann was repeatedly portrayed by the media and indeed presented himself as a model "European" seeking to fit in to, rather than take on, English social mores. Not surprisingly, this path has continued to have an influence upon the way he is currently represented by followers of football in England.

1) *Winning over the sceptics* (August-September, 1994)

On the 29th of July 1994, the Spurs management unveiled the surprise signing of Jürgen Klinsmann on a two year contract. As a German, Klinsmann immediately had to deal with "the particular emotional load carried by the idea of Germanness within British discourse" (Blain, Boyle & O'Donnell, 1993: 192).[16] In addition, as a German international player, he was already known to English fans both as a skilful centre-forward and a bit of a cheat because of his tendency to "dive" in order to obtain penalty kicks for his side.

The first obstacle was reduced by the player himself through his proficiency in English but also his "gentlemanly" demeanour during press interviews. Indeed, much was made by journalists of Klinsmann's capacity to speak not only English but French and Italian, proof that wherever this player went he would adapt himself to the country of his hosts. As *The Times* put it: "there is nothing insular about Klinsmann...he has already begun to cross the divide just by being here" (8.8.94). Whether this was the reason or not, many Tottenham fans came to Klinsmann's first games clad in replica German shirts (a particularly symbolic act for some given that Tottenham is reputed to attract the support of North London's Jewish community).

What *The Times* labelled as Klinsmann's own "charm offensive" sought to tackle the second obstacle head on. Anticipating questions from the press about his penchant for falling in opposition penalty areas, the player quipped "are there any diving schools in London?" (*Daily Mail*, 5.8.94), a form of self-deprecation designed to appeal to the English sense of humour. In the same vein, Klinsmann also underlined: "I don't want to be a star? I don't try to be a star. I have come here expecting to play for my team-mates, not for them to play for me. That's my way" (*Daily Mail*, 5.8.94). Indeed, in the same edition of this newspaper, an article headed "Klinsmann the perfect gentleman" appeared opposite a page devoted to Eric Cantona's latest sending-off under the headline "Cantona the unrepentant". Klinsmann's welcome was finally and dramatically confirmed by his scoring three goals in Spurs' first two league matches, a feat rendered even more memorable by his being stretchered off in a 4-3 victory at Sheffield Wednesday.

2) *Everyone's favourite* (October, 1994-April, 1995)

Over the rest of the 1994-95 season Klinsmann's popularity with English football followers proceeded to grow from strength to strength. If the quality of his on-field play guaranteed idolisation by Tottenham fans, its alliance with frequent post-match interviews and other TV appearances (such as his work as a commentator for the BBC) rapidly won the respect of neutrals and even opposing fans. Reports of Klinsmann's private life (his work with Bosnian orphans, his driving a Volkswagen Beetle, his membership of Greenpeace, etc.) confirmed the image of a star who was not "big-headed" or obsessed with money. Indeed, his on and off-field appeal was confirmed by the fact that wherever Tottenham played that season the ground was full, largely because neutral fans turned up specifically to see this particular player. As part of a wider trend within football crowds which has seen more affluent spectators choose their games on the basis of the players they want to see, rather than the clubs they support, Klinsmann's impact is particularly striking. One incident related to me by an intensely loyal Aston Villa supporter serves to underline this point: "When Spurs came to the Villa Klinsmann got injured after 10 minutes in a collision with our 'keeper. The next day you had some supposedly lifelong Villa supporter writing to the local paper suggesting he should get his money back because he had been robbed of 80 minutes of Klinsmann!" (interview). Perhaps the respect of opposing fans for Klinsmann can in part be attributed to the fact that Spurs are not seen as a serious threat in the way that Manchester United now constantly are. Nevertheless, the nationwide liking for this player seems particularly noteworthy.

3) *A surprising departure* (May, 1995)

Indeed, this sentiment appears to have been sufficiently strong to overcome any feeling of betrayal that might have emerged over Klinsmann's rapid exit from Spurs and the English game at the end of the 1994-95 season. Leaving because of reported differences of opinion with Spurs' contested chairman, Alan Sugar, as well as a relative lack of success on the field (they finished 7th in the league and thus failed to "qualify for Europe"), Klinsmann's last match, in the classical footballing tradition more usually reserved for the retirement of club stalwarts, involved him leading the team out and receiving bouquets of flowers. As the *Daily Mail* concluded, "Few footballers could have inspired such respect and prompt a party atmosphere when they were leaving after just one year (...) Auf wiedersehen, Jürgen" (15.5.95). Ever the diplomat, Klinsmann himself was "all smiles" and, saying all the things expected of him, managed to convince the *Mail*'s journalist that his departure was not really of his choosing, rather it was "inevitable ... there is nothing we can do".[17]

Impacts of Foreign Players upon English Selfness and Otherness

The purple prose and hyperbole of many sports journalists, as well as the recollections of individual fans, of course need sifting through if anything of importance is to be interpreted from the Cantona and Klinsmann stories. Indeed, much of what has been observed needs relating to the wider questions of my study into the Europeanisation of English and French football and rugby. However, a few cautious comparisons and remarks can already be made around the effects these particular foreign players have had upon English football and society.

First, however, it is necessary to compare both narratives in the light of distinctions between different types of supporter. Rather than falling back on class dominated categories which see the middle class as "interested" spectators while the working class are "committed" fans (Blain, Boyle, O'Donnell, 1993: 6), today it is more useful to separate "the diehards" from the "neutrals" on the basis of their biographical links to territory and club. For the former, foreign players remain epiphenomena, given that the meaning of football is related above all to the club they support and, indirectly, to the territory that this club represents. For the neutral, however, foreign players do very much contribute to a trend which Stephen Wragg suggests has the following effect: "Potentially - through television and globalisation - European football in part severs links with place and local cultures and enters the world of 'Eurovision'". (Wragg, 1995b: 122)

With these thoughts in mind, and in full knowledge that even "the diehard" harbours visions of the self and the other, a rapid comparison of the Cantona and Klinsmann narratives reveals the following tentative conclusions.

Beginning with English selfness, three points merit repeating or making. Firstly, today it seems eminently plausible to argue that, each in his own way, these players contributed to a wider movement of English people becoming more at ease and even reidentifying with their nation's football. By showing conclusively that creativity pays in terms of results, Cantona's on-field performances in particular reinjected a certain grace to a game which in England had often become more physical than skilful. More importantly still, the repeated comments of both men on the quality of English football boosted self-esteem and thus helped to lighten a collective inferiority complex as regards continental football.[18] As Pociello has said of sporting heroes in general, "they are embraced because they exalt the qualities and values of a group and thus allow fans to admire themselves while admiring their champions" (1983: 251).[19]

Secondly, although partly a coincidence, the move to England of both these players foreshadowed that of many continental players and even managers. Accelerated by the effects of the Bosman ruling, the abandon of limits on EU players and the recapitalisation of many leading clubs, English football is today no longer a purely British arena. In sports parlance, the adjective "cosmopolitan" has consequently had to be extended to cover descriptions of cultural difference which are not primarily ones of skin colour.

A final point concerns football fans themselves. Foreign players obviously come to England for the extra money now available, but they also join English clubs for the intensity of the support that these enjoy. Having spent much of the 1970s and 1980s apologising for the behaviour of a minority of their supporters, as born out by success of the Euro 96 tournament, many English people now seem able to embrace the foreign-validated qualities of the majority of fans who have never been involved in crowd violence.

Not surprisingly, Klinsmann's willingness to assimilate into English society has led to him having more support amongst fans, particularly the neutrals, because neither his words nor his body language challenged established codes of behaviour. Indeed, in a sense his image reaffirmed the importance of "gentlemanly" values that are so often portrayed as having disappeared in recent years. In this way Klinsmann reassured many Englishmen that not only their football but their society was something to be proud of. In contrast, Cantona made little effort to adopt the social graces of his hosts and conform to the role of the respectful visitor. Although frequently elogious of English football, his occasional interviews and omnipresent demeanour consistently marked out his cultural differences. Consequently, although one might be tempted to conclude that Klinsmann's impact on English selfness has been the greater, if one takes a more complex view of the foreigner's contribution to identity the converse might well be more accurate.

Indeed, in embracing such a perspective, changes in English selfness can also be perceived through shifts in depictions by the English of the other. The importing of foreign players is already an indicator of modification in such attitudes. Continental players are now far less often stereotyped as "brittle" and insufficiently "hard". Previously reviled Italian football is now even the subject of a much-watched weekly television programme.[20] Indeed, whereas previously English football had sheltered behind "the national myth" of its invention of the game,[21] the progressive introduction by the English national team of tactics associated with continental football (complex formations, slower build-ups, more sophisticated defending) is probably an even better indicator of change, since tactics reflect many deep-seated priorities and prejudices (Archetti, 1996). The fact that the present (Hoddle) and previous (Venables) managers of the national side have either played or coached on the continent provides some explanation here, but such men would simply not have been appointed in a previous social context. Europeanisation of this societal type is thus about evolution of the underlying, as opposed to the immediately visible, variety.

In this respect, the general conclusion amongst fans of Klinsmann's greater impact compared to Cantona again needs closer inspection. To a certain degree, the path trod by the former actually led to his Germanness being downplayed to a great extent in favour of non-national or even universalist depictions (the polyglot, the team man, the good sport, the charity worker). Cantona in contrast never disguised his Frenchness and thus made football followers confront cultural difference in a way that Klinsmann did not. Of course, my purpose here is not to pursue comparisons between these two players, fascinating as they may be. Instead, these comparisons serve to underline the importance of conducting research into sociological difference from a perspective that actually deals with, rather than diminishes, the cultural adventure of greater contact between the peoples of Europe.

Conclusion

One day soon the England XI could revert to its traditional game, hooligans may return with a vengeance and Glen Hoddle might be sacked for having "gone native" during his French playing days. Nevertheless, some lasting displacement in the conception of the non-English seems to have already taken place around the sport of football. Large reserves of latent xenophobia towards continental people doubtless still exist in England, but the Cantona and Klinsmann narratives suggest that the ongoing Europeanisation of the sport has played a part in easing its intensity.

From a more general perspective this point raises the question: *what is Europeanisation?* At first glance, this chapter seems more concerned with Englishness, Frenchness and Germanness than with England's *rapport* with Europe and European integration. However, a socio-anthropological approach to territorial identification is not only rigorous and stimulating, but also an indispensable stepping stone to reflection upon problems different peoples have with politically and economically driven European integration projects. In contrast to existing identities, "European" has little symbolical or mythical foundation and consequently no popular resonance. Of course, politics involves the creation and dramatisation of power by elites who instrumentalise collective identities both as political resources and as a dimension of their social roles (Abélès & Jeudy, 1997). In this respect public actors inevitably consider that they can create territory and thus create

"Europe". However, as social scientists we need to be aware that impositional styles of creating territory are logically opposed to awareness of societal roots and tolerance of cultural difference. Put another way, given that "Europe" has almost universally been depicted as an elite-led construction, the dominant research question has been: "why don't the people follow their leaders?". However, from a socio-anthropological position a more pertinent question seems to be "how do the different peoples of Europe see themselves and their geographical neighbours at a time when contact, but not necessarily understanding, is increasing?"

In a recent book aptly entitled *En attente d'Europe*: ("Waiting for Europe"), Marc Abélès concludes that the fundamental challenge for the European Union is one of politics coming to terms with a cultural pluralism that is not solely centrifugal. Instead this pluralisation can involve an element of "deterritorialisation which is a factor of enrichment and innovation" so long as reactualised and meaningful visions of territory emerge to take the place of what is lost (1996: 130). In a similar vein, the approach I have outlined here is centred upon a "peoples' Europe", a term that currently needs rescuing from well-intentioned ambiguity. In contrast to many proponents who confuse the term with calls for a more active EU role in social policies (a people's Europe), a "peoples' Europe" postulates that the political and societal dimensions of European integration are logically distinct. The best one can therefore hope and work for is a reappraisal of the meaning, and therefore the limits, of what common parlance reduces to "mutual understanding" and "roots". By harnessing them to objects of study that are of importance to the daily lives of Europe's inhabitants, the twin concepts of selfness and otherness offer perhaps the best way forward for future research.

References

Abélès (Marc) 1996: *En attente d'Europe*, Paris, Hachette.
Abélès (Marc) 1997: "De l'Europe en particulier et de l'anthropologie en général", *Cultures et Conflits*, hiver.
Abélès (Marc) & Jeudy (Henri-Pierre) eds, 1997: *Anthropologie du politique*, Paris, Armand Colin.
Anderson (Benedict) 1991: *Imagined communities*, London, Virago.
Archetti (Eduardo) 1996: "In search of national identity: Argentinian football and Europe", in J. Mangan, ed., *Tribal identities. Nationalism, Europe, Sport*, London, Frank Cass.
Belot (Céline) & Smith (Andy), 1998: "Europe and collective identity: a challenge for the social sciences", in U. Hedetoft, ed., *Political symbols, symbolic politics: Europe between unity and fragmentation*, London, MacMillan.

Blain (Neil), Boyle (Raymond), O'Donnell (Hugh), 1993: *Sport and national identity in the European media*, Leicester, Leicester University Press.
Bromberger (Christian), 1995: *Le match de football. Ethnologie d'une passion partisane à Marseille, Naples et Turin*, Paris, Éditions de la Maison des sciences de l'homme.
Coddington (Anne), 1997: *One of the lads. Women who follow football*, London, HarperCollins.
Elias (Norbert) & Dunning (Eric), 1986: *Quest for excitement. Sport and leisure in the civilizing process*, Oxford, Basil Blackwell.
Ferry (Jean-Marc), Thibaud (Paul), 1992: *Discussion sur l'Europe*, Paris, Calmann-Lévy.
Geertz (Clifford) 1973: *The interpretation of culture*, New York, Basic Books.
Habermas (Jürgen) 1992: "Citoyenneté et identité nationale. Réflexions sur l'avenir de l'Europe", in J. Lenoble & N. Dewandre, eds, *L'Europe au soir du siècle. Identité et démocratie*, Paris, Editions Esprit.
Haynes (Richard) 1995: *The football imagination. The rise of football fanzine culture*, Aldershot, Arena.
Hedetoft (Ulf) 1996: "Constructions of Europe: territoriality, sovereignty, identity", paper presented to the conference *Identité collective et représentation symbolique*, Paris, July.
Holt (Richard), Mangan (J.A.), 1996a: "Prologue: heroes of a European past", in R. Holt, J. Mangan., P. Lanfranchi, eds, *European Heroes. Myth, identity and sport*, London, Frank Cass.
Holt (Richard), Mangan (J.A.), 1996b: "Epilogue: heroes for a European future", in R. Holt, J. Mangan., P. Lanfranchi, eds, *European Heroes. Myth, identity and sport*, London, Frank Cass.
Hornby (Nick) 1994: *Fever pitch*, London, Indigo.
Hornby (Nick), dir. 1997: *My favourite year. A collection of new football writing*, London, Indigo.
Muller (Pierre) 1995: "Un espace européen de politiques publiques", in Y. Mény, P. Muller, J-L. Quermonne, eds, *Les politiques publiques en Europe*, Paris, l'Harmattan.
Poche (Bernard) 1994: "L'Europe ne se compose que de minorités", paper to the conference *Le rôle culturel des minorités dans la nouvelle réalité européenne*, Trieste University, 22-26 September.
Poche (Bernard) 1995: "Le groupe territorial et son identité. Le lien social au-delà de la crise du politique", in N. Marouf, ed., *Identité-Communauté*, Paris, l'Harmattan.
Poche (Bernard) 1996: *L'espace fragmenté. Éléments pour une analyse sociologique de la territorialité*, Paris, l'Harmattan.
Pociello (C.) 1981: *Sports et société. Approche socioculturelle des pratiques*, Paris, Vigot.
Russel (David) 1997: *Football and the English. A social history of Association Football in England 1863-1995*, Preston, Carnegie Publishing.

Simmel (Georges) 1979: "Digression sur l'étranger", in Y. Grafmeyer et I. Joseph, eds., *L'Ecole de Chicago, naissance de l'écologie urbaine*, Paris, Champ Urbain.

Tassin (E). 1994: "Identités nationales et citoyenneté politique", *Esprit*, n° 1, January.

Taylor (Charles), 1989: *Sources of the self. The making of the modern identity*, Cambridge, Cambridge University Press.

Wagg (Stephen) 1995a: "The missionary position: football in the societies of Britain and Ireland", in S. Wagg, ed., *Giving the game away. Football, politics and culture on five continents*, Leicester, Leicester University Press.

Wagg (Stephen) 1995b: "On the continent: football in the societies of North-West Europe", in S. Wagg, ed., *Giving the game away. Football, politics and culture on five continents*, Leicester, Leicester University Press.

Wallace (Helen), 1995: "Les relations entre la Communauté et l'administration britannique", in Y. Mény, P. Muller, J-L. Quermonne, eds, *Les politiques publiques en Europe*, Paris, l'Harmattan.

Notes

1   My research intentionally targets England rather than Britain.
2   More precisely, although football in particular has recently spawned accounts of the increase in women fans (Coddington, 1997), or fanzines (Haynes, 1995), other than in historical analyses (Russel, 1997), clubs, teams, and players tend to overwhelm research into links between supporters and their passion.
3   This research is limited to spectators and television viewers in France and England. The following of two sports, football and rugby, is studied in four cities where these codes are reputedly supported to differing degrees: Bordeaux, Montpellier, Coventry and Birmingham.
4   In the past at least, sport as a field of sociological research suffered from the impact of binary oppositions such as work vs leisure. Norbert Elias and Eric Dunning summed this situation up in their inimitable fashion: "sociologists have neglected sport principally because few of them have yet detached themselves form the dominant values and modes of thinking of Western societies to be able to grasp the social significance of sport, the sociological problems that it poses, or the scope that it offers for exploring areas of social structure and behaviour that are, for the most part, ignored in conventional theories" (1986: 4).
5   Sport as a spectacle is thus not simply a "quest for excitement" (Elias et Dunning, 1986). Instead partisanship "is itself a necessary condition which founds the dramatic interest of a sporting contest" (Bromberger, 1995: 110). Seen in this way, partisanship has three layers: "to give emotion its head

while becoming an actor oneself (going from 'they' to 'us'); asserting one or several senses of belonging, adhering to a nebulous yet consistent system of values incarnated by the style of "his' or 'her' team and 'his' or 'her' favourite players" (Bromberger, 1995: 111). For fascinating insights into the passions which surround English football see Nick Hornby's autobiographical book *Fever Pitch* (1994) and a collection of essays he has also edited (Hornby, 1997).

6   Harry Pearson, a "new football writer" and Middlesborough fan, provides an amusing account of the feelings generated by a race for promotion in 1990-91: "By the time we got to Upton Park, Boro had moved to third in the table. West Ham were top. It was ten days before Christmas and the ground was packed. In the away end, the low roof of the stand reverberated with the noise, the air was chill with the sharp crackle of frost and anticipation; the pitch glistened under the floodlights. It's at moments like these that you know for certain why you come to football. Then the game starts and ruins everything" (in Hornby, 1997: 44).

7   Even specialists of collective identities such as Ulf Hedetoft surprisingly give credence to the "sport as a substitute for war" thesis (1996: pp 12-14).

8   This definition is similar to Bromberger's analysis of the "ambiguity of fandom" (...) "at one and the same time a visible assertion of social and territorial affiliations and an autonomous template classifying the world according to particular criteria" (Bromberger, 1995: 110).

9   Poche accepts that self definition of territory can intervene at several levels. However, he stresses that the scale of identification is strongly restricted by parameters that are both top-down and bottom-up (1996: 202).

10 The Welshman John Charles played for Juventus from the mid-1950s onwards. More frequently, Argentinians have played in the Italian championship, and even for the national team, since the 1930s (Archetti, 1996).

11 Bromberger relates many examples of "mimicry" (such as the Englishman Chris Waddle's haircut during his days at Marseille). However, he concludes that "this mimicry is only of limited impact and that footballers have only ever inspired partial ways of looking and behaving: their glory is too ephemeral, their notoriety too closely linked to that of their team, meaning that for fans their aura fades away as soon as they leave 'their' club. Lastly, and above all, footballers as opposed to the stars of show business do not offer images of total existence, models or counter-models of *'savoir vivre'*, being and loving. Identification with footballers thus operates in a more indirect fashion" (Bromberger, 1995: 343).

12 These two narratives have been reconstructed from 25 interviews with sports followers in the cities under study as well as newspaper accounts. Methodical analysis of the *Daily Mail* and the *Coventry Evening Telegraph* over the

period 1992-97 has been supplemented by unsystematic reading of *L'Equipe, Libération, The Guardian, The Independent* and *The Financial Times*.

13 Writing before acts 2, 3 and 4 of this narrative, Holt and Mangan conclude however that Cantona has reinforced the "equation that the French are undisciplined and impetuous - the Latin stereotype (...). it is not clear that a man so successfully idealised and demonized by different groups has done much to foster mutual understanding" (1996b: 173-174).

14 Had Cantona punched rather than kicked the spectator media reaction may well have been much milder.

15 Replying to a questionnaire in the influential sports daily *L'Equipe*. 83% of those responding sought Cantona's reinstatement.

16 Interestingly, the German media were particularly worried about this point and sent TV camera crews to cover Klinsmann's reception during pre-season friendly matches (*Daily Mail*, 8.8.94).

17 Just after this chapter was prepared. the Klinsmann story underwent a new twist as he returned to Tottenham for six further months. During this time Klinsamann helped them escape relegation and helped get himself back in the German world cup squad.

18 An inferiority complex which was heightened by the Heysel stadium incident in 1985 where many Italian fans died fleeing from Liverpool supporters. Guilt over football violence was reinforced by the penalty of a subsequent five-year ban on English clubs playing "in Europe".

19 On this idea see also Bromberger (1995 pp. 121-153).

20 Indeed, the content and reception of this programme would in itself constitute an interesting research object. In passing Stephen Wragg has identified three basic paradigms for the content: 1) Italy as a place of style and high culture where elegance, passion and discernment are valued; 2) Italy as the land of quick temper and extravagant gestures; 3) Italian football as difficult terrain for the Englishman abroad (Wragg, 1995b: 121-122).

21 A national myth described by Wragg in the following terms: "the British popular media have in recent years developed a kind of national melodrama wherein the England team has the role of the missionary. on which a host of former tutees and subject peoples has now turned" (1995a: 1).

17 Afterword: Studying "Britain"

MICHAEL WILDING

It was a colleague of mine in an English department in an English university who first raised my anxiety about 'studies'. Whenever the word studies is attached to a discipline, he said, it always marks the degradation of the original. Drama becomes Drama Studies, French becomes French Studies (with no language compulsion), English becomes English Studies. When a title had to be found for my chair at the university of Sydney and a fellow professor suggested English Studies, I was deeply, and I suspect properly, suspicious.

But then whatever might have been meant by English Studies was not at all what is meant by British Studies. The apparent interchangeability of English and British in so many contexts does not apply in this context. English has always been a subject of its own, indeed an empire of its own, which no doubt explains its suspicions of British Studies. English (the subject) was always the language of English and the literature written in that language. The national provenance of the literature was not perceived as explicitly significant: so English was the banner under which American literature was taught, and later Commonwealth Literature, and later again the New Literatures in English. English as the subject's title is still redolent of those days when the language was the only qualifier of Literature, or Writing, not the nationality. The days when I grew up wanting to be a writer, not an English writer or a Worcestershire writer or an expatriate writer or anything but a writer. But those days seem to have gone. I remember David Lodge asking me in puzzlement not so long ago, What are you? Are you an English writer or an Australian writer? I found I couldn't clearly answer him. As far as I was concerned I was just a writer, I felt no need to attach a national label. But the world, or certain forces in the world, have felt the need to attach national labels. It is one of the huge paradoxes of the contemporary moment that in an economic phase of globalisation of markets and investments, in a period of the domination of the transnationals, themes of nationality and nationalism have revived so stridently.

Now in one aspect, the injection of the idea of British studies into the teaching of English literature can be a very salutary thing. The way in which English (the subject) transcended mere nationality was part of the way in which it transcended pretty well everything and attempted to inculcate those elusive 'purely literary values.' English has always been bedevilled by a refusal to contextualise itself, in terms of nationality, history, politics, class, economics, psychology or indeed anything else. English has been characterised at many institutions, certainly at the University of Sydney, by a series of negations. The old style professorial pronouncements went along the lines of, We are teaching English, not politics, not history, not psychology, not biography, not religion. It didn't leave you with much after all the exclusions. Issues that might have made clear the issues of the literature were taboo. This was the whole project of the old 'New Criticism' and this has continued to be the project of the larger part of the new 'theory.'

So I for one would welcome the possibility of British Studies influencing the study of English literature in the direction of understanding the Britishness of English literature, the whole complex history and culture embedded in the writing. It would be, of course, a huge task. And it would be rather more than the old cliche of pointing out to Australian students that midsummer in Britain is in June, not December, that the seasons are the other way round, and other such things. It would be rather more than filling in a catalogue of flora and fauna, too. After reading Rachel Carson's *The Silent Spring* about the destructive effects of DDT, Aldous Huxley remarked that we were losing half the subject matter of English poetry. It was not a trivial observation and I don't want to trivialise Huxley's response. But it does continually need to be stressed that there is more to English literature than catalogues of flowers and the memorialisation of that English paradise. Indeed you have only to turn to the play in which the English paradise is celebrated, Shakespeare's *Richard II*, to see that when John O'Gaunt refers to Britain as 'This other Eden, demiparadise' he is celebrating something which was under attack, that the paradise was deeply divided amongst competing political and social forces; and you have only to explore a little of the context of Shakespeare's own time to see that the supposedly historical play Richard II was dealing with contemporary political divisions, and that after it was performed at request on the eve of Essex's unsuccessful rebellion, Shakespeare and his company tactfully and rapidly left town for a while. As Queen Elizabeth put it, 'Know that I am Richard.'

One of the many failings of the last political administration in Australia was its introduction of racial politics to cover up its betrayal of its socialist constituency. So to be British in Australia was something of a liability. If you were British you had sent young Australians to their death in Gallipolli, you had starved the Irish in the potato famine, you had surrendered Singapore to the Japanese, and you wanted to retain a monarchy. To be blamed for the atrocities of the British ruling class in Australia is something many of us find very galling. Indeed, it was to get away from that very ruling class that many of us came to Australia.

What a British studies programme could valuably do in Australia is show how divided a society Britain is and always has been. The United Kingdom is a phrase that has always seemed to me a misnomer. D'Israeli over a century ago popularised the concept of the two nations, but I think he was underestimating. During the seventeenth-century the concept of the Norman Yoke encapsulated how oppositional groups felt about British politics, that the ruling party were not really British but occupying Normans. A. E. Housman's poem 'The Welsh Marches' encapsulates the earlier conflict between the Anglo-Saxon and Celt:

> The flag of morn in conqueror's state
> Enters at the English gate:
> The vanquished eve, as night prevails
> Bleeds upon the road to Wales.

And the poem encapsulates, moreover, the way the conflict continues within the single individual.

> In my heart it has not died,
> The war that sleeps on Severn side;
> They cease not fighting, east and west,
> On the marches of my breast.

But these ethnic stereotypings within Britain are in large part metaphoric for divisions based on region, on class, on ideology.

There have always been strong oppositional voices in Britain. After all, the English Revolution was the great model for the French Revolution and the Russian Revolution, even if Mrs Thatcher, commenting on the French bicentennial celebrations of 1789, said rather oddly that Britain had never had nor needed a revolution. Wrong on both counts, surely. To go back to England's treatment of Ireland, governmental policy has never commanded total support. There was vocal opposition within Britain to Cromwell's campaign in Ireland. As a Leveller pamphlet put it:

> For consider, as things now stand, to what end you should hazard
> your lives against the Irish: have you not been fighting these seven

years in England for rights and liberties that you are yet deluded of? and that too, when as none can hinder you of them but your own officers, under whom you have fought? and will you go on still to kill, slay and murder men, to make them as absolute lords and masters over Ireland as you have made them over England?'

There was vocal opposition to the military strategies and policies of the First World War. Indeed there was vocal opposition to everything. 'A headstrong, moody, murmuring race,' Dryden called his fellow British. (*Absalom and Achitophel*, 1 450.)

Even within English (the subject) good work has been done in exploring this area. John Lucas's splendid *England and Englishness* (Hogarth Press, 1990) looks at just these complexities in the idea of nationhood in English poetry. For all the nationalistic implications of a programme like British Studies, it is a programme that can undo simplistic nationalistic sloganising; it can demonstrate the oppositional forces and critical forces and dissident forces within the national; indeed, it can demonstrate that the national is only the policy of a particular group that has seized power at a particular time; and that the nation contains a much greater richness and diversity and decency than that. And it can also indicate the great positive achievements of these forces of dissent and opposition. It might still not be too late to recall that trades unions, free education, a national health service and the welfare state were pioneered in Britain - even if these are all rapidly becoming concepts fading from contemporary reality and found only in the historical records. And if this can be done, then 'British studies' will have represented not that degradation of academic study I mentioned to begin with, but instead have contributed a significant enhancement of scholarship, education and understanding.

Notes on Contributors

Andrew Bonnell is Lecturer in the School of Humanities, Griffith University. He has written a number of articles on German history, specialising in the history of German Social Democracy, and recently co-edited *Power, Conscience and Opposition: Essays in German History in Honour of John A. Moses*.

a.bonnell@hum.gu.edu.au

Conal Condren is Professor of Political Science, UNSW. His most recent book was on the semantics of political argument in seventeenth-century England, plotting changes in language use and the consequences of this for the interpretation of early modern political texts. Forthcoming is a study of notions of satire and lying in seventeenth and early eighteenth-century Britain, *Satire, Lies and Politics* (Macmillan, 1997). He is presently working on a book on Thomas Hobbes and on a large scale study of the presuppositions of argument in the early modern period.

c.condren@unsw.edu.au

Roger Covell is Australia's leading music critic, the author of a number of path-breaking works on the history of Australian music, and *Generalmusikdirektor* at the University of New South Wales.

r.covell@unsw.edu.au

Grant Fleming is Lecturer in Economics at the Australian National University where he teaches Australian economic history and the history of economic thought. His current research interests lie in the history of macroeconomics, focusing on the economic and social research of the International Labour Organisation. Previous research has appeared in journals such as *Business History, International Labour Review, New Zealand Economic Papers*, and the *Australian Economic History Review*.

grant.fleming@anu.edu.au

John Gascoigne is Associate Professor in History at UNSW and was educated at Sydney, Princeton and Cambridge Universities. He has recently completed a two volume study of Joseph Banks and his intellectual and political context. The first volume appeared in 1994 as *Joseph Banks and the English Enlightenment. Useful Knowledge and Polite Culture;* the second, *Science in the Service of Empire. Joseph Banks, the British State and the Uses of Science in the Age of Revolution* is due to be published by Cambridge University Press in 1998. His earlier work focused on the relations between science, religion and politics in the eighteenth century and the character of the early modern university, and he is now beginning work on a book entitled *A Nation Rationally Conceived? The Enlightenment and the Foundations of Australian Society 1788-1851*.

j.gascoigne@unsw.edu.au

Dick Geary is Professor of Modern History at the University of Nottingham, Editor of *Contemporary European History* (CUP), a Fellow of the Alexander-von-Humboldt Foundation and Research Associate of the Institut zur Erforschung der europäischen Arbeiterbewegung at the Ruhr-Universität (Bochum). He is currently researching unemployment in interwar Europe and Brazilian labour history. His books include *European Labour Protest, 1848-1939* (1981 - German edition 1983); *Karl Kautsky* (1987); with Richard J Evans (eds), *The German Unemployed* (1987); (ed.), *Labour and Socialist Movements in Europe before 1914* (1989); *European Politics from 1900 to the Depression* (1991); *Hitler and Nazism* (1993 - Slovene edition 1995); and *Hope and Impotence: Aspects of German Labour, 1871-1933* (late 1997).

Dick.Geary@nott.ac.uk

Hans Joachim Meyer, Professor of English at the Humboldt University in Berlin since 1985, was Minister for Education and Science in the first freely elected government of the German Democratic Republic in 1990 and a member of the GDR team which negotiated the Unification Treaty. He is now State Minister of Higher Education, Research and Culture in the Saxon State Government in Dresden.

John Milfull arrived at European Studies via many years in German Studies and nine years as Dean. He is now Professor of European Studies and Director of the Centres for European Studies and Intercultural Jewish Studies at the University of New South Wales. His main research interests are the German-Jewish experience and culture and society in the vanished German Democratic Republic. The seed of the **Britain in Europe** project was sown in his fallow brain in conversations with elderly ladies on buses during a period of study leave at the University of Sussex in 1995.

j.milfull@unsw.edu.au

James Mitchell is Professor of Politics at the University of Sheffield. His main interests are in territorial politics: the politics of identity and nationalism; regional and urban policy; and relations between different levels of government. He is the author of *Conservatives and the Union* (1990); *Strategies for Self-Government* (1996); and co-author of *Politics and Public Policy in Scotland* (1991) and *How Scotland Votes* (1997). He is completing a book on *Regionalism and Regional Policy in the European Union and Devolution in the UK*.

James.Mitchell@sheffield.ac.uk

John Murphy, born Bolton, Lancashire in 1936, educated at Leeds University and the University of East Anglia, has lived abroad since 1964 in Turkey and Denmark, returning to England briefly in the early 1970s to write a doctoral thesis in Economic History on the "Town and Trade of Great Yarmouth, 1740-1850". Has been a senior lecturer in British Studies at the Copenhagen Business School since 1981. Current interests are Britain in Europe and English local government, with emphasis on York.

Murphy/ENG@cbs.dk

Elim Papadakis was recently appointed to the Chair of European Studies at the Australian National University. He was previously Professor of Sociology at the University of New England.

papael@artalpha.anu.edu.au

Peter Shearman is Senior Lecturer in the Department of Political Science at the University of Melbourne. He previously taught at the University of Essex (1984-1990). His main research interest is in the field of Russian politics and international relations, and his most recent publications include articles on the Russian Far Right, NATO Expansion and the Russian Question, and Britain's Changing Relationship with Europe. He was active in British politics in the early 1980s in the (old) Labour Party, and stuck with Labour despite disagreements with the party's stance on Europe in the hope and expectation (now realised) that it would change.

shearman@politics.unimelb.edu.au

Andy Smith, English by nationality, is a reader in political science at the Institut d'Etudes Politiques de Bordeaux. Since completing his PhD thesis in 1995 (published as *L'Europe politique au miroir du local. Les fonds structurels en France, en Espagne et au Royaume Uni*, Paris, l'Harmattan, 1995), he has pursued two dimensions of European integration. The first is centred upon its intertwining with changes in traditional centre-periphery relations ("Studying multi-level governance. Examples from French translations of the structural funds", *Public Administration*, forthcoming). The second deals with the question of identity.... (with Celine Bélot: "European integration: from political to social legitimacy", forthcoming in U. Hedetoft, ed., *Political symbols, symbolic politics: Europe between unity and fragmentation*, forthcoming, 1997).

smith@rsiep.iep.u-bordeaux.fr

Rodney Smith is Senior Lecturer in the School of Political Science at the University of New South Wales. His research interests include political culture and political parties. His most recent research in these areas includes a forthcoming chapter 'Australia—An Old Order Manages Change', in P.J. Davies and J. White (eds), *Political Parties and the Collapse of Old Orders*, Albany, SUNY Press, forthcoming (1998).

rod.smith@unsw.edu.au

Helen Wallace, Professor of Contemporary European Studies and Director of the Sussex European Institute, has lived the story of Britain and the EU as a citizen, and since her doctorate on the entry negotiations, she has written widely on European political integration, has sometimes advised the European Commission, and has worked in the British public service.
h.wallace@sussex.ac.uk

Michael Wilding holds a personal chair in English & Australian Literature at the University of Sydney. His critical studies include *Political Fictions, Dragon's Teeth: Literature in the English Revolution,* and *Social Visions.* His fiction includes the novels *Living Together, Pacific Highway,* and *The Paraguayan Experiment,* and the short story collections *Great Climate, This is for you,* and *Somewhere New.*
michael.wilding@english.su.edu.au

Heidi Zogbaum trained as a historian and now teaches Russian and German 19th and 20th century politics in the Department of Politics at La Trobe University.
hishz@luff.latrobe.edu.au

For Product Safety Concerns and Information please contact our EU representative GPSR@taylorandfrancis.com
Taylor & Francis Verlag GmbH, Kaufingerstraße 24, 80331 München, Germany

www.ingramcontent.com/pod-product-compliance
Lightning Source LLC
Chambersburg PA
CBHW052031300426
44116CB00024B/1371